KT-509-734

B.
N|

B.S.U.C. - LIBRARY

00210443

God's Place in the World

God's Place in the World
Sacred Space and Sacred Place in Judaism

Seth D. Kunin

CASSELL

London and New York

Cassell
Wellington House, 125 Strand, London WC2R 0BB
370 Lexington Avenue, New York, NY 10017–6550

© Seth Kunin 1998

First published 1998

All rights reserved. No part of this publication may be reproduced or transmitted
in any form or by any means, electronic or mechanical, including photocopying,
recording, or any information storage or retrieval system, without permission in
writing from the publishers.

British Library Cataloging in Publication Data
A catalogue record for this book is available from the British Library

ISBN 0–304–33748–X

Typeset by York House Typographic Ltd
Printed and bound in Great Britain by Bookcraft (Bath) Ltd, Midsomer Norton

BATH SPA UNIVERSITY
COLLEGE
NEWTON PARK LIBRARY

Class No.
296.6 KUN

Phil Dutch | 28. APR. 2000

DISCARD

Contents

Acknowledgments

My thanks are due to the many people who assisted me during the writing of this book. My colleagues in the Theology Department at the University of Nottingham were always willing to discuss and debate many of the themes discussed here, and were also willing to listen to and critique a paper on pilgrimage which was a draft of the chapter presented below. Special thanks are due to Professor Douglas Davies, Dr. Morris Casey and Dr. Carl Trueman who willingly gave their time in reading many of the chapters. Dr. Nicholas De Lange was helpful in setting me on the right track in respect of pilgrimage. I would also like to thank the Jewish Theological Seminary and the Department of Anthropology at New York University for their hospitality during my study leave; their libraries were indispensable. Finally, thanks are due to Rabbi D. Kunin, Lawrence Kunin, and Dr. Carolyn Kunin, who patiently read and proofed the final versions of the book.

Dr. Seth D. Kunin
Department of Theology
University of Nottingham

February 1998

1 Introduction

From the very foundations of Jewish myth, ritual, and history, sacred space has been an important way of recognizing the presence of God in the community and relating to God. Over the past 3000 years the models used for conceptualizing sacred space have developed and been transformed in response and relation to transformations and developments in the cultural community. In many respects these models of space are useful markers in understanding the broader levels of transformation and conceptualization. Several interrelated aspects of sacred space and the uses of it are examined in order to distinguish the nature of the models and the patterns of transformation.

Many aspects of sacred space have been studied by anthropologists and other social scientists, often leading to encompassing, cross-cultural perspectives. This is true of the work of M. Eliade, H. Turner, and V. Turner.[1] Each one of these theorists proposes a conceptually limited, broadly applicable explanation of aspects of sacred space.

Eliade's analysis of the general phenomena of sacred space clearly defines, on what appears to be a universal basis, the key features of sacred space. These features are assumed to figure in any particular example. He suggests that all sacred spaces are perceived as being centers of the universe, places where the divine and human can meet. He also argues that they are equivalent to the cosmic navel, and join together the three domains, that is, the underworld (hell), the earth, and heaven. Although some Israelite/Jewish texts from different periods do suggest symbolic associations of these kinds, in many cases they are the exceptions rather than the rule.[2] The primary problem with Eliade's approach, however, is found in respect of its understanding of the relationship between myth, culture, and time. He overemphasizes the cyclical understanding of myth and time, seeing many aspects of the sacred and sacred space as attempts to mirror this cycle, with myth, ritual, and sacred space seeking to return time to its sacred mythological beginnings. This concept shapes many aspects of his analysis of sacred spaces. Although the understanding of time in biblical and rabbinic texts shares some aspects of this model, with past and future being related, it is not essentially cyclical. The future and past affect each other, but they do not repeat each other.

Harold Turner, in a fascinating phenomenological and theological analysis, proposes a model which distinguishes between types of sacred spaces (cross-culturally), *domus dei*[3] and *domus ecclesiae*. The model itself is useful in that it highlights the differences in use and understanding of two common forms of sacred space, which are analogous to the Temple and synagogue respectively. There is, however, built into Harold Turner's analysis a strong element of theological ethnocentricity. He consistently displays a preference for the *domus ecclesiae* model.

Victor Turner's analysis of pilgrimage suggests that there are common elements, for example, liminality and *communitas*, within all forms of pilgrimages. Unlike the other two approaches Turner's model is flexible, presenting pure, ideal types which can be subtly varied in reality. One of the aims of this study is to address the question of the applicability of these models to Israelite/Jewish sacred space. The models will be tested both in respect of their applicability to ethnographic material and in the light of a broad structuralist analysis of Israelite/Jewish culture.

This book is primarily interested, due to its basis in structuralism, in the models of thought used at different times in Israelite/Jewish history. It focuses on the synchronic aspects, that is, the models used in a particular period, and the diachronic, that is, the way that the models change over time (and space). Although each chapter examines the details of particular ethnographic uses of sacred space, the particular details are secondary to the conceptualization of them. Thus in the chapter on pilgrimage, the analysis focuses on the way that pilgrimage was conceptualized rather than on the experience of particular pilgrims. The analysis of individual experiences and motivations is, in any case, impossible as this type of material is not available for study from the biblical and rabbinic periods.

This book demonstrates the relationship between the structural models developed in biblical myths and that developed in regard to sacred space. On the basis of structuralist theory, it is argued that the same underlying structure will be found in all phenomena created within a single culture or subculture. This is demonstrated here on the synchronic level. The models of sacred space developed in the biblical text are structured in the same way as in the narrative texts. Similarly, the transformations in rabbinic narrative texts are also mirrored in rabbinic sacred space. Structuralist theory also suggests that diachronic transformations in underlying structure should be consistent at each synchronic point. This latter thesis is the primary argument addressed and demonstrated in this volume.

The analysis of sacred space is divided into a number of conceptual categories which are examined separately. The second chapter examines the models used in biblical texts, the centralized and decentralized models. It suggests that these two models are ultimately based on the same underlying structure, with, however, a difference in emphasis, based on different though interrelated cultural contexts. The chapter also examines the work of Levinson, particularly in respect of his application of Eliade's models to biblical sacred space.[4]

The third chapter examines the development of these models within rabbinic texts. It focuses on the transformations in model which accompanied the destruction of the Temple in Jerusalem and the establishment of the synagogue as the primary sacred space. This chapter examines the role of cultural transformation in underlying structural transformation. It examines the interrelationship between the model of sacred space and the conceptualization of the divine, demonstrating that the transformations in the understanding of God reflect the reemphasis on the decentralized model. The work of Harold Turner (1979) is also assessed. The analysis suggests that although Turner's model is broadly applicable to the transformations within Israelite/Jewish sacred space, his ethnocentric presuppositions in favor of the *domus dei* lead him to misinterpret some of the data.

Chapter 4 examines the role of pilgrimage within Jewish sacred space. It is written as an extended critique of Victor Turner's model, touching, however, on the work of other anthropologists as well. It examines the applicability of Turner's concepts of liminality, transformation, and *communitas* to pilgrimage from different points in Jewish history, that is, biblical, rabbinic, Hasidic, Moroccan, and modern pilgrimages. The analysis suggests that due to the underlying structural model, which does not allow movement between categories, the three elements are not significant or essential characteristics of pilgrimage in Israelite or Jewish cultures.

The fifth chapter examines the use of sacred space in modern synagogues. Although it is based on ethnographic fieldwork and thus includes a degree of descriptive material, it is primarily concerned with the models employed which are exemplified in the use of space. It focuses on the differences between the use of sacred space in Orthodox and non-Orthodox synagogues. It suggests that within modern synagogues there is a transformation back to a form of the centralized model (exemplified by the Temple), which leads to a greater exclusivity in access to sacred space. Although this transformation is more pronounced in Liberal and Reform synagogues, which have a higher degree of openness, and therefore weaker boundaries, it is also found in Conservative and Orthodox synagogues.

Chapter 6 uses gender as a means of examining the diachronic development of conceptual models of sacred space. It argues that within centralized sacred space women are excluded on the basis of intrinsic qualities, while in decentralized sacred space they are excluded due to extrinsic qualities. It also argues that within modern sacred space many aspects of women's access are returning to using intrinsic qualities as the basis for exclusion or inclusion, mirroring the return to centralized sacred space discussed in chapter 5.

The overall theoretical perspective which underlies this book is a variant of French structuralism. Although it is largely based on the work of Claude Lévi-Strauss, it is also shaped by that of Leach, Hugh-Jones, T. Turner, and Wagner.[5] The primary interests of the book are therefore the underlying structural equations or patterns of Israelite/Jewish culture. The particular ethnographic aspects of the discussion are of secondary importance.

In Lévi-Strauss's work, structuralist analysis has mainly focused on mythology. The scope of mythology has been extended to include other aspects of cultural classification, for example, totemism. This book moves in a different direction. Although models of space and geography are encompassed in the general rubric of cultural classification, they also include a strong material and ritual (actional component).[6] Ritual, however, may be seen to belong to a different category of phenomena than myth or cultural classification. This is implied by Lévi-Strauss's suggestion that myth and ritual work in opposing directions. He suggests that myths create disunity while rituals create unity. Other scholars, however, argue that the two are complementary modes of communication.[7] From this point of view both myth and ritual are means of manipulating and organizing information based on the underlying structural equations.[8] This latter understanding of the relationship between myth and ritual, at least within the Israelite/Jewish framework, is supported by my previous research into Hebrew mythology and ritual.[9]

It is suggested here that like myth, ritual can be broken down into components, termed ritemes, which are comprised of actions or behavior associated with liturgy or ideology.[10] Ritemes are combined in various configurations which express or are based on the underlying structure. It is through the combination of the ritemes and the oppositions of sets of ritemes that the ritual communicates.[11]

On this basis a particular riteme has no one set meaning or role in the pattern of opposition. The meaning and the role are contextually determined by the structural configuration. Like phonemes and the combination of phonemes into a word, the meaning assigned to a particular riteme or a set of ritemes is arbitrary – there is no absolute or necessary association between the two. It is both cultural and contextual, and it is liable to transformation. In this sense the relationship between the riteme and meaning is analogous to the relationship between the signifier and the signified. It is culture and context specific. Because components of ritual are both materially and ideologically based, they tend to change in relation to transformations in material culture. Using the analogy of the *bricoleur*, the ritemes will be composed of those things and concepts which are available. It is the configuration rather than the ritemes themselves that is structurally significant.[12]

For the sake of clarity, elements of culture, for example ritual or myth, can be examined on four interrelated levels: S^1, S^2, S^3, and N. Each one of the levels is progressively more culturally specific and more conscious. S^1 is the most abstract and universal level of structure. Lévi-Strauss argued that at its most fundamental level, underlying structure is based on biological structures of the brain. As such, these structures are the common genetic inheritance of all human beings. S^1 is completely abstract and contentless. It has the potential to organize information, rather than either actual categorization or a method of categorization. Although Lévi-Strauss suggests that these basic structures are binary, it is likely that there may be more complex possibilities as well.

S^2, the next level of underlying structure is still abstract. It is a basic equation with no specific content. It is at the S^2 level that the nature of the relationship between categories is established. In a binary system there are three main types of relations between categories: positive (+), negative (-), and neutral (n). These relations are ideal types along a polar axis, with a wide range of gradations between each type. Positive qualitative valence means that information will be shared by the categories, that is, they will overlap either completely or partially. Negative qualitative valence means that the two categories are mutually exclusive, that is, there is no overlap between them. Neutral qualitative valence means that there is no necessary relation between the categories. A piece of information may be in both or may not be. S^2 is the level at which the nature of the relationship between the categories is set, but no information is placed in the categories. S^2 is culture or culture area specific.

S^3 is the level of structure at which information is added into the categories based on the qualitative valence established at S^2. Any type of information, whether material or symbolic will be categorized at this level. It is this level where ritemes are developed in relationship to ritual and mythemes in myth. Because this level is related to specific information, it is highly culture specific.

N, or the narrative level, is the highest. It is the level of the narrative of a story or the progression of actions in a ritual. N is highly culturally and chronologically specific. It is created out of cultural elements which are available in a particular time and place. The N is also the conscious level of the phenomena.

Although all these levels are significant to anthropological research, structuralist analysis is particularly interested in S^2 and S^3. Through the analysis of S^3 in a wide range of phenomena – for example myth or ritual – from a single cultural community, the cultural equation can be abstracted. Although structuralist theory suggests that there will be an unlimited number of examples at S^3 (this level can encompass any new information), there will be a limited set of equations at S^2 (these equations may possibly be reducible to a single basic equation in each culture or subculture). These equations can be compared cross-culturally with related and unrelated societies or communities, or diachronically in terms of transformations within structure in a single cultural community through its historical development.

Both with respect to underlying structure, transformations occur on the upper three levels, S^2, S^3, and N. Transformations on the N level will occur frequently, perhaps any time that the myth is told (unless it is written down) or the ritual is performed. These transformations are not structurally significant and do not necessarily reflect structural transformations. Transformations at S^3 occur due to changes in context, for example historical or geographical. Thus for example, at one point in time a neighboring nation may have a particular valence because it is significant, perhaps as an enemy or a friend. If, however, this significance changes (perhaps they have no relationship at all) then their structural categorization may change. They may move to the other category or not be categorized at all. On a geographic level, changes in external environment may lead to objects being differentially categorized; underlying structure uses what is available to it. Transformations at the level of S^2 are much rarer. This level of structure tends to be conservative. It can transform in two ways, either through emphasis or in respect of the qualitative valence. While the latter form only occurs in response (or in relation) to significant cultural transformations, transformation in emphasis is more frequent and can result from small cultural developments.

One feature of structure that is especially significant is mediation. Mediation refers to the way in which intermediate elements which are not easily categorized are dealt with or considered. It is closely related to the qualitative valence of the equation and allows subtle shading in respect of it. Mediators typically include elements of both categories and thus, depending on the system, may allow elements to pass from one category to the other. In systems with positive or neutral qualitative valences, mediators will usually be viewed positively, because the systems are built on either interchangeable categories or on non-exclusive permeable categories. In cultures with negative qualitative valence, mediators will tend to be negated or removed because they imply that the categories may not be mutually exclusive.

The aspect of transformation of structural elements due to historical changes in cultural context is one of two areas of transformation. Transformation can also occur within a myth or a ritual. Traditional structuralism de-emphasizes this aspect of transformation by focusing on the metaphoric aspect of cultural phenomena. This approach emphasizes categories built on similarity, joining together those elements which are similar and examining the categories which they are opposed or related to. The primary aim of the analysis is the nature and quality of the relation – all such relations are viewed synchronically and thus the aspect of internal transformation is ignored. A second avenue of analysis is the metonymic. This approach focuses on the way in which elements are combined, and the order of presentation. The metonymic analysis of ritual focuses on the progression of actions within a single ritual. This approach allows the analysis to reveal patterns of transformation, in riteme, mytheme, or actor. This question is especially relevant in respect of pilgrimage (or any rite of passage) which both on the N and S^3 levels involves transformation. Both the metaphorical and metonymic elements are used in the structuralist approach used here.[13]

One aspect of structuralist theory, and critique of structuralist theory which needs to be addressed, is the question of nature and culture. Although this dichotomy has been emphasized in some structuralist analyses, it is not assumed that it is universal or the basic structural opposition. As suggested above, it is argued here that the levels of S^1 and S^2 are contentless and therefore at its widest level there is no necessary opposition between any two elements. At S^3, the first level at which this dichotomy could be found, the relationship between the categories, that is whether nature and culture are opposed or overlap, will depend on the particular culture which is being studied. Although many cultures may include nature and culture in their categories, the nature of the relation is culture specific – with no universal specification.

Part of the problem may lie in a confusion of terms. In the *Logic of Incest* it was suggested that the structuralist theory of culture is based on a 'myth of societal development' (Kunin, 1996: 23–4). This myth is based on a perceived disjuncture between potential and actual, that is, between what is humanly possible and what is culturally acceptable. This disjuncture, which is the basis of the crisis underlying cultural phenomena, may be considered in some cases or cultures to be a nature–culture dialectic and therefore, opposition, but it need not be. Nature may be understood to be as controlled as is human society.

Within Israelite culture, which is based on categories with impermeable boundaries, the symbolic complex which can be defined as nature is used in a variety of ways, depending on the other symbols or mythemes with which it is associated. In a wide range of texts there is no essential difference between nature and culture. They are organized and structured in the same way. Thus animals and time are categorized based on the same conceptual equation of A (not) B. In other cases they are used to emphasize the difference between elements. Thus Esau and the nations are equated with nature and Jacob and Israel are equated with culture (Kunin, 1996: 112–19). Thus the nature–culture dialectic is not intrinsic to Israelite culture, but is used contextually depending on the structural or narrative needs.

The methodology used for structuralist analysis of ritual is similar to that of myth. A wide range of related rituals, in this case connected with sacred space, are analyzed. Each ritual is broken down into its constituent units or ritemes, which are then associated with similar ritemes from other rituals. The relationship of categories or bundles of ritemes are then examined in order to abstract the underlying structural equations. The transformation of particular ritemes within a single ritual, and the development of the ritemes and the relationship between ritemes as rituals transformed over time are also then analyzed.

Several aspects of the Israelite/Jewish underlying structures found in narrative myths are necessary for the understanding of sacred space. Israelite structure, S^2, is based on mutually exclusive categories with a negative relation. Each category is absolutely distinct with no overlap and no movement between categories. Within this structure mediators are negative, as positive mediators would suggest that categories are permeable.[14]

At the S^3 level of Israelite structure two of the primary areas which are emphasized within the structure are the relation between Israel and the nations, and endogamy. These two areas represent the same structural phenomena with, however, a difference in emphasis. The opposition between Israel and the nations, that is, that the two are qualitatively and categorically distinct reflects the macro-level of opposition. It emphasizes a strong external boundary, while minimizing internal divisions. Endogamy when taken to its logical conclusion – as it is in many myths in Genesis –

emphasizes the smallest internal units, the family, and the need to marry as closely to the family as possible.[15] Many of the narrative myths in the Bible emphasize endogamy, suggesting that it was more culturally problematic. It is likely that this is due to the problem of cultural cohesiveness of the community after the return from exile.

In the rabbinic period S^2 goes through a zero transformation. The underlying structural equation remains A (not) B. The emphasis on S^3 in respect of Israel/nations and endogamy, however, shifts. Endogamy no longer appears to be a significant cultural problem. The expectation remains, but its fulfillment no longer is an issue. The element of Israel and the nations is emphasized on the individual level, with texts emphasizing individual transformation and rebirth. These texts emphasize the qualitative difference between Israel and the nations in spite of outward appearances.

Although it is not suggested that models of sacred space will transform for exactly the same reasons, it is argued that they will transform according to the same pattern. Just as the S^2 level remains consistent through both the biblical and rabbinic periods in respect of myth, so it should remain constant in respect of sacred space. Patterns of emphasis, however, on the S^3 level will change in response to external context. Sacred space, *qua* geography, is closely related to the concepts of nationhood, thus endogamy is a factor in its transformation. It is argued that the emphasis in models of sacred space will be related to the nature of external boundaries and possibility of movement from one domain to the other.

Notes

1. See for example: Eliade, M. (1971) *The Myth of the Eternal Return, or Cosmos and History*, Princeton: Princeton University Press; Turner, H. *From Temple to Meeting House: The Phenomenology and Theology of Places of Worship*, The Hague: Mouton Publishers; Victor Turner and Edith Turner (1978) *Image and Pilgrimage in Christian Culture*, New York: Columbia University Press.
2. One good example is Ezekiel 5:5. This text often used to show that the navel symbolism is found in the Bible. The translation of the term טבור as 'navel,' however, has been challenged (see Talmon, Sh. (1976) 'הארץ" והשיטה המשווה טבור"' [Tabûr Ha'arez and the Comparative Method] in *Tabriz* 45, 163–77). Even if the translation of the word is correct, a more literal reading, i.e. as center, might be a more appropriate understanding, without importing concepts foreign to the text. Talmon argues that none of the significant elements discussed by Eliade are supported by the biblical text.
3. The *domus dei* is essentially characterized by many of the elements developed in Eliade's work.
4. Levenson, J. (1985) *Sinai and Zion: An Entry into the Jewish Bible*, San Francisco: Harper and Row.
5. See for example: Lévi-Strauss, C. (1963) *Structural Anthropology*, New York: Basic Books; (1969) *The Raw and the Cooked*, New York: Harper & Row; (1976) *Structural Anthropology II*, New York: Basic Books; (1988) *The Jealous Potter*, Chicago: University of Chicago Press; Leach, E. (1961) *Rethinking Anthropology*, London: Athelone Press; (1967) *The Structural Study of Myth and Totemism*,

London: Tavistock Publications; Leach, E. and Aycock, A. (1983) *Structuralist Interpretations of Biblical Myth*, Cambridge: Cambridge University Press; Hugh-Jones, S. (1979) *The Palm and the Pleiades: Initiation and Cosmology in Northwest Amazonia*, Cambridge: Cambridge University Press; Turner, T. (1985) 'Animal Symbolism, Totemism and the Structure of Myth' in G. Urton (ed.), *Animal Myths and Metaphors in South America*, Salt Lake City: University of Utah Press; Wagner, R. *The Invention of Culture*, Chicago: University of Chicago Press.

6. See: Tambiah, S. J. (1985) *Culture, Thought and Social Action: An Anthropological Perspective*, Cambridge: Harvard University Press.

7. For discussions of the question of whether ritual is a form of communication see: Bell, C. (1992) *Ritual Theory, Ritual Practice*, New York: Oxford University Press; Humphrey, C. and Laidlaw, J. (1994) *The Archetypal Actions of Ritual*, Oxford: Clarendon Press. While it is agreed that ritual is not necessarily a conscious form of communication, and Bell's focus on practice is particularly oriented to the conscious level, it is suggested that ritual communicates unconscious patterns and relationships.

8. Smith's definition of ritual adds a further component, on the conscious level, which is related to Lévi-Strauss's definition of myth, and applicable to the understanding of ritual developed here. He suggests that 'ritual is a means of performing the way things ought to be in conscious tension to the way things are in such a way that this ritualised perfection is recollected in the ordinary, uncontrolled, course of things' (Smith, J. Z. (1982) *Imagining Religion*, Chicago: University of Chicago Press, p. 63).

9. See: Kunin, S. *The Logic of Incest: A Structuralist Analysis of Hebrew Mythology*, Sheffield: Sheffield Academic Press, p. 279.

10. The distinction between actions and actions associated with myth or liturgy is important. Although many ritemes do have a conscious mythological or liturgical component, which often functions as implicit myth, there are also ethnographic examples of rituals with no conscious explanation or liturgical elaboration. See for example the discussion of Dorze ritual in: Sperber, D. (1975) *Rethinking Symbolism*, Cambridge: Cambridge University Press.

11. This is not to suggest that rituals do not have significant elements other than cognitive models. Rituals also clearly include communal, emotional, and actional elements. See for example: Turner, V. (1967) *The Forest of Symbols: Aspects of Ndembu Ritual*, Ithaca: Cornell University Press. A good summary of this issue is presented in Bloch, M. *From Blessing to Violence: History and ideology in the Circumcision Ritual of the Merina of Madagascar*, Cambridge: Cambridge University Press. Elsewhere, Bloch focuses on another level of interpretation, suggesting that the significant feature of ritual and religion as a whole is the exercise of power. See: Bloch, M. (1989) *Ritual, History and Power: Selected Papers in Anthropology*, London: Athlone. A sophisticated discussion of ritual and symbolism which underlies much of the analysis presented here is found in: Sperber, 1975.

12. Lévi-Strauss coined the words *bricolage* and *bricoleur* to describe the process through which content is added to structure. Like the *bricolage*, whatever is available in the cultural context (new or transformed) can be used to exemplify the underlying structural patterns. See Lévi-Strauss, C. (1966) *The Savage Mind*, Chicago: University of Chicago Press, pp. 16–36.

13. See Kunin, 1996: 21; Turner, T. (1977) 'Narrative Structure and Mythopoesis: A Critique and Reformulation of Structuralist Concepts of Myth, Narrative and Poetics,' in *Arethusa* **10.1**, p. 111.

14. A good example of this pattern is found in respect to Israelite food rules. Each type of food or animal is placed in one category or the other. Thus category A includes animals which chew their cud and have cloven hooves; category B includes all animals which do not. Movement between A and B is impossible. A pig appears to be a mediator; it contains elements of each category, that is it has cloven hooves (A), but does not chew its cud (B). Since mediators are negative within the Israelite system, the pig cannot remain a mediator. It is transformed to strongly negative in order to emphasize the boundaries. See Douglas, M. (1975) *Implicit Meanings: Essays in Anthropology*, London: Routledge & Kegan Paul, pp. 249–73.

15. Whether the Israelites actually practiced endogamy in a strong sense, or indeed at all, is questionable. It is certainly very difficult to demonstrate prior to the return from the Babylonian exile. The redacted version of the biblical text, however, does imply that there was an ideological preference for endogamy (See Kunin, 1996: 49–61). By the rabbinic period endogamy was increasingly enforced both internally and externally. This pattern has significantly changed only in the twentieth century, in which increasing numbers of Jews are not marrying within the Jewish community.

2 Biblical Sacred Space

The biblical text lays the foundation for models of sacred space developed by Jewish culture as it has developed and been transformed diachronically and geographically.[1] Although the centralized model, focusing on the Tabernacle or Temple, is the primary model developed in the text, evidence of other models, for example the decentralized or localized models, are also presented. This chapter examines all of the variant models and shows how they represent related transformations of Israelite underlying structure. It suggests that the particular model emphasized reflects Israel's wider cultural context, that is, where the external boundaries are strong, internal boundaries are fragmented, and where the external boundaries are weak, internal boundaries are centralized.

The biblical text develops centralized sacred space through two related models: the dynamic and the static.[2] The dynamic model is presented primarily in Exodus, Leviticus, and Numbers. Although it centers on the Tent of Meeting, it includes the entire Israelite camp. The sacred place exemplified by the camp is not tied to any particular location, rather as the camp moves the sacred place moves. The static model, the Temple of Solomon, is described in 1 Kings. Unlike the dynamic model it is in a fixed unique location, that is, the Temple Mount in Jerusalem. In spite of this difference both variations share the same underlying structure.

Dynamic Sacred Space

Biblical dynamic sacred space was characterized by five qualitatively distinct zones.[3] The plan of the Tabernacle and Court is depicted in Figure 2.1.[4] The Holy of Holies (קדש קדשים) was the most sacred zone. It was a curtained-off section on the western end of the Tabernacle (משקן) or the מועד אהל) which housed the Ark of the Covenant.[5] The next zone, the eastern section of the Tabernacle, was called 'the Holy' (הקדש) in Exodus 26:33. The Tabernacle itself was entered through a door on its eastern wall. The Tabernacle was surrounded by the Court (החצר) which also had an entrance on the eastern wall (see Exodus 27:9–19). The Court itself may have been further subdivided into zones of greater and lesser holiness.[6]

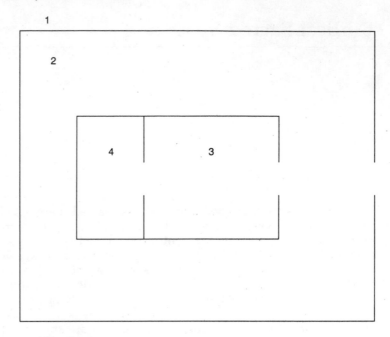

1 The Camp
2 The Court
3 The Holy
4 The Holy of Holies

Figure 2.1 Dynamic Centralized Sacred Space

These zones can initially be characterized by a set of concentric circles (depicted in Figure 2.2) with the Holy of Holies in the center and the larger circles representing the progressively less holy zones. The utilization of the category of purity (טהורה), used in several texts as a limiting factor in respect of access to different levels of sacred place, regarding the camp, suggests that the camp be included in this model as the largest extension of sacred place. Purity or impurity is the element which can lead to exclusion from holy precincts.

Several texts indicate that a certain degree of purity was expected within the camp. In those cases where the impurity came through contagion, for example contact with a corpse, the impurity could be cleansed in a seven-day process (see for example Numbers 19:14–20). The text states that anyone who fails to cleanse himself will be cut off from the congregation because that person has made the holy place unclean. More permanent forms of impurity, for example leprosy, however, led to exclusion from the camp on the basis of that impurity. This is emphasized in Leviticus 13:45 through the repetition of the word טמא, 'impure,' which said at the time that the leper is excluded from the camp.

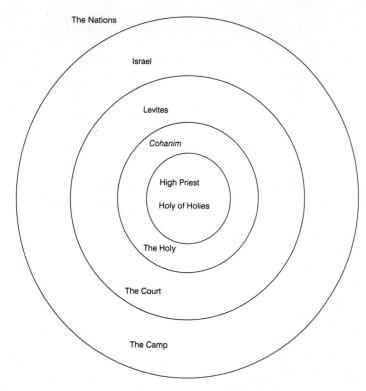

Figure 2.2 Concentric Model of Sacred Space

The structural relationship between the zones is highlighted through analysis of access and exclusion. Each of the zones, concluding with the boundaries of the camp, was progressively more exclusive. Access to the Holy of Holies was restricted to the High Priest. He, however, was only allowed to enter it in a ritual context on the Day of Atonement. Only priests were allowed to enter the Holy. As in the case of access to the Holy of Holies, this was only permitted in the context of cultic ritual. Only ritually clean laity were permitted into the court. There is, however, some scholarly debate about access of laity to the court. Milgrom argues that the laity were given full access to the court. Haran, however, suggests that the court was divided into a zone open to the laity and one, between the altar and Tabernacle, which was restricted to the priests.[7] Those who were unclean were excluded from the camp. This use of categories of purity as a basis for inclusion or exclusion suggests that just as the structural elements of the camp and Tabernacle are increasingly holy, human beings are analogously categorized as relatively pure or impure, the High Priest being the most pure and the laity being the least pure. The nations of the world, those people outside of the camp, are impure, that is, in opposition to the relative or progressive purity of Israel.

Thus the texts present a model of sacred place consisting of progressively smaller domains which are opposed one to another on the basis of holiness and purity. Each ring is more exclusive and holy with respect to the ring outside of it, and less exclusive and holy with respect to the ring inside of it.

The texts suggest that the widest zone of holiness and purity is the camp itself. It is set into structural opposition with the world, which is the realm of the profane and the impure. There is no suggestion in the text that the circles of relative holiness extend beyond the camp's boundaries. If a similarly structured model is extended to people, other than those Israelites who have become impure either permanently or temporarily, it is likely that the nations or people of the world are categorized as permanently impure, analogous to the leper. They are structurally equivalent to the world outside of the camp which is set in qualitative opposition to Israel. Just as the circles of holiness end with the camp, those of purity end with the Israelites.

The opposition between Israel and the nations, and the camp and the world reflects the same underlying structural pattern. In each case the categories are exclusive and unbridgeable. Each category is so defined that it excludes the other. The camp, for example, is the realm of the pure and the world that of the impure. Any element which seems to mediate or bridge the two categories must be transformed to fit fully in one category or the other. Thus the impure, persons or objects, cannot remain in the camp; they must be purified or removed. The leper must either be proven not to be a leper to be allowed to remain in the camp, which represents the category of the pure and Israel, or he must be shown to be a leper and excluded from the camp, which represents the category of the impure and the nations. The opposition between unbridgeable categories exemplifies the structural equation A (not) B. Structuralist analysis suggests that this equation is characteristic of Israelite culture as a whole.[8]

The structural oppositions between the camp and the world, holy and profane, Israel and the nations, suggest a refinement in the model of sacred space presented thus far. Structuralist theory suggests that structural models tend to be repetitive, with each level exemplifying the same type of structural relationship or equation. Thus since the structural relationship at the widest level reflects a pattern of opposition based on the equation 'A (not) B,' it is likely that the internal oppositions will also reflect this structural relationship.

If the elements which make up the inner circles are examined, a similar pattern is evident. In each case the internal circles include all members of the next largest circle. Thus at the widest level the camp is opposed to the world. At this widest level the camp includes all of the different elements which make up the Israelite community from the Ark to the boundary of the camp. Within the camp the constituent elements are divided into two opposing categories: the court is set in opposition to the rest of the camp. Within the court, the Tabernacle is opposed to the rest of the court, and within the Tabernacle, the Holy of Holies is opposed to the Holy. This final opposition is supported by the names given to each zone; the terms emphasize a qualitative difference and relationship.

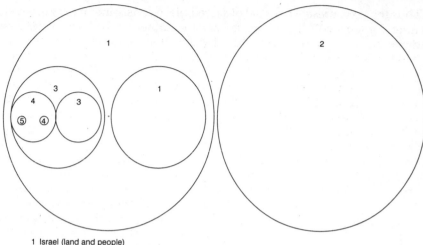

1 Israel (land and people)
2 Nations (lands and peoples)
3 Levites and Tabernacle Court
4 *Cohanim* and The Holy
5 High Priest and the Holy of Holies

Figure 2.3 Segmentary Model of Sacred Space

This structural model is also found in respect to the divisions within the Israelites and their respective access to sacred space. A structural diagram of both of these realms is presented in Figure 2.3. On the widest level the Israelites are in opposition to the nations. At this widest level the term Israelite is inclusive including the tribes, the Levites, and the priests. The Levites (including the priests) are set in opposition to the rest of the Israelites. The process culminates with the High Priest. As in the case of categorization of space, the final terms, priests and High Priest, suggest both difference and relationship.

This model presented here is similar to that used by anthropologists to diagram the phenomena of segmentary opposition. In many respects, Israelite models of space and humanity reflect this sociological phenomena.[9] Segmentary opposition describes a system in which elements within similar cultural categories, depending on the circumstances and cultural context, are either set in opposition to each other or joined together in opposition to elements within a higher level category. This model is best understood using a genealogical metaphor. This genealogical framework is presented in Figure 2.4. At the highest level, A and B, the group is divided into two opposing segments; these may be two families, lineages, or clans. At each lower level the segment is subdivided into two smaller segments, for example A1 and A2.[10] People included in the lowest level segment A1a are in direct opposition to those included in A1b. If, however, a person from A2 is in conflict with someone from A1a, then A1a and A1b will combine in opposition to all of the segments (not illustrated) of A2. Similarly, if some

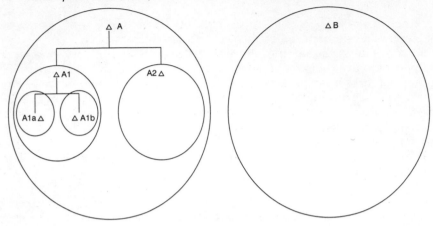

Figure 2.4 Segmentary Opposition

one from B harms someone from A1a, all of the segments of A will unite in opposition to B.[11] Thus the level called into play depends on the level of the opposing unit, the higher level the segment, the higher level the opposition. This model, however, does not depend on actual conflict or opposition; it can also be used, as it is here, to depict a method of relating distinct categories cognitively. Each category is structurally opposed to a category of the same cultural level. Figure 2.5 depicts the abstract segmentary opposition model of sacred space.

The model is superior to that of concentric circles in several ways. First, it provides a diagrammatic presentation of the structural equation and illustrates the application of the equation at varying cultural levels. This is in

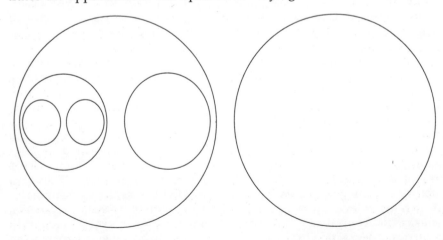

Figure 2.5 Abstract Segmentary Model

keeping with the expectations of structuralist analysis which suggests that all levels will be structured by the same underlying equation.

Second, it demonstrates the nature of the oppositions. Each category is set in opposition to a category at the same cultural level. Thus it is structurally appropriate to set Israel in opposition to the nations, or the camp to the world, but inappropriate to set the High Priest in opposition to the nations. The concentric circle model only depicts the aspect of graded holiness. It does not indicate the nature of the structural relationship between the different categories or levels.

Third, it clearly indicates the relationship of the part to the whole. The wider circle includes the inner circles. The inner circles, that is A1 and A2, are together equivalent to A. The concentric model implies that the inner circles are separate and distinct from the respective larger circles. It suggests that the Levites are separate from Israel and the priests from the Levites. The segmentary model, however, indicates that Israel includes both the Levites and the non-Levites; both are Israel when opposed to the nations. Similarly, the camp includes everything within it when opposed to the world. The category only comes into play based on the level of opposition.

Finally, the segmentary model avoids one significant pitfall suggested by the concentric model, that is the extension of graded holiness outside of the camp. The concentric model creates the possibility that circles of relative holiness may continue indefinitely beyond the boundaries of the camp; this blurs the distinction between categories and thus blurs the structural equation. The segmentary model, which opposes unbridgeable categories, emphasizes and strengthens the underlying structural equation.

Thus far, this discussion has brought together several different cultural categories, that is holiness, purity, space, and communal organization. Each of these categories is closely related in defining and exemplifying the oppositions upon which the system is built. Thus, the Holy of Holies, a category in space, is associated with the highest degree of holiness (emphasized by its name), the High Priest, and the highest level of ritual purity. These categories are set in structural opposition to categories of the same cultural level, for example, in space and holiness the Holy of Holies is in opposition to the Holy, and communally the High Priest to the priests. In both these examples the names of the categories emphasize the oppositions. In his discussion of graded holiness Jenson also discusses aspects of the sacrificial cult and time. Jenson argues that each of these categories is based on a similar conceptualization (1992: 130–5). His argument is consistent with the expectations of structuralist analysis which suggests that all areas of culture will be similarly structured.

The oppositions within the personal sphere are developed on several levels in respect of its relation to sacred place. This is clearly developed in the placement of both the Levitical families and the tribes around the Tabernacle and the court.[12] This is illustrated in Figure 2.6. The Levites are divided, on the basis of genealogy, into four groupings, Aaronites (Kohathites descended from Aaron), the remaining Kohathites, Gershonites, and Merariites. Each group is positioned on a different side of the Tabernacle.

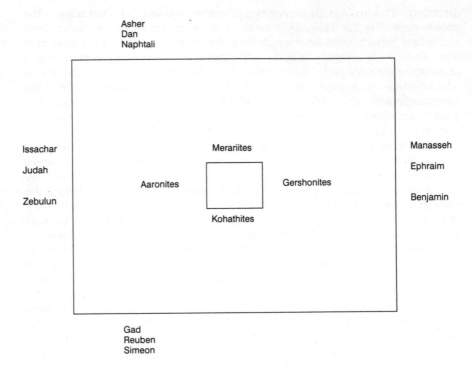

Figure 2.6 Placement of Levitical Families and Tribes around the Tabernacle

The Aaronites are on the eastern side of the Tabernacle (Numbers 3:38). The remaining Kohathites are on the south. The Gershonites are on the west and the Merariites are placed on the north. It is likely that these placements have symbolic value both in respect of the Israelite categorization of space and of the Levitical groups. Priority is given to the Aaronites who are placed on the eastern side of the Tabernacle. Jenson suggests that the family of the Kohathites and particularly those descended from Aaron are given hierarchical priority due to the presence of Aaron. It is perhaps of equal value to ask why Aaron was placed in this particular family in the genealogy, that is, descended from the second son of Levi rather than the first, as might have been expected, based on the principle (or expectation) of primogeniture found in many biblical texts. This genealogical placement, however, is consistent with the structural and narrative model developed in Genesis, in which the chosen line always descends from a younger son, for example Jacob, as opposed to Esau.[13]

Although Jenson suggests that the eastern side is the privileged side he does not present an argument explaining this valuation, other perhaps than its location, closest to the entrance of the Tabernacle (which faced an easterly direction). This answer, however, begs the question as it does not resolve the problem of why the Tabernacle faced that particular direction rather than any other. Structuralist analysis of Hebrew myth suggests that each direction had a qualitative value in Israelite culture.[14] Movement (and orientation) in a westerly direction was positive, while movement to the east was negative. Thus the placement of the Aaronites on the eastern side of the Tabernacle reflects a positive or preferential valuation because they face west (toward the Tabernacle) and move in a western direction to enter it.

It is possible that the Gershonites were placed on the western side (oriented in an eastward direction) due to their descent from the eldest son, a structurally negative genealogical position (mythologically, the first born were excluded from the chosen line of descent). The placement clearly indicates their structural opposition to the Aaronites. The Kohathites, on the southern side (oriented to the north) of the Tabernacle create the possibility of mediation, a situation which is antithetical to the structural equation because it suggests that the categories are bridgeable. They are descended from the same line as Aaron and therefore appear to be, at least in part, in the same category. Structural integrity between categories is created and emphasized, on the narrative level, through the texts relating to Korah's rebellion (Numbers 16–17).[15] These texts create qualitative distance in the place of genealogical distance. The Merariites, on the northern side (oriented south), are not structurally problematic as they descend from a distinct genealogical line.

The placement of the tribes around the court reflects a similar structural pattern.[16] Judah, the tribe of the Davidic dynasty, is placed directly facing the entrance of the court, that is on the eastern side. As Jenson suggests, this placement may reflect a conscious political agenda (1992: 137). Judah is set in direct opposition to Ephraim, who may represent the Northern Kingdom.[17] The eastern side as a whole is composed of Leah's youngest sons, fourth through sixth in order of birth, that is, Issachar, Judah, and Zebulun. The western side is composed of Rachel's children or grandchildren, all of whom are either first or second born, that is, Manasseh, Ephraim, and Benjamin. The opposition may reflect both the pattern of relative rejection of the first born and a rejection of the favored line – both of which are consistent with structural models developed in Genesis.

The symbolic value of Leah and Rachel, however, is inverted. In Genesis, Rachel's position as younger daughter was emphasized and her children, primarily Joseph, represented the chosen line of descent (Kunin, 1995: 120–3). This symbolic value was part of a more general structural set in which the younger son was set in structural opposition to the elder. In this text, however, Leah's youngest sons are given the privileged position. This possibly reflects the element of *bricolage* which is essential to the process of expression of underlying structural patterns. Conscious political realities of the editorial present shaped the qualitative valuation of tribes, with Judah being the most positive and significant.[18] This valuation is used within the underlying structure to emphasize the opposition between those tribes placed on the east and west sides of the court.

The tribes placed on the north (Asher, Dan, and Naphtali) and south (Gad, Reuben, and Simeon) are also consistent with the Levitical placement and structural expectations. In the Levitical placement, the southern side had a negative component, that is, the rejection of Korah.[19] This negative aspect is preserved in respect of the tribes placed on the southern side with the exception of Gad. Gad, as a child of one of the concubines appears to be structurally less significant than either the children of Rachel or Leah. Gad is placed on the south to fill a space (that is, each side has three tribes) rather than due to any intrinsic symbolic significance. Similarly, as in the Levitical case, the tribes on the north, all descended from concubines, are structurally insignificant. Both Reuben and Simeon, however, are children of Leah and thus create a similar structural problem to that created by the Kohathites. As in the case of the Kohathites, Reuben and Simeon are possible mediators, bridging categories. Similarly, they are presented negatively in Genesis (for example, Reuben in Genesis 35:21–2, 49:4, and Simeon in 49:5–6). Thus the negative texts create and strengthen boundaries not created by the genealogical relations. The placement of both the Kohathites, and Reuben and Simeon in the south suggests that movement in a northerly direction had a negative component. As suggested, those tribes placed on the northern side of the court, Asher, Dan, and Naphtali, all descendants of Bilhah and Zilpah, seem to be structurally insignificant, which further suggests that movement south was not structurally negative.

Jenson's discussion, however, emphasizes the concentric aspects of the model. Thus, in his discussion of the 'personal dimension' he lists the different categories in hierarchical order. The model begins with Moses in the center and culminates with the nations as the furthest from the cult (1992: 117). Although Moses is certainly unique and the founder of the cult, his inclusion in the model actually clouds the relations between the levels of hierarchy, both in a concentric and the opposition model. The High Priest is associated with the central aspect of the cult, that is the Holy of Holies, with no figure equivalent to Moses in opposition to him. Jenson actually recognizes this distinction when he distinguishes between Moses and Joshua, on the one hand, as political leaders, and Aaron and Eleazar, on the other, as leaders of the priestly hierarchy (1992: 117). His concentric emphasis focuses on the hierarchical aspects of the structure without analyzing the structural relations between the different categories, and thus on occasion imports elements from one structural category to another. Moses, primarily, stands at the head of the set of political relations, while Aaron stands at the head of the set of priestly relations.

Jenson's discussion of 'Israel and the Nations' (1992: 145–7) raises a significant challenge to a purely concentric model. It suggests that rather than being related as concentric circles, suggesting an opposition of part to the whole, Israel, as a whole, is in opposition to the nations, as qualitatively and structurally distinct units. Jenson uses the analogy of animals (also used by Mary Douglas (1975: 267–8)) to emphasize the distinctions. The priests are aligned with those animals fit for sacrifice, the Israelites with clean animals, and the nations with unclean animals (Jenson, 1992: 146). The category of unclean animals is distinct from that of clean animals. It cannot be modelled using concentric circles, rather it must be modelled using unbridgeable categories (circles) set in structural opposition one to the other. The category of unclean animals, as the extension of a concentric model can never include clean animals; the two categories are conceptually distinct. Thus his argument supports the move to the alternative segmentary model.

Jenson limits his model and concept of conceptual categorization to P. He argues, in effect, that the model is a conscious conceptualization which emerges from a single textual source. This suggests that the model is both culturally limited to P and consciously imposed on the text. If, however, the model is abstracted to its underlying structural equation, A (not) B, and examined at the level of underlying structure rather than conscious conceptualization, it can be shown that this structure is characteristic of Israelite culture as a whole or, at the very least, the editorial present of the text. *The Logic of Incest: A Structuralist Analysis of Hebrew Mythology* demonstrates that the equation 'A not B' is found consistently in all the sources out of which Genesis was created (Kunin, 1995: 269–70). This suggests that the model is either characteristic of all the sources or imposed on all of them, including P, by the editorial present.

The dynamic aspect of the model of sacred place exemplified by the Tabernacle and camp is significant, both in respect of understanding the nature of biblical sacred place and the models of sacred place developed in the subsequent periods of Jewish history. By definition, dynamic sacred place is not confined to any particular location or even kind of location.[20] There is, for example, no reason to assume that the camp was always built on one type of geographic feature rather than any other. This distinguishes the model from other variations developed in the text in which sacred places were associated, for example, with hills or groves. Nor is sacred place associated with a historical or mythological experience of the divine. Sacred place is directly tied to the people and moves with them through the wilderness. In this respect it fits with the narrative nomadic model developed by the text. Dynamic sacred place is temporary and disassociated from physical space. It is based on the conjunction of other significant categories, objects, people, and activities, rather than locations.

The discussion of the various models or sets of categorization discussed above, in respect of space and humanity, argued that the models share the same underlying structure. The dynamic aspect of sacred space suggests that the models are not only similar, but are fundamentally related. Sacred place comes into being through the presence of the people, that is, the camp, and its structural hierarchies are interrelated with the people and their hierarchies. The camp comes into being and is defined by the presence of the Ark and the zones of holiness related to it, which in turn serve to structure the social and communal hierarchies.

Although the Ark in and of itself does not create sacred space, it provides an important unifying factor. Dynamic sacred place without the Ark is unthinkable. Thus its singularity emphasizes the singularity of dynamic sacred place. In spite of the splits and rebellions described in the text, for example the rebellion of Korah, the camp itself is never divided into two separate camps. This is because, conceptually and structurally, without the Ark as its center there could be no camp.

The dynamic aspects of this model suggest a very fluid notion of sacred place. Any place can become contextually sacred. The presence of the people and the Ark are two significant factors, assuming that they are organized and separated into their particular zones. Time and activity may also be significant factors. Jenson suggests that time is organized by the same principles as are the other cultural domains (1992: 37). This suggestion is supported both by structuralist theory and analysis.[21] Access to sacred place is determined not only by social status but also by time. The High Priest, for example, is in principle only allowed to enter the Holy of Holies on the Day of Atonement (יום הכפורים). Time was also a determining factor in respect of the rituals of the cult. Thus sacred place in this context owes very little to location. It is determined by the structural organization of holy spaces within the camp, the organization of the people, the organization of time, and the cultic activities. In effect, sacred place is created by the imposition of the structural model on time, activity, and place. Location is not significant; structure of that location is what makes it significant. These elements, particularly time and cultic/ritual activity, become the distinguishing features of functional sacred space in the rabbinic period.

In respect of its singularity, dynamic sacred place is similar to the primary model of static centralized sacred space exemplified by the Temple of Solomon. Although, as discussed below, there were at different periods in Israelite history different sacred places, and even several temples existing simultaneously, the editorial present of the text emphasizes a unitary, centralized model with the Temple of Solomon eventually being depicted as the sole forum of direct communication to God through the sacrificial cult.

It is likely that the two models, dynamic and static, share the feature of singularity due to the fact that the description of the camp and Tabernacle is an idealization, perhaps based on the Temple itself. It projects back on the mythological formative period of Israel, a model of sacred space which was culturally significant at either the time the texts were written or at the editorial present of the text. Removed from an actual physical reality, the ideal model allows the significant elements of the oppositions to be clearly developed. It presents sacred place as it was thought to be, rather than as it existed.

This aspect of idealization is essential to understanding dynamic sacred place. If the model is taken out of its narrative context, that is the wilderness, it can be understood as an abstract representation of space, with no necessary direct connection with sacred place as it actually existed, or was used. It provides a model which can be more generally applied to the understanding of geography, and to the position of the Temple and Israel in respect of the world. The ideal aspect of the model also emphasizes the need to evaluate the symbolic valences of the categories and elements which it structures. Ten of the tribes, for example, no longer existed at the editorial present of the texts. Thus rather than merely representing the actual tribes, they are symbolic markers defining and qualifying the value of elements of the structure. It is the symbolic value of the tribe, or any other element, within the oppositional structure that is significant, rather than the particular tribe or element itself. The ideal model allows the exemplification of cognitive structural models rather than being bound by the concrete of historical situations.

Static Centralized Sacred Place

The Temple of Solomon exemplifies the Israelite model of static centralized sacred place. Detailed descriptions of the Temple are found in 1 Kings 5–9 and 2 Chronicles 3–5. The plan of the Temple mirrors that of the Tabernacle and court. The Temple building itself was surrounded by a court: 2 Chronicles 4:9 identifies this area as the Court of the Priests. Although the texts do not directly indicate the direction of the entrance to the Temple or the court it is likely that it faced east. This is suggested by the placement of the molten sea to the southeast of the Temple, most likely near the entrance of the Temple (1 Kings 7:39). The use of the term ימין in that verse suggests that it is equivalent to east. This suggests that the door mentioned in 1 Kings 6:8 was on the eastern side of the Temple, in the same directional location as that of the Tabernacle. The Priest's Court was surrounded by the Great Court (2 Chronicles 4:9). First Kings uses the terms Inner and Outer Court respectively (6:36; 7:9). The Temple itself was divided into two sections, the Inner Sanctuary, דביר, and the Outer, הקל. The Ark of the Covenant was placed in the Inner Sanctuary.

Both the account in Kings and that in Chronicles use several of the same terms as that found in respect of the Tabernacle. The terms Holy of Holies, קודש הקדשים, and The Holy, הקודש, are used for the Inner and Outer Sanctuaries (see for example 1 Kings 6:16; 8:6; 8:8). Although scholarly consensus suggests that these terms as well as several other additions are due to priestly redaction, both the application of the terms and the structure presented suggest an analogous plan to that of the Tabernacle.[22]

Although there is relatively little information about how the Temple of Solomon was used it may be assumed that the descriptions of the use of the Tabernacle are at the very least idealizations of the use of the Temple. Thus the descriptions of access to the Tabernacle and its court may also be applicable to the Temple. The Temple's architectural plan, and the names used for different areas are also suggestive of a cognitive model if not the actual functional use of space. In certain respects the Temple of Solomon must be regarded as exemplifying an idealized model as opposed to a functional model. Although aspects of its description may have originated while the Temple still stood, the descriptions found in the Bible are also the product of redactors who lived after the Temple's destruction.[23] This is significant in respect of the descriptive terms found in 2 Chronicles, a text written during the postexilic period.[24] The term Priest's Court, for example, is not found in texts which are considered to be preexilic. This and related terms suggest boundaries in respect of access which in all probability are idealizations.

The ideal model presented is structurally identical to that developed in respect of the Tabernacle. The Holy of Holies is set in structural opposition to the Holy; the Temple (or House) is in opposition to the court. The Inner (or Priest's) Court itself is in opposition to the Outer Court, the set of opposition concluding, in all probability with that between Judah and the world. The terms found in 2 Chronicles make a direct association between the structure of space and society. The term Priest's Court suggests that, at least ideally, this area was the preserve of the priests, with the laity being excluded. It may be assumed that in the ideal model access to the Holy of Holies was limited to the High Priest, the Holy limited to the priests (and High Priest), the Priest's Court to the Levites (and priests), and the Main Court to the Israelites as a whole.[25]

J. Z. Smith's analysis of models of sacred space found in Ezekiel emphasizes many of the similarities between the biblical models of dynamic and static sacred place.[26] He suggests that Ezekiel's first map (Ezekiel 40:1–44:3) categorizes space in respect of sacred and profane. As in the case of dynamic sacred place this can be seen as circles set in opposition to each other. Smith states, for example: 'This is elaborated in a series of segmentations characteristic of sacred/profane hierarchies. With respect to the temple mount, the land is profane; with respect to the temple, the temple mount is profane . . .' (Smith, 1987: 56). He also suggests that these qualitatively distinguished areas (at least within Ezekiel's idealization) are distinguished by relative height – with those of greater holiness being progressively higher.[27]

The second aspect of the first map, discussed by Smith, presents the relationship of human beings to sacred space. It highlights the distinction between people on the basis of sanctity, with a direct association between the degree of sanctity and the degree of access, culminating in the High Priest, the only person allowed into the Holy of Holies (Smith, 1987: 57–60).

This aspect is developed in a related way in Ezekiel's second map (44:4–31). Smith suggests that this model is based on relative purity. This model has implications for both access and ritual action. Like the first map (and that presented above in respect of the Tabernacle) there is a direct association between the level of purity and participation and access to the cult and Temple (Smith, 1987: 62–3). As in the segmentary model of the Tabernacle (see page 16) these categories can be seen as oppositional, which, depending on the context either unite or divide categories.

Thus, in many respects its structure is very similar to that of the dynamic model. The significant difference between the two lies in its fixed location of the Temple and thus the nature or source of its holiness. First Chronicles 21:18–30 presents a justification for the site of the Temple which is similar to that given for the establishment of other holy places, for example, Beth El in Genesis 28:22. The site of the Temple, Ornan's threshing-floor, is the location of God's promise to end a plague. David builds an altar there, which is called by an angel, 'the house of the Lord God,' and 'the altar of burnt-offering for Israel.' A similar narrative is found in 2 Samuel 24:15–25. The text in Samuel is more indirect in respect of divine participation. David is commanded to build the altar by a prophet, Gad, rather than an angel, and the text omits the statement of the angel at its conclusion.[28] In spite of these differences, both texts provide a miraculous justification for the establishment of the Temple and the sanctity of its location. The sanctity of the Temple is further enhanced in 2 Chronicles 3:1. This text makes a direct association between the threshing-floor of Ornan and Mount Moriah, which was the site of the sacrifice of Isaac, Genesis 22.

The divine or miraculous justification for the establishment of the Temple is the basis of the cognitive transformation from a dynamic to a static model. The dynamic model relied on the presence of God (in either a strong or a weak sense), symbolized by the Ark, the formal structure created by the organization of the camp and its opposition to the world, and the ritual or cultic activities which actualized or recognized the divine presence. The static model includes all of these elements in its definition of sacred place.[29] They too are presented in a static form. The Ark is no longer carried before the people. It is placed in the Holy of Holies as a permanent dwelling place, emphasized by the term בית, house, which is used in the text for the Temple. The Tabernacle, court, and cultic elements (e.g. the altar) which were intrinsically portable structures are replaced by permanent structures. The organization of Israelite society is also formalized in space. Ideally each tribe is allotted a section of the land as its permanent inheritance, with Jerusalem and the Temple being placed in the midst of Judah. The relation between the community and sacred place is also formalized in time. Whereas the relation between the community and the Tabernacle in dynamic sacred space was constant, that found in respect of static space is structured. Particular points in time are selected for general access or connection to sacred place. Thus the three pilgrimage festivals are emphasized as the points in time when Israel (the people) shall approach their God.

The static and divinely validated aspect of sacred space is also significant in respect of the place of the Temple in relation to the land and the world. During the mythological period characterized by dynamic centralized sacred space, there was no significant relationship between the camp and its location. The location by definition was mobile, and that area outside of the camp can be uniformly placed in the category of 'the world.' In the static model, however, the Temple is the center of a much larger conceptualization. Sacred place does not end with the Outer Court or even the walls of Jerusalem. The Temple is the center of the promised land, all of which contains an aspect of the holy. Unlike the dynamic model which does not provide a firm foundation for the characterization of geography, the static model with its center fixed in Jerusalem provides a firm basis for the cognitive understanding of the land of Israel and the world.

Selection or emphasis of any particular sacred place cannot be entirely separated from other sociological phenomena. The selection of Jerusalem as the site of the Temple on the basis of social and political considerations, and therefore the role of centralized sacred place in creating a religious, communal, and political identity cannot be overemphasized. Although the Temple of Solomon may never have exercised the religious dominance suggested in the biblical text, its role as a centralizing force is developed in several texts. For example, 1 Kings 12:25–33 indicates the perception of Jerusalem and the central role of the cult in creating social and political identity. The text directly associates the pilgrimage to Jerusalem with the people's political identity. It states:

> Now will the kingdom return to the house of David. If this people go up to offer sacrifices in the house of the Lord at Jerusalem, then will the heart of this people turn back unto their lord, even unto Reheboam king of Judah (1 Kings 12:26–8).

The text suggests that on the basis of this consideration Jeroboam decided to build two new holy places for pilgrimage. In addition, 1 Kings 12 indicates that Jeroboam also restructured both the people, creating a new priesthood (12:31), and time, ordaining new festivals (12:32), as part of his creation of static sacred places for the Kingdom of Israel. Although this text may not reflect a historical event it does indicate a perception of the role of sacred place in both cultic and political identity.

The emphasis on Jerusalem and the Temple as unique holy places in all probability also had economic implications. This may be true both prior to the exilic period, when the cult may not have been totally centralized, and certainly true in the postexilic period. The economic aspects are associated both directly and indirectly with the cult. The purchase of sacrificial animals and other necessary ritual elements would be a significant direct economic factor. The movement of large numbers of people in and out of Jerusalem, both at the pilgrimage festivals and at other times in the year, would also be additions to the economic structure of Jerusalem as a whole.

The perception of the role of sacred place in creating political identity may also be a factor in the emphasis on centralized models in the biblical text. If, as suggested, the descriptions of both the Tabernacle and the Temple of Solomon, as presented, are essentially ideal models extensively redacted after they no longer existed, then their centrality in the text may be a response to exile, the sociological context in which they were created. The centralized model, with its focus on a single center, provides a basis for the development of strong external boundaries.

The centralized models of sacred space are directly related to identity and boundary creation. Within the Israelite underlying structural equation of 'A (not) B' they create both a religious center and a strong external boundary. Both the center and the boundary are significant because they define the presence and extent of the place of the sacred in the world. The presence of the holy is necessary because it defines the quality of space and its opposition to the profane (i.e. the extent of sacred place). Ultimately both the static and dynamic models at their widest extent create an opposition between

Israel, symbolized by the camp, or the idealized national boundaries and the world. Although the boundaries are at one level geographic, they are essentially cognitive. They create a means of categorizing and defining self in opposition to the other. The strong centralized element, with its focus on the center, provides a constant unifying force, pulling the boundary toward the center. With its emphasis on unbridgeable oppositions it strengthens the external boundary and thereby cultural and religious identity.

Non-centralized Models of Sacred Place

Although, as indicated, the centralized model is emphasized by the final redaction of the biblical text, many individual texts suggest that the Israelites also employed, in perhaps historically distinct periods or simultaneously, a decentralized model consisting of many different sacred places. This model is evident in many texts throughout the biblical canon. Some texts, for example Genesis, only include examples of the decentralized model.

Several different holy places are depicted in Genesis. In many cases these places are associated with one of the patriarchal figures. In some of the texts there is a direct association between the patriarch and the founding of the sacred place. In other texts the patriarch may merely be narratively connected with a particular site. Thus for example Beth El is associated in two different texts with Jacob (Genesis 28:10–22; 35:1–14). In Genesis 28, Jacob dreams of God's presence, and as a result declares that the place is sacred. The text concludes with Jacob setting up a pillar and naming the holy place. The narrative of Genesis 28 suggests that prior to Jacob's dream of the ladder the site was not qualitatively distinct. Its sacredness was due to the experience rather than prior to it. It is not suggested that the text actually describes the foundation of the sacred place, rather it describes or justifies Israel's explanation for the holiness of the place, which may have been a holy site long before it was appropriated by the Israelites. Although Genesis 35:9–16 offers both an alternative and complementary explanation for the establishment of a holy place at Beth El, and for the name Beth El, verses 1–8 of the same chapter imply that the site is already known by the name Beth El. It also directly associates the sanctity of the place with the narratively earlier story, that is, Genesis 28:10–22. This connection is presented in 35:1 and 7. For example, verse 7 states: 'He built there an altar, and called the place El Beth El, because there God was revealed to him, when he fled from the face of his brother.' The narrative suggests that the sanctity of the place was highlighted or created in Genesis 28 and the place was established as a holy place in Genesis 35. The second part of the chapter, however, presents a different explanation for the establishment of Beth El. Verses 9–16 describe a vision of God, in which God makes various promises to Jacob and his descendants. It centers around the change in Jacob's name to Israel.[30] The text concludes with Jacob building a pillar (as in Genesis 28) and changing the name of the place of Beth El. In spite of the narrative differences among the different versions, the basis for the holiness of the place is identical. In both cases it is directly associated with a vision or revelation from God. Other holy places are mentioned in the biblical text without a narrative explaining their establishment. Thus for example, 1 Kings 18:20–40 indicates that Mount Carmel was an established holy place. Elijah is described as rebuilding the altar rather than building it.

The significant element in all of these texts is the absence of implied singularity or uniqueness. In each case there is no suggestion that the holy place is in any way distinct from other holy places. This suggests that the structural model upon which these texts are based is different from that discussed above. The decentralized model allows for a multiplicity of sacred places and therefore a multiplicity of centers.

If the concentric model were correct in respect of centralized sacred space, then centralized and decentralized sacred space would be unreconcilable. The concentric model relies on each level being singular and there being a single unique center. The segmentary model, however, can accommodate multiplicity. In the centralized form, the emphasis is on duality. The duality at each level naturalizes and emphasizes the pattern. Ultimately this creates a very strong external boundary. If the external boundary is less important, then greater internal segmentation is possible.

The discussion of the application of the structural equation to kinship in *The Logic of Incest* suggest that two different but related cultural models could be applied to the same data depending on the cultural context. If external boundaries were significant, then a linear model, equivalent to the dyadic segmentation model, would be used. Significance, in this case, refers to the need to maintain the integrity of the boundary. If, however, external boundaries were insignificant, that is their integrity was maintained externally, then a multiple segmentation model would be used. The first model emphasizes the unity of the community in respect to the world, while the second emphasizes the divisions within the community in respect to itself.

In respect of the genealogical data, the multiple segmentation variation of the model works at the lowest genealogical level. Although the subtle distinctions in level emphasized by the dyadic model are still in effect, the central focus is on the lowest, most highly segmented level of opposition. The model emphasizes the structural opposition between individual families, and the need for endogamy. The logical extension of the Israelite preference for endogamy is marriage as close to the immediate family as possible.[31] In this respect endogamy is a strong inward force. Unchecked it emphasizes segmentation and division.

A similar cultural pattern may be evident in respect of sacred place. In historical (or ideological) contexts which emphasize the external boundary, the dyadic segmentation model is used. This model emphasizes the nature of oppositions and the impermeability of categories, and therefore creates (or supports) a strong external boundary. In a context, however, in which the external boundary is less significant, because its maintenance is not problematic, then the dyadic aspect is de-emphasized and the multiplicity of oppositions at the lowest level can be expressed. As in the case of genealogy, the fullest expression of the structural opposition, A (not) B, creates a multiplicity of structurally distinct and opposing units.

There are several possible explanations for the presence of these two differing applications of the structural equation to place, and equally to genealogy. They may reflect two distinct periods in Israelite history preserved in the strata of the texts. It might be suggested that, on the one hand, the decentralized model reflects the preexilic period. The centralized model, on the other, reflects the postexilic period. This explanation draws support from both the text itself and many modern reconstructions of Israelite history. Many scholars argue that the preeminence of the Temple only occurs after the return from exile. Similarly, much of the material which describes the Tabernacle and Temple are attributed to P, a source which is generally considered to have been completed during the postexilic period. Many of the alternative holy sites mentioned in the text would also not have been included in the territory of Judea under Persian rule and thus may reflect an earlier historical period. This explanation would also be in keeping with the anthropological model. During the preexilic period strong external cultural boundaries existed. These boundaries were essentially nonproblematic. Thus some form of the multiple segmentation model might be expected. During the postexilic period, when Judea was part of the Persian empire, it is possible that the external boundaries were problematic, that is not clearly impermeable, and thus required structural support. In such circumstance the dyadic model, which emphasizes the cultural logic, might be expected.

Although it is possible that the two variations in the expression of underlying structure are artifacts of different historical periods, it is also possible that they reflect two different views of the editorial present, one functional and the other ideological. It is possible that the multiple segmentation model, and the multiplicity of sacred places, depict sacred place as it existed, using the 'historical' narratives to justify both the model and particular places, in Israelite society, while the dyadic or centralized model reflects an ideological position, that is, sacred place as it should ideally be. The description of the Tabernacle clearly fits this ideological characterization as it is unlikely that it existed at the time of description (if indeed it ever existed). It is also not unlikely that the descriptions of the Temple were written, in perhaps idealized form, after its destruction.

This type of conflict between ideological and functional models is evident in the text itself. Second Kings 23 describes an attempt by Josiah to centralize the cult in Jerusalem. It depicts him as gathering all of the priests into Jerusalem and destroying many of the alternative holy places. In Deuteronomy there is also a clear opposition to multiple holy places. The text of Deuteronomy develops an idealized centralized model for many aspects of Israelite culture.

The distinction between ideological and functional models is similar in several respects to a model proposed by Victor Turner in relationship to pilgrimage. He distinguishes between pilgrimage shrines which tend to be singular and focuses of wider group identity, and political shrines which are local, emphasizing a narrower focus of group or political identity. The ideological model shares many of the elements of the pilgrimage shrine. Its unique and centralized aspect emphasizes the widest extent of Israelite cultural identity. It differs from Turner's model only in respect of its placement. Turner argues that pilgrimage shrines will tend to be placed on the periphery of cultural space. The ideological model, however, centers on Jerusalem, which represents the center of cultural and political space. The functional model is similar in many respects with the local shrine. In many cases it appears to be connected with smaller political and social units, thus only creating local identity. It may, however, have also had a wider pilgrimage function separate from its local political aspects, e.g. Beth El.

Liminality

One of the key features shared by many of the biblical sacred places is liminality.[32] This term was applied by van Gennep to *rites of passage*, referring to the ambiguous phase between two statuses – this margin was called the limin. Victor Turner's work has extended the understanding and applicability of the term.[33] The liminal refers to those areas which form a bridge between different or opposing categories. In many cases this inter-mediate area is one of danger or possibility. Thus the threshold which joins the domains of inside and outside is in some cultures considered to be a dangerous place. It is not unlikely that the placement of a *Mezzuzah* on the doorway of a Jewish house owes something to liminality.[34] One significant feature of the liminal is the merging of qualities of both categories. Since the liminal is neither fully one type of space (category) or the other, it will take on aspects of both; it is this indeterminacy of quality and therefore predicta-bility that creates the aspect of danger.

The indeterminacy which is a central characteristic of liminality is also creative, allowing the combinations of new forms and new relations.[35] Within ritual it allows the participants to encounter one another free of status roles or hierarchies. In respect of geography it allows the contact between different realms and the human and divine to develop in ways not usually possible. Thus both direct communication between God and man, and death and rebirth usually occur in liminal spaces.

Within the Israelite understanding of space, various types of locations bridged different domains. This is most clearly seen in respect of raised and lowered spaces. Both of these aspects of space possessed liminal qualities. They are commonly used for both symbolic rebirth and in respect of raised space communication with the divine. It should not be assumed, however, that these sites are understood to be intrinsically liminal. Not every moun-tain, for example, is a mountain of God. The sites may possess a potential for liminality which can be actualized by a particular narrative or cultural context. Mountains and other raised locations do, however, have a strong association within the biblical text as sacred places. This element is clearly seen in frequent use of the term במה, 'high place.' Although the term is at times used to mean mountain, for example Ezekiel 36:2, it is often used to mean place of worship.[36] These high places were associated both with Israelite worship (see 1 Samuel 9:12–25) and those of the nations (see Numbers 33:52). The term itself suggests that there is an association between the sanctity of the particular place and its natural or artificial geographic features.

Mountains and other raised locations bridged the domains of heaven and earth. This merging of domains suggests the possible connection or joining of the human and the divine. It creates an intermediate area in which the divine may communicate with the human and the human with the divine. It also sometimes creates or suggests ambiguity between the categories of human and divine. This possibility and the liminal aspects of mountains are hinted at in Genesis 11, that is, the 'Tower of Babel.'

The nature of raised liminal space can best be discussed using examples from mythological narrative in the biblical canon. Genesis 22, the 'Sacrifice of Isaac' develops many of the themes characteristic of raised liminal space. In Genesis 22 God commands Abraham to offer up his son as a sacrifice on a certain mountain. Initially, in the narrative, the particular mountain is not indicated, perhaps suggesting that it is a liminal location, outside of human control. The location is described as a mountain in the land of Moriah, later associated with the location of the Temple in Jerusalem. Upon arriving at the mountain, Abraham's two servants are left at the bottom of the hill while Abraham and Isaac ascend the mountain to worship God. At the top of the mountain Abraham prepares to offer up, *la'haalot*, Isaac as an offering. As he is about to slaughter Isaac an Angel (or God) stops him and a ram is provided in Isaac's stead.

The liminal aspects of the location and the text are developed in several respects. The text as a whole is one of transformation and rebirth. Isaac is symbolically sacrificed and symbolically reborn of divine rather than human descent.[32] Liminality is thus developed in respect of a transformation in Isaac, moving from one domain to another. This liminality is mirrored and strengthened by the narrative location and action. Mountains, as suggested, bridge the earthly domain with the firmament and perhaps the divine domain. They do not properly fit into either domain but share features of both. It is possible, and according to structuralist analysis of the text, likely, that the opposition between Abraham and Isaac, on the one hand, and the two servants, on the other, reflects this liminal quality. Only Abraham and Isaac, who are of the chosen line, are fit to go up into contact with the realm of the divine. The act of sacrifice also emphasizes the liminal quality through its emphasis of raising up. One raises up a sacrifice to bring it into contact with the divine.

The liminality developed in Genesis 22 has a clear symbolic valence. It can be defined as positive liminal space. All of the elements of Genesis 22 are symbolically positive within the Israelite system. The narrative is shaped by God's command, and thus the commanded action, if followed, is intrinsically positive. The type of death described by the text is sacrifice.

Sacrifice was understood to be a positive purifying death. The positive aspect of the space is confirmed at the conclusion of the text by God's blessing.

Other examples of raised liminal space confirm this positive valence. The most significant of these is found in respect of the Ten Commandments and the covenant at Mount Sinai. Mount Sinai (perhaps like Mount Moriah) is a doubly liminal site. It is both a mountain and in the wilderness – and between settled areas. It is the location where Moses and the people come into direct contact with God, and a permanent relationship is established. In several respects it functions in a similar narrative (or structural) way to Mount Moriah. Both are sites of divine communication and more importantly both are sites of transformation. Israel at Sinai is transformed into a covenant people with God.[38]

The aspect of positive symbolic death or transformative death which is associated with raised liminality in Genesis 22 is also developed in several other texts. On a structural level this type of death is associated with symbolic divine rebirth. Several other deaths occur in the biblical texts on mountains. These texts share the common aspect of passing on the mantle of leadership to the next generation. This aspect mirrors the structural role of divine rebirth which is related to the passing of the divine seed within the genealogical framework.

In Numbers 20:25 Aaron is taken up Mount Hur to die. One key element emphasized in the text is the passing of his position unto his son Eleazar. Both verses 26 and 28 state that Aaron's garments should be removed and given to Eleazar who then becomes the High Priest. Similarly Moses dies on Mount Nebo (Deuteronomy 34). As in respect of Aaron one key element is the passing on of the divine mantle. The chapter is preceded, upon the announcement of Moses' death (Deuteronomy 31:14), with the appointment of Joshua, which is also mentioned in Deuteronomy 34:9. The statement in 34:9 is particularly significant as it suggests the passage of Moses' relationship with God to Joshua.

The aspect of divine transformation and the passage of authority from one generation to the next is developed in 2 Kings 2:11. This text also focuses on raised liminal space. The text states: 'And it came to pass, as they still went on and talked, that, behold, there appeared a chariot of fire, and horses of fire, which parted them both asunder; and Elijah went up by a whirlwind into heaven.' The text suggests that through this ascent Elijah is transformed into a semidivine figure. The text includes elements which suggest sacrifice. As in a sacrifice Elijah ascends to heaven through the medium of wind and fire. Fire is directly associated with sacrifice in the Elijah narrative in 1 Kings 18:20. As in the case of the deaths of Moses and Aaron this text also includes the element of passage of authority, which is described in similar terms to that between Aaron and Eleazar. Elisha's transformation into Elijah's role is emphasized in 2 Kings 2:14 when he removes his own clothing and takes up Elijah's mantle. It is also emphasized by his causing

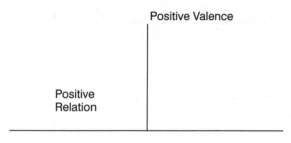

Figure 2.7 Raised Liminal Space

the same miracle, the parting of the waters of the Jordan, as Elijah had prior to his ascent.

An interesting variation on this theme is developed in respect of Saul. Saul's death is described in 1 Samuel 31. Like those described above, a mountain is mentioned in the text, that is, Mount Gilboa. It is not clear from the text, however, where the action occurs, and where Saul actually dies. The preposition used is בְּ, usually meaning 'in.'[39] Although it can also be used to mean 'on', there is no sense in the text that Saul and his men necessarily ascended the mountain. In the case of both Moses and Aaron the verb עָלָה (to go up) is specifically used. There is a similar transformation in respect of Saul's armor. Rather than passing it on to David, his successor, the armor is taken by the Philistines. This variation fits in with many aspects of the Saul narrative in which Saul acts in variance to textual expectations.[40] In respect of the mantle (in a literal sense) it is likely that this has narratively already symbolically passed down to David (or been removed from Saul) in several texts, for example, 1 Samuel 17:42; 24:5. The structure of raised liminality is illustrated in Figure 2.7. One significant feature of raised liminality emphasized by the diagram is its positive valence. This aspect is discussed below in respect of the conflict between liminal categories and Israelite/Jewish underlying structure.

Pits and other lowered spaces bridged the categories of earth and '*Sheol.*' This type of location, like raised features, are liminal places and thus also allow movement or mediation between categories. The best example of this type of liminality is found in Genesis 37. This text, the 'Murder of Joseph,' is a structurally inverted version of Genesis 22. Joseph is placed in the pit while a goat is killed in his place. Structuralist analysis suggests that this text, like Genesis 22, is a rebirth text, with the descent into the pit symbolizing death.[41]

There is a consistent association in the biblical text between descent and death. In Genesis 37:35 Jacob states that the death of Joseph will cause him to 'go down to the grave.' The Hebrew verb root 'יָרַד' (to go down) is used by the text. This root is used in association with death in several other texts from the Joseph narrative, usually by Jacob.[42] It is also used by Judah with the same association in Genesis 44:31. In the context of the Joseph narrative as a whole the root יָרַד is used frequently in respect of descent into Egypt. It is structurally likely that this descent is also a symbolic death.[43] The association between descent and death is also developed in Numbers 15:30. As in the texts in Genesis the terms ירד and שאול are closely associated.

The use of descent as symbolic of death and rebirth may also be developed on a broader scale in the descent of Jacob's family into Egypt and the ascent out of Egypt as the nation of Israel. This possibility is supported by the use of the term ירד and by the transformation which occurs. Jacob descends to Egypt with an individual covenant with God, the Israelites leave Egypt as a nation, and at Sinai take on a national and eternal covenant.

The aspect of rebirth is also suggested by the comparison of the Exodus with three structurally similar narratives; Genesis 12, 20, and 26. The structural pattern of the Wife/Sister texts is very similar to that of the descent into Egypt and the exodus. All of the significant narrative and structural elements are common to both.[44] The significant mythological element developed in the Wife/Sister texts was the death and rebirth of the wife and her transformation into sister. This transformation mirrors that of Israel. Prior to the exodus narrative Israel has a temporary individual relationship with God, similar to that created by a wife (that is, between two families). After the exodus Israel has a new permanent relationship with God which is analogous to that of a sister – that is the genealogical relationship is ongoing. Thus the underlying structure of the narrative supports the characterization of descent as equivalent to symbolic death and there for the element of liminality.[45]

The descent form of liminality also includes the element of communication, albeit with the dead rather than God. The primary example of this is found in 1 Samuel 28:8–25. This text describes Saul's attempt to contact the ghost of Samuel. The liminal aspect is developed in several respects. The action of the narrative takes place at Ein Dor. The word עין (*Ein*) means 'well', and may represent a link between this world and the underworld (*Sheol*). The witch uses the term 'bring up', in respect of calling Samuel's ghost. Thus, like raised liminal space, communication between domains is possible. Lowered liminal space is diagrammed in Figure 2.8.

Both raised and lowered liminal spaces, and liminality as a category, are structurally problematic within Israelite culture. As suggested above, Israelite culture is based on the structural equation 'A (not) B.' One significant aspect of the Israelite variant of the equation is in respect of mediation. Mediators, like liminal categories, bridge culturally distinct domains. Their existence suggests that the categories are not actually mutually exclusive and impermeable. Such bridging of categories challenges the basis of the structure. Within Israelite culture the strategy for dealing with mediation and liminality is transformation of the symbolic valence.

Symbolic valence of liminal categories is equivocal. Within the Israelite system this ambiguous valence is transformed in either direction, that is, to positive or negative. In respect of raised liminal spaces the symbolic valence is always positive. Thus in Genesis 22 the type of death associated with

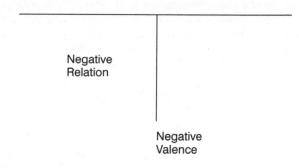

Figure 2.8 Negative Liminal Space

raised liminal space is sacrifice. Sacrifice, within the biblical framework, is a purifying positive act. The positive association between raised liminality and sacrifice regarding symbolic valence is indicated by the Hebrew word for sacrifice, להעלות, that is, to raise up. This valence is confirmed in respect of the type of communication found in raised liminal space, that is divine–human.

The typology of the deaths which occur on raised liminal space also respects this transformed symbolic value. As suggested above, many of the deaths include the element of genealogy, whether real or symbolic. This is emphasized by the passing of the mantle, represented by clothing, from one generation to the next. This type of death and connection between generations is an essential element of Israelite structure which emphasizes the passage of the divine seed (or relationship) from one generation to the next. The transformed positive valence of the liminal location emphasizes the positive valence of the relationship between generations.

Lowered liminality is correspondingly transformed. It moves from the equivocal to the negative. On the narrative level this is developed in Genesis 37. In that text the death which occurs in lowered liminal space is murder rather than sacrifice. Murder is the symbolic opposite of sacrifice. It is a polluting rather than purifying death.

The biblical text includes a third type of liminality which retains some ambiguous features. This liminality is not characterized by a specific geographic feature, rather it is defined by geographic location. These locations are either between culturally settled domains, that is, wilderness, or bridge different types of domains, for example, the fork of a river. These liminal areas tend to have both positive and negative symbolic valence. They also often include elements of both the raised and lowered liminal types.

There are several interesting narrative examples of this type of liminality. The location of the action in Genesis 32:23–33 is liminal in several respects. The location is described as being a ford in the river, a place where land and water meet. It is also possibly liminal as a mediating point between the lands of Aram and those of Israel (suggested by the conclusion of the previous chapter). The events described in the narrative contain elements of both murder and sacrifice. The murder element is emphasized by the wrestling – which makes an allusion to the struggles between Jacob and Esau in the womb (Genesis 25:22). Thus this narrative element works on the horizontal level, that is the level typically found in the narratives which occur in lowered liminal space. The conclusion of the text, that is Jacob's symbolic rebirth – emphasized by the change in name from Jacob to Israel – fits into the raised liminality pattern.

Exodus 4:20–6 is another example of this type of liminality. Like Genesis 32, this narrative includes elements of both forms of liminality. The text includes the element of murder, that is, in verse 24: 'the Lord sought to kill him.' It also includes the element of sacrifice symbolized by the circumcision which concludes the text (verse 25).[46]

Both of these texts contain ambiguous elements which might suggest a reason for the type of liminality. Jacob, himself, is an ambiguous figure. The narrative creates problems both on the horizontal level, between Jacob and Esau, and on the vertical level, between Jacob and Isaac. The type of liminality used allows both of these elements to be dealt with. The wrestling creates structural distance between Jacob and Esau, and the rebirth and change of name allow the passing of the divine seed from one generation to the next.

Exodus 4:20–6 also contains ambiguous elements. These include the structural relationship between Moses and Aaron. Which brother is the inheritor of the divine seed? The roles of Ziporah and Moses' children are also ambiguous.[47] Thus the ambiguity of the liminal space reflects the narrative and structural ambiguities. The symbolic valence of this type of liminal space, unlike the other two, is not transformed in either qualitative direction. Elements of both qualities are included. It is likely that this type of liminality was structurally less problematic because of the nature of the domains which it bridged. Raised and lowered liminality bridged the natural with different aspects of the supernatural, while this type only bridges different aspects of the natural and the cultural. In spite of this, ambiguous liminal space provides the same type of merging which allows transformation and communication.

Direction

As suggested above in reference to the Tabernacle (see page 43), direction, or more specifically movement in different directions, was associated with varying qualitative valences. The directions with the strongest valences are eastward and westward. In Genesis all movement in an eastward direction is negatively valanced. This type of movement is first found in Genesis 3:24, where Adam and Eve are expelled eastward from the garden. Genesis 4:16 depicts Cain as moving eastward, to the east of Eden, after murdering Abel. It also states that he built a city there, suggesting that the origins of city life are based on sin. The builders of the Tower of Babel move to the east before building their city (Genesis 11:19). In each of these cases movement to the east is associated with descent into sin (either before or after the movement).

Other examples make it clear that the eastward movement is set in structural opposition to westward movement. When Abram and Lot, representing Israel and the nations respectively, divide the land (Genesis 13:5–12), Lot takes the eastern side while Abram takes the western. The text emphasizes the qualitative aspects through mentioning the evil of Sodom. The association of Israel with the west and westward movement and the nations with the east and eastward movement is also found in Genesis 25:6, in which Abraham divides the land between his descendants, Isaac, representing Israel stays in the west while the other sons, representing the nations move to the east.

It is possible that this qualitative understanding of directionality is related to Israel's geographic position. Israel's placement on the shores of the Mediterranean Sea, in effect on the borders of civilization, meant that it was as far westward as possible, with all other nations (that is, those which were culturally significant) placed to the east. It is also likely that the directionality found in the Temple and the Tabernacle is related to this qualitative understanding of space. Thus it is therefore less likely that the structure of the Temple was intended to mirror the cosmos, that is the movement of the sun, as suggested by some scholars.[48]

The symbolic valences of northward and southward movement are less strongly valenced. The biblical text suggests that northward movement was associated with finding a wife, and southward movement with transforming her into a sister.[49] The qualitative valences of northward and southward movement appear to be slightly negative and neutral respectively. These qualities are reflected in the placement of the tribes and Levitical families around the Tabernacle. It is possible that these qualitative valences were related to the placement of the Israelite tribes with Judah being the southernmost tribe. The weakness of the valences might be due to the need to keep all tribes relatively positively valenced.

Sinai and Zion

Within the literature there is a wide range of discussions comparing Sinai and Zion as either competing holy places or models of holiness within the Israelite system. Several of these analyses rely on the work of Eliade.[50] Aspects of Eliade's approach to sacred space have been mentioned above (see page 1). Aspects of his approach as they are applied to Sinai and Zion, the concept of 'cosmic mountain' are examined here.[51] Eliade's analysis focuses on several interrelated elements. These include, centrality,[52] *axis mundi*, and assimilated centrality. Other significant elements include Eliade's understanding of mythology and mythological time. All of these elements are applied by Levenson and Cohn to the Israelite conceptions regarding both Sinai and Zion.

Smith argues that the three central aspects of this model are not supported either by current understanding of Near Eastern material, nor is their universality supported by ethnographic evidence (1987: 14–23). His discussion focuses primarily on the relationship between the 'cosmic mountain' and holy places, but is applicable to the analyses of Israelite material in which these two categories appear to be merged.

In respect of centrality and *axis mundi*, that is, the place of the 'cosmic mountain' in the center and foundation of the cosmos, Smith argues that this concept was based on a misunderstanding of Near Eastern ideology. He suggests that the essential aspect of this concept is that of a 'world mountain.' Yet, the concept of 'world mountain' joining the underworld, the world, and the heavens within Mesopotamian mythology, he argues, is not supported by the evidence.[53] The third element of assimilated centrality derives from the other two aspects, and its cognitive value is based on theirs.

Within the Israelite model of space, the role of neither Mount Zion nor Mount Sinai depends on their intrinsic holiness. If the place is not intrinsically holy, but contextually holy, then the concept cannot be usefully applied. Levenson applies Eliade's model to Mount Zion. In his discussion he divides the concept of cosmic mountain into five elements and uses biblical quotations to support the application of each element to Mount Zion.

The first element which he examines is centrality (Levenson, 1985: 115). Although Levenson admits that this concept is more fully developed in rabbinic texts, he also argues that it can be traced in biblical cosmology (Levenson, 1985: 122). His argument in respect of the Bible rests on the interpretation of two texts both of which are from Ezekiel (5:5 and 38:12). The first of these texts is suggestive, speaking of Jerusalem being in the midst of the nation. The nature of this centrality, however, is not explained or emphasized. Levenson himself cites S. Talmon's contention that this centrality was due to importance rather than geography (Levenson, 1985: 115). The second text includes the word '*tabbur*' which is translated by Levenson as 'navel.' Levenson indicates that this translation is also contested by Talmon, who argues that this usage was found in the postbiblical period.[54] Levenson concedes the plausibility of Talmon's arguments but concludes that it is doubtful that the Israelites would be sophisticated enough to distinguish between spiritual centrality and geographic centrality.

Levenson's argument relies on the Israelites ignoring geographic reality and the view of their own history (as they describe it in biblical texts). The texts suggest that the building of the Temple in Jerusalem was contingent on the conquest of Jerusalem and its selection by David as his capital city. Jerusalem does not appear to be intrinsically holy, but rather becomes holy through the establishment of the Temple. It also ignores the dynamic aspects of sacred space represented by the Ark and Tabernacle. The Ark was by definition portable, suggesting that sacred space was not intrinsically static. His arguments also ignore, perhaps as a function of dividing the concept up, a significant aspect of Eliade's argument, that is, centrality, which refers to centrality in the cosmos as well as merely geographic centrality. Neither of the texts cited support this characterization.

Levenson picks up this thread in his discussion of *Axis Mundi*. He initially discusses the vision of Isaiah in the Temple. He convincingly argues for the aspects of the Temple which serve as a locus of communication between the human and the divine. His argument, however, neither demonstrates that this aspect was the sole province of Mount Zion, nor does it include the aspect of fulcrum joining the three realms of heaven, earth, and Sheol.[55]

The element of mountains serving as loci of communication with the divine is not contested. Many texts in the biblical canon support this characterization, as suggested above in the discussion of liminality. There does not appear, however, to be any particular priority given to Mount Zion in respect of this type of communication. Mount Sinai would seem to be a more paradigmatic location for revelation. This element can more convincingly be explained by the concept of transformed liminality than Eliade's concept of cosmic mountain.

The types of communication which occur on Mount Zion and other locations, particularly but not exclusively Mount Sinai, are also essentially different. The Temple, that is, Mount Zion, is associated with communication between humanity and God in an upward direction, primarily through the means of sacrifice. Although some visions occur in the Temple, visions are secondary to its primary purpose for existence. Mount Sinai, however, is associated with downward communication. It is the place where God speaks and reveals to Moses.

In respect of sacrifice, although the Temple eventually is given cultic priority, this appears to be primarily due to political and religious reformation rather than purely theological or cosmographical grounds. Prior to this centralization, sacrifices were offered in many locations, sometimes associated with the Ark and sometimes not. There is no reason to assume that sacrifices offered in these other locations, for example, in the wilderness of Sinai during the 40 years of wandering, were perceived as less efficacious than those offered in Jerusalem. If the aspect of cosmic mountain and *axis mundi* were significant some qualitative distinction might be expected throughout.

This is not to suggest that Jerusalem was not eventually seen as the most important holy place. As discussed above, the centralized model becomes the primary model developed in the text. This, however, does not necessarily support the *axis mundi* or cosmic mountain explanation offered by Levenson. It merely points to the development or enhancement of certain cultural models or structures which, in order to create a strong internal identity, emphasize a single religious center.

It is in this light that Levenson's suggestion that one aspect which distinguishes Jerusalem and the Temple from other holy places is that even after the destruction of the Temple, the site still retains some aspect of holiness (1985: 125), thus perhaps supporting Mount Zion's intrinsic holiness. Both texts which are cited are exilic, and therefore possibly after the reformation of the cult and its centralization only in Jerusalem, and the developing ideology that sacrifices only be offered in Jerusalem. The continued focus on Jerusalem can therefore be explained by the perceived sanctity of Jerusalem and its ideological centrality rather than any concept of *axis mundi*. Although Jerusalem, within Israelite religion, has become the ideological center, there is insufficient evidence to support its characterization as a cosmic mountain or *axis mundi*.

Levenson's third attribute is one of the most problematic. It is based on Eliade's understanding of the difference between mythological and historical time. He suggests that while historical time is linear, mythological time is non-linear.[56] Although Levenson is not suggesting that Israelite, or biblical, thought and symbolism are entirely mythological or entirely historical he does use the mythological model for explaining or describing features of sacred space.

This approach rests on a qualitative distinction between myth and history. Myth for Eliade and mythical time are in a real sense timeless. They owe their origin to creation in this timeless period and stand outside of history (Eliade, 1971: 20). While the mythological concept of time contains a circular or recursive element, the historical view of time is linear. Eliade's dichotomy is not confirmed by general ethnographic analysis nor is it confirmed within the biblical text itself. The biblical text itself contains a very strong linear model, with no clear conception of elements created in a pre-temporal mythological period. The dichotomy is also problematic in that it suggests a perhaps evolutionary and perhaps qualitative relationship between the two models of time. Modern anthropological evidence suggests that different cultures create variant models for describing and experiencing time, which are not necessarily related in an evolutionary scheme.[57] The terms mythological and historical used for describing different concepts of time are also problematic in that they suggest a differing degree of objectivity. It can be argued, however, that both 'myth' and 'history' are equally subjective.

Structuralist analysis suggests that models of time are closely related to underlying structure. Different models of time, for example circular, linear, or spiral, do not appear to be related to particular modes of thought or periods in universal human cultural consciousness. Thus the nature of the Israelite model and its application to notions of myth and history must be analyzed in respect of the particular underlying structure rather than a model based on universals of human thought.

In a certain respect Sinai includes aspects of several types of liminality. It is described as both a mountain and a wilderness, and is particularly not in the land of Israel. The location of the mountain itself is ambiguous. Levinson points out that this geographic ambiguity is not primarily one of topography, but is due to the 'extraterrestrial quality of the mountain.'[58] In other words he is highlighting the aspect of liminality. Levenson also suggests that the divine abode is not merely the mountain but also much of the wilderness area (1985: 20).

Conclusions

This chapter examines the models of sacred space developed in the biblical text. Two main types of models are developed, the centralized model exemplified by the Temple in Jerusalem and the decentralized model exemplified by the multiple smaller holy places scattered throughout the biblical text. Although the decentralized model is found in many sections of the Bible, it is the centralized model which predominates, and is that which is emphasized by the editorial hand(s).

The centralized model is found in two variations, the static and the dynamic, the Temple and the mobile Tabernacle respectively. The model of dynamic sacred space is the most complex and highly developed, due, in all probability, to its ideological character. It is based on a segmentary model of impermeable categories, which at their widest extent create a structural opposition between the Israelites and the nations. The structure is inter-related with concepts of purity which define access to the different categories of sacred space.

The centralized model is based on the underlying structural equation, A (not) B. Each level of segmentation fits into one of these categories, A or B, based on the level of opposition. The complex development of the structure recapitulates and thus revalidates it at each level. It is suggested that the strongly centralized model is related to a need for strong external bound-aries; although the model allows for some internal segmentation (only into two categories at a time), the emphasis is placed on the external bound-ary.

The decentralized model is also based on both the segmentary model and the underlying equation. It, however, places the emphasis at a different level. It emphasizes internal segmentation and takes the external boundary for granted. The logical extension of the segmentary model (with endogamy as one of its features) is the focus on the smallest level of segmentation – without external opposition the system breaks down into its smallest units, each of which is conceptually an impermeable category. It is possible that the texts which reflect the decentralized model emerged from a historical context in which the boundaries, culturally and genealogically, were exter-nally maintained.

The aspect of liminality is also a significant feature of biblical sacred space. Yet, liminality does not act as mediatory space. Rather, liminal spaces, that is between heaven and earth, or between earth and underworld, are transformed in qualitative value. In effect there are three qualitative categories, the heavens (positive space), the earth (neutral space), the underworld (negative space). Liminal spaces are transformed in one direc-tion or the other, in order that they not mediate and bridge categories. Thus although liminality is significant, it cannot remain liminal within the system.

All of the features of biblical sacred space set the foundations for the models of sacred space used during the following periods. Both the cen-tralized and the decentralized models are developed with the emphasis shifting, in response to new cultural contexts, to the decentralized model. Many aspects of rabbinic sacred space consciously replicate structures found in the Temple. Liminality also continues to be a significant if problematic feature, especially in respect of pilgrimage and transformation.

Notes

1. For an interesting discussion of other aspects of the biblical understanding of the land as a symbol of the covenant, see: Orlinsky, H. (1986) 'The Biblical Concept of the Land of Israel' in Hoffman, L. *The Land of Israel: Jewish Perspectives*, Notre Dame: University of Notre Dame Press, pp. 27–64.
2. The analysis presented here is particularly concerned with the editorial present of the biblical text, that is in its final canonical form. This is due to theoretical issues concerning the transformation of structure. Underlying structure is not an artifact; it is transformed when a text is edited or translated. Thus, although earlier structural elements may be preserved, it must be assumed that the structures and models are those of the periods of redaction rather than the times in which the texts were originally written.
3. It should be noted that some scholars suggest that dynamic sacred space is found in two forms in Exodus, the complex form discussed below and a simpler form, which ultimately through the redacting process was assimilated to the complex form. This simple form comprised of the Tent of Meeting which, they argue, was placed outside of the camp, rather than at its center These arguments are based on texts from the Pentateuch including: Exodus 33:7; Numbers 12:4; and Deuteronomy 31:14 (see for example: Haran, M. (1960) ' "Ohel Moedh" in Pentateuchal Sources,' in *Journal of Semitic Studies*, **5.1**, 50–65). Many of the discussions are based on a premise that individual, non-priestly, or hierarchical worship is the purer form. They associate this with the Tent of Meeting, which is sometimes identified as the prophetic form of sacred space as opposed to the priestly (Haran, 1960: 56). On this basis they also argue for its historical priority, even suggesting that the texts, as opposed to the texts describing the more complex tabernacle, preserve remnants of Mosaic practice.

    It is argued here that although this variation may indeed reflect a decentralized model of sacred space, this does not necessarily allow the model to be dated at a point earlier than the other model. There is no clear evidence to suggest that either model was based on historical practice. Both models may be contemporary idealizations, reflecting the two types of models of sacred space. See also Turner, H., 1979: 88–96.
4. The plan depicted here is based on the accepted reconstruction as depicted by Jenson. Jenson, P. P. (1992) *Graded Holiness: A Key to the Priestly Conception of the World*, Sheffield: Sheffield Academic Press, p. 90.
5. See, for example, the description of the Holy of Holies in Exodus 26:33.
6. See for example, Haran, M. (1978) *Temples and Temple-Services in Ancient Israel: An Inquiry into the Character of Cult Phenomena and the Historical Setting of the Priestly School*, Oxford: Clarendon Press, p. 184, in which the court is divided into the zone between the Tabernacle and the altar, and between the altar and the entrance to the court.
7. See Haran, 1978: 184; Milgrom, J. (1970) 'The Shared Custody of the Tabernacle and a Hittite Analogy,' in *JAOS* **90**, 204–9; and Jenson, 1992: 92.
8. See Kunin, 1995: 257–78.

9. It is also possible that aspects of Israelite social organization were based on a similar model. See for example, Kunin, 1995: 261–5.
10. Segmentation need not be binary; it can be based on any number of divisions. Binary divisions are used here to facilitate understanding of the model, and because the oppositions analyzed (and therefore the segmentation of sacred place) are binary in structure.
11. For a wider discussion of segmentary opposition see for example, Barth, F. (1981) *Process and Form in Social Life*, London: Routledge & Kegan Paul, p. 17.
12. See for example Jenson's discussion of this issue (1992: 130–8).
13. See for example, Kunin (1995: 258) where it is argued that ideological distance – created by qualitatively negative narrative material – is used to deal with the problems created by genealogical closeness.
14. See Kunin, 1995: 273–5. It is also discussed in detail on page 36.
15. Jenson touches on this distinction (1992: 133).
16. See Numbers 2:1–34.
17. This opposition reflects the historical period after the division of the kingdom into Israel and Judah. Ephraim was one of the preeminent tribes of the Northern Kingdom of Israel.
18. I am not suggesting that conscious particular political realities shape underlying structure. Contemporary symbolic values are inputted into the underlying structure in order for its cognitive model to be meaningful within its cultural context. The *bricoleur* uses the tools and objects which are available to create structure at the S^3 level.
19. See Numbers 16 for a description of Korah's rebellion.
20. This is supported by Milgrom in his discussion of the court. He suggests that it was the objects rather than the location which were the source of holiness (1970: 207).
21. See for example, Kunin, 1995: 164.
22. See Tomes, R. (1996) '"Our Holy and Beautiful House": When and Why was 1 Kings 6–8 Written' in *JSOT*, **70**, 34.
23. Even though Tomes, for example, argues that the description in 1 Kings was written while the Temple still stood (1996: 47–8) he also mentions the priestly additions to the text (1996: 34) which are generally regarded as being post-exilic.
24. See for example Fohrer, G. (1968) *Introduction to the Old Testament*, London: SPCK, p. 238.
25. It is important to emphasize that a micro set of oppositions is encompassed in the macro set. Thus for example the High Priest is included with the priests in opposition to the Levites.
26. See J. Z. Smith (1987) *To Take Place: Towards Theory in Ritual*, Chicago: University of Chicago Press, 56–73.
27. See the discussion of the biblical understanding of direction, e.g. up or down, on pages 31–2. It is argued that upward movement or space is positive liminal space.
28. The owner of the threshing-floor also has a different name, Araunah rather than Ornan, in 2 Samuel.
29. It must be emphasized that it is not being argued that the Temple replaced the Tabernacle diachronically, rather two ideal models of space are being compared with no diachronic reference. They both are described in an editorially synchronic text.
30. An alternative explanation for this change is found in Genesis 32:28–30.

31. This is found in the practice of parallel cousin marriage, and mythologically in the preference for incest (see Kunin, 1995).
32. Some aspects of the role of the liminal in the biblical text are discussed by Nanette Stahl (1995) *Law and Liminality in the Bible*, Sheffield: Sheffield Academic Press. Her use of the term is very broad, meaning little more than narrative points of transformation characterized by 'an attempt at divine–human communication and interaction' (1995: 13). In her discussion of liminal moments, however, a wide variety of textual material is reviewed which owes very little to liminality and in the rare cases that it does, it adds very little to the discussion. Her examination of Moses suggests a misunderstanding of the term. Although her description of Moses as a mediator, with semidivine attributes, reveals a classically liminal figure, i.e. between two statuses, she seems unaware of this aspect of liminality, describing Moses as the 'only protagonist who is not undercut in the biblical depiction of a liminal moment' (Stahl, 1995: 73). It should be noted that although liminality figures significantly in the title, it plays little role in the interests of the book which are rooted in the narrative role of the law.
33. See for example, Turner, V. (1969) *The Ritual Process: Structure and Anti-Structure*, Chicago: Aldine; and (1974) *Dramas, Fields and Metaphors*, Ithaca: Cornell University Press. See also, Ashley, K. (ed.) (1990) *Victor Turner and the Construction of Cultural Criticism*, Bloomington: Indiana University Press, p. xviii.
34. The placement of the *Mezzuzah* may reflect a transformation in the qualitative symbolic valence of the threshold. As suggested below, the Israelite system of A (not) B does not allow for true liminal space; such space would suggest mediation and movement from one domain to the other. Thus liminal space needs to be transformed into nonliminal space. The *Mezzuzah* may effect this type of transformation, bringing the threshold into the house, one of the centers of the performance of mitzvot.
35. See for example, Turner, 1974: 255–6; and Alexander, B. (1991) *Victor Turner Revisited: Ritual as Social Change*, Atlanta: Scholars Press, pp. 17–19.
36. See Brown, F., Driver, S. and Briggs, C. (1979) *The New Brown–Driver–Briggs–Gesenius Hebrew English Lexicon (BDB)*, Peabody: Hendrickson Publishers, p. 119.
37. For discussions of the aspects of symbolic rebirth and death see Kunin, 1995: 94–103.
38. The liminal aspects of the Sinai period and the events at Mount Sinai are discussed in Cohn, R. (1981) *The Shape of Sacred Space: Four Biblical Studies*, Ann Arbor: Scholars Press, pp. 7–23.
39. The primary definition of ב given in *The New Brown–Driver–Briggs–Gesenius Hebrew-English Lexicon* is 'in' (Brown *et al.*, 1979: 88). It is also occasionally used as 'on', e.g. Exodus 24:18.
40. Robert Alter briefly discusses the incomplete use of the betrothal type scene in 1 Samuel 9:11–12. See Alter, R. (1981) *The Art of Biblical Narrative*, New York: Basic Books, p. 60.
41. For a structuralist comparison between Genesis 22 and 37 see Kunin, 1995: 95–103; and 'The Death of Isaac: A Structuralist Analysis of Genesis 22,' in *JSOT* **64**, 57–81.
42. See for example, Genesis 42:38.
43. This is emphasized in the Joseph story by the consistent use of double structure. Thus the symbolic death in the pit is mirrored by that suggested by the descent into Egypt.

44. See Kunin, S.·(1994) 'Perilous Wives and (Relatively) Safe Sisters' in *Journal For Progressive Judaism* 2, 16–17, 32–4.
45. The relationship between God and Israel is described in many ways in the biblical text. Several texts pick up the theme of marriage. See for example, Malachi 2:14 and Hosta 2:16–25. Other texts emphasize the eternal aspects of the covenant, for example, Deuteronomy 5:1–3. The two aspects of covenant are discussed in detail by Levenson in *Sinai and Zion*, 1985: 75–86.
46. This text is discussed in detail in Kunin, S. (1996) 'The Bridegroom of Blood: A Structuralist Analysis' in *JSOT* 70, 3–16. It is suggested there that the liminality is closely related to the general pattern of inversion which characterizes the text, and the Moses narrative.
47. See Kunin, 1996: 3–4.
48. See for example, Turner, 1979: 58–9.
49. Kunin, 1994: 15–34.
50. See for example: Levenson, 1985: 113–37; Cohn, 1981, explicitly in pp. 63–79 and implicitly in 43–61.
51. Many aspects of Eliade's approach are cogently critiqued by J. Z. Smith (1987), in *To Take Place: Towards Theory in Ritual*, Chicago: University of Chicago Press.
52. Eliade, M. (1961) *The Sacred and the Profane*, New York: Harper and Row, pp. 36–47.
53. Smith, 1987: 16. His argument is based on that found in Clifford, R. J. (1972) *The Cosmic Mountain in Canaan and the Old Testament*, Cambridge: Harvard University Press.
54. Levenson, 1985: 116; see also Talmon, 1976: 163–77.
55. Levenson's only argument for this aspect is based on an interpretation of Isaiah 14:12–15. His interpretation rests on a hardly convincing parallel use of the term 'upmost peak of Zaphon' in Psalms 48:3, where the term is parallel to Zion, and an assumption that the fact that in the text the description of Sheol (which is the opposite of the mountain) implies that it is below the mountain as necessitated by an *axis mundi*. Even if the mountain is indeed Mount Zion, the description of Sheol only creates a structural opposition, i.e. that Zion and Sheol are opposites, rather than suggesting a connection between the two. Sheol is clearly described in numerous texts as being below many areas, e.g. Numbers 16.
56. See Levenson, 1985: 103, 127. See also Eliade, 1971: 20; 1961: 68.
57. See for example Leach, E. R. (1961) *Rethinking Anthropology*, London: University of London Press, pp. 124–36. For a more recent though conceptually problematic discussion of time re anthropology see Gell, A. (1992) *The Anthropology of Time: Cultural Construction of Temporal Maps and Images*, Oxford: Berg.
58. Levenson, 1985: 21. See also Cohn, 1981: 43.

3 Rabbinic Sacred Space

Rabbinic sacred space is characterized by two primary models, ideological centralized and functional decentralized sacred place. The ideological model is essentially a retrospective model, reflecting the Temple in Jerusalem which had been destroyed prior to the editing of the primary rabbinic texts. The functional model, which is still the essential model of space used today, is associated with the establishment of the synagogue as the primary focus of Jewish ritual and communal life. It is suggested that the fundamental difference between the two models lies in the nature of the sanctity of the space: within centralized sacred space it is essentially qualitative and intrinsic, while within decentralized space it is relational and based on use.

Idealized Sacred Space

Although the ideological aspect of centralized sacred space is already found in the Bible, because most of the texts describing it were written or edited after the destruction of the First Temple it is more fully developed in the rabbinic texts. The rabbinic texts extend the model of space to create a model of geography encompassing the entire world. It creates an abstract model of space in which the biblical model of the camp or the Temple becomes a micro-model which can be applied to the macro-level.

M. *Kelim* 1:6–1:9 presents a clear depiction of the ideological model:

> There are ten degrees of holiness: the land of Israel is holier than other lands. And what is its holiness? They bring from it the Omer,[1] and the first fruits,[2] and the two loaves,[3] which cannot be brought from all other lands. The walled cities are still more holy than it (the rest of the land), because they had to send lepers from them ... Within the walls of Jerusalem is still more holy than they are (that is the walled cities) ... the Temple Mount is still more holy ... the Women's Court is still more holy ... the Israelites' Court is still more holy ... the Courtyard of the Priests is still more holy ... Between the Sea and the Altar is still more holy ... The Sanctuary is still more holy ... the Holy of Holies is still more holy, for none may enter into it except for the High Priest on the Day of Atonement.

This text presents a model for organizing space into a pattern which while based on the biblical models discussed above, expands the model and presents a clear basis for the qualitative distinction between categories. The model contains both the macro- and the micro-levels. It begins with the relationship of the land of Israel to the world and then progressively works inward to the opposition between the Sanctuary and the Holy of Holies.

The macro-level of the model, which culminates with the Temple Mount, is defined by general categories of holiness and purity. At the widest level the land of Israel is qualitatively distinct from the world on the basis that it alone can produce three basic holy products, the loaves, the Omer, and the first fruits (*m. Kelim* 1:6). This type of distinction extends to the opposition between Jerusalem and the rest of the walled cities. Only in Jerusalem can the lesser holy things (sacrifices) be eaten (*m. Kelim* 1:8).

The macro-level also emphasizes the qualitative distinction between people, and includes a clear indication that the distinction is based on purity. As the text moves toward the center, the Holy of Holies, the number of people who are allowed to enter the holy space is progressively reduced. At the first level, between Jerusalem and the Temple Mount, the aspect of purity is clearly emphasized. Men who are impure due to sexually related diseases[4] and women who are menstruating or have borne a child are forbidden from entering. Each one of these is a category of ritual impurity. It is likely that the exclusion of women, even those without some specifically defined aspect of impurity, from spaces beyond the Women's Court is also due to purity. It is argued below (chapter 6) that within the centralized model women were perceived as intrinsically impure and thus forbidden from access to significant sacred spaces. It is therefore likely that the progressive exclusions from the more significant levels of sacred space are also based on relative purity. After the initial exclusions based on extrinsic impurity, access to increasingly sacred spaces is determined by intrinsic purity.

The model of space and geography presented in *m. Kelim* is based on the same underlying structural pattern as was centralized space in the biblical text.[5] Although one reading of the texts suggests a concentric rather than an oppositional model, it is likely that the oppositional structure of A (not) B is implied. On the widest level there is a clear opposition, Israel is set in direct opposition to the rest of the world. There is no suggestion that the levels of holiness extend beyond the boundaries of the land. Only Israel can be the source of produce fit for the Temple, thus this macro-level is characterized by the A (not) B equation. This pattern is carried on through the other levels of geography. At each level the previous level is subdivided into two exclusive categories one holier than the other. In each case the holy aspect is unique and exclusive to one category in opposition to the other.

The kinds of spaces exemplified by the Temple are ideological (at least within the rabbinic texts) in several respects. By the time that the rabbinic texts were edited (and for the most part written) the Temple and the ritual and spacial structure which it supported had been destroyed by the Romans.[6] The community itself was also becoming predominantly a diaspora community. Thus the descriptions and the models which underlie them are idealizations.

Although as discussed in chapter 4, Jerusalem and the land continued to be sites of pilgrimage by Jews throughout the diaspora, for the majority of the community Jerusalem as ideological sacred space took on a symbolic messianic character. This aspect is hinted at in the conclusion of the Pesach Seder. The text of the *Hagaddah* states, 'Next year in Jerusalem, next year we will be free.' Jerusalem in this context is usually understood to refer to the heavenly Jerusalem, a symbol of the age of the messiah, rather than the earthly city. Thus the ideological level becomes a space in time as well as in geography.

It is possible that the conceptual transition between prophecy and rabbinic authority is also related in part to the transformation from actual to ideological sacred space. Prophecy, a mode of communication and authority based on the divine selection of an individual who became qualitatively distinct from the rest of the community, is structurally related to the centralized model of sacred space. The prophet often addresses the largest possible unit. Prophecy was considered by the rabbis to occur at set times and more particularly only in intrinsic sacred space. The rabbinic mode of authority is based on the segmentary conceptual model. The difference between rabbi and non-rabbi is relative rather than intrinsic. The model is essentially nonhierarchical and open to any (male) member of the community. The roles of rabbi and prophet (and priest) reflect the nature of their contemporary sacred space, that is, the synagogue and Temple respectively.

Functional Sacred Space

The primary model of sacred space developed in rabbinic texts is functional decentralized sacred space. This model is related to the decentralized models found in the biblical text. Although it is based on the same logical structure, that is, A (not) B, it focuses on the relation between units at the lowest micro-level rather than those at the macro-level – for example between Israel and the nations. In respect of the segmentary opposition model, it deals with the relationship between the level of segmentation into the smallest units.

Functional decentralized sacred space is also dynamic. The dynamic aspect is tied in part to the dispersion of the community.[7] A single static sacred center would not serve the needs of the community as a whole. Sacred space was moved to the lowest social level, the *minyan*, ten men which were the minimum number of men necessary for a community. The *minyan* can be seen as the communal equivalent, the family, and thus the lowest level of social segmentation. Although synagogues were formally established, with buildings set aside for the purpose, the sacredness remained dynamic. It was based on the presence of the community and the use of the building. Any building (in principle) could become a sacred space, either temporarily or permanently. Unlike centralized sacred space which is intrinsic, decentralized sacred space is conditional and extrinsic.

The Synagogue

The synagogue was one of two significant loci of decentralized sacred space. It was based on the communal level of segmentation and is minimally based on the *minyan*. Although synagogues existed prior to the destruction of the Temple in CE 70, it is at that time that they perforce replaced the Temple as sacred spaces.[8] Synagogues were products of a different conceptual model, that is, the segmentary model, hence their use and structure are significantly different from that of the Temple.

The most obvious difference between the synagogue and the Temple in respect of sacred space lies in its essentially decentralized character. Unlike the Temple which was unique, the synagogue is ubiquitous. Every community and even many subcommunities had their own synagogues. The synagogue was a defining element of each segment of the community, while the Temple was that of the people as a whole.

This transformation was also reflected in the mode of worship found in each institution. The Temple service was based on sacrifice. By the time of the Second Temple, sacrifices were the sole preserve of the *Cohanim*. Ordinary Israelites could bring sacrifices to the Temple, but only the priests could offer them to God (and consume them afterwards). Thus the Temple worship emphasized the structural opposition between *Cohen* and Israelite. The *Cohanim* were qualitatively and structurally distinct, with an impermeable boundary between them and the rest of the Israelites. The mode of service found in the synagogue was prayer. Rabbinic prayer was immediate with no mediation or mediator. Thus all members of the community were equal in respect of prayer. Although the decentralized model is based on impermeable boundaries, and relies on the accepted (and enforced) distinction between Israel and the nations at the widest level, the internal hierarchies are no longer categorized in the same way. The opposition between the rabbis and the community was qualitative not categorical. The rabbis were not a caste which was qualitatively distinct (see page 56 for further discussion of this point). In principle, any person with the requisite training and knowledge could become a rabbi. Decentralized sacred space is thus essentially democratized and de-hierarchized (in respect of men but not women, see chapter 6).

This nonexclusiveness in respect of access is found even in respect of the most significant elements of the synagogue service. There is no indication, for example, that any part of the service was specifically reserved for the rabbi or other officials. Although the descendants of the priests were given some privileges, for example the first Torah blessing (see below chapter 5), this was done for the sake of maintaining peace in the community rather than any significant qualitative distinction.[9] Developments in respect of the Torah reading are significant. Originally (at least ideally) any member of the community, including women and children, were permitted to be called to read the Torah.[10] Later it was limited to the adult men (on the basis of extrinsic rather than intrinsic reasons). The person called was expected to read from the scroll, suggesting that the only limiting factor was the ability to do so. Eventually, due to the diminution of this ability, an additional reader was appointed who would read on behalf of either those who were unable to do so or all of those called up. In spite of this, the person who receives the merit of the reading was the congregant who was called up rather than the reader (Elbogen, 1993: 140–1).

Although, as discussed below, there were aspects of synagogue construction, especially by the Medieval period, which reflected hierarchies of holiness, the original construction minimizes this aspect. The early rabbinic texts include no specific rulings about the size or shape for the buildings. The archeological evidence suggests that all of the congregants sat along the walls with no clear divisions in respect of access.[11] Although some of the synagogues have a *bimah* a raised platform from which some of the prayers may have been led, initially there seems not to have been a set place for the Ark (the cabinet in which the Torah was kept).[12]

The synagogue, was, however, set in structural opposition to the houses around it. The *Tosefta* states that a synagogue should be built at the city's highest point (*t. Megillah* 4:22). Talmudic texts state that at the very least the synagogue should be taller than the roofs of houses.[13] This pattern of visible distinction and opposition continued until it was prohibited by Christian and Islamic authorities.[14] Thus, the synagogue is set in opposition to the houses. This opposition, however, unlike that created by centralized sacred space, is relative.

Several aspects of the synagogue create a direct association with the Temple and the models of sacred space developed in the biblical text. On the level of worship a direct association was made between the service of the Temple and that of the synagogue. One of the major rabbinic innovations after the destruction of the Temple was the transformation in the means of creating or using sacred space. The *Avodah*, the sacrificial cult, was replaced by *Avodat HaLev*, prayer. The rabbis state that service of the heart, prayer, replaces sacrifices in the Temple.[15] The association of the two types of sacred space was made by the association of terms. The synagogue replaced the Temple as the space where one could communicate with the divine.

The synagogue was also divided hierarchically into spaces of relatively greater holiness. The building itself has an element of sacredness. This aspect is seen in those laws which limit the purposes for which a building that had been a synagogue could be used if it was sold by the community. *M. Megillah* 3:2 states that a synagogue could not be sold to be used as a bathhouse, a tannery, an immersion pool, or a urinal. Even if the building is in ruins, there are limitations as to how it should be treated. The laws which limit those activities which are allowed to be done in a synagogue also demonstrate its relative sanctity. This holiness, however, is of a different kind than that found in respect to the Temple. The Temple was intrinsically holy, and there would be no situation which would allow its use for other purposes. In spite of the restrictions found respecting synagogue buildings, they could be used for other purposes, provided that there was no disrespect to the building. The synagogue's holiness is relative rather than intrinsic and exists only so long as the building functions as a synagogue.

The relative holiness of the synagogue is also indicated by the laws concerning the *mezuzah*.[16] The medieval codes state that a synagogue is exempt from this requirement. Although this exemption is in part due to the fact that certain things were not done in a synagogue, for example eating or sleeping, it is also due to the holiness of the building. It does not need a *mezuzah* because the synagogue itself, *qua* building, will act as a *mezuzah*, that is, to remind those who go in and out of their obligations to God.

The internal structure of the traditional synagogue[17] was also organized hierarchically into areas of increasing holiness which are similar to those of the Temple. The building was divided into a men's and a women's section. The women's section was often in the form of a gallery or a section separated by a *mehitzah*, a small wall or partition. This section is compared to the Women's Court of the Temple. The men's section was subdivided into three divisions. The first was the area in which the community sits. This area was generally nonhierarchical, though leaders or respected members of the community might be given seats of honor which are often placed near the Ark (Elbogen, 1993: 362). The second subdivision was the *bimah*, a raised platform from which the service was led. In ancient times the *bimah* was often placed along the northern side, facing the entrance (Elbogen, 1993: 346). By the Middle Ages, however, it was customary to place the *bimah* in the center of the building.[18] The Ark was the final subdivision and the holiest part of the synagogue. The Hebrew term that has come to be used, *aron hakodesh* (the Holy Ark), makes a clear allusion to the Ark in the Temple. The *Tosefta* calls it the *kodesh*, the holy, emphasizing its sacred character.[19] The Ark contains the Torah scrolls. Since the Middle Ages, the Ark was usually placed on the eastern wall of the synagogue facing Jerusalem. The orientation of prayer was also toward the Ark and Jerusalem.

The hierarchy of sacred spaces, with the exception of women, is different from that of the Temple. Each area of the Temple was progressively more exclusive, with progressively fewer individuals allowed to move into the sacred center. These hierarchies were based on a model of intrinsic purity. The synagogue, however, has no such restrictions. All male members of the community are allowed access to all areas of the synagogue. The particular holiness of the *bimah* and the Ark, however, is emphasized or differentiated by the practice of calling up readers and others who will play a role in the service. The *Tosefta*, for example, states that even the leader of the community could not go up to the *bimah* (for the reading of the Torah) without being invited by the congregation.[20] Thus access to sacred space in the synagogue is determined by the congregation (as an honor) rather than being due to an intrinsic quality.

The decorations of the Torah scrolls are also directly connected with the Temple. Although there is a high degree of variation, some aspects are fairly consistent (Elbogen, 1993: 355). In Ashkinazic communities the Torah is adorned with a breast piece which is worn in the same manner as that of the High Priest. The breast piece often has as part of its decorations a depiction of the two pillars, Yachin and Boaz, which stood in front of the Temple.

Other decorations include pomegranates and bells which were also part of the vestments worn by the High Priest.

The synagogue also includes other reflections of the biblical under-standing of sacred space. The aspect of height, or raised areas, as a significant feature of positive sacred space is already indicated by the location of the synagogue, originally in the highest part of the city. Raised areas are also used to indicate the most sacred parts of the synagogue. The *bimah* is usually a raised platform. Thus the most important aspects of the service, especially the reading of the Torah, symbolic revelation, are always led from a symbolic mountain, that is, positive liminal space. The positive, and significant, aspect of going up is emphasized by the term used to describe being called to participate in the Torah service: *aliyah*, that is 'going up.'[21] Like the *bimah*, the Ark is always built in a raised position, usually higher than the *bimah*.[22]

The aspect of directionality is also related to models found in the biblical text. In the biblical text positive value was attributed to the west while negative value was attributed to the east. This valuation seems to be inverted in most diaspora communities. In most synagogues the Ark was placed on the eastern wall and this was also the orientation of prayer. This orientation is directly associated with the Temple, as it is meant to be toward Jerusalem. In some synagogues in other parts of the diaspora (non-European) the Ark faces in other directions, depending on their geographic relation to Jerusalem.[23]

This variation in the valuation of geographic directionality is important in understanding the nature of cultural symbols and their transformation. Symbols are never static; they can change on several levels. Minimally they have a large cone of ideas, memories, and feelings which they evoke and that, in conjunction with other symbols, are used to create conceptual patterns. This cone of evocation is constantly changing and developing both on the individual and cultural level. If, however, the cultural context changes significantly, then the meaning or use of the symbol may also change to reflect the new cultural circumstance. This is found here in respect of direction. The direction west had a certain qualitative value in biblical Israel (and perhaps Babylonia) perhaps due to the geographic placement of Israel. With the diaspora, especially into Europe, that qualitative valence was no longer culturally significant, thus the valence is inverted to reflect the new cultural conditions and conceptualization of geography.

Relation of the Divine to Sacred Space

Although the theological basis of rabbinic models of sacred space is related to that of the Bible, it is significantly transformed in association with the development of the decentralized model of space. The biblical model was based on God's unique presence, either historically or ahistorically. Sites like Beth El owed their sanctity to a historic revelation, while the Temple in Jerusalem owed it to an ongoing and absolutely unique presence (either in a strong sense as a literal place for God to dwell or as a place where God's glory manifested itself). It is the later model that predominates in biblical theology. Although rabbinic texts, especially those which focus on the Temple, include elements of the unique presence model, they also extend the model to encompass multiple decentralized sacred spaces. Some of the biblical texts already suggest a transformation in the understanding of God and God's relation with particular places and the world as a whole. This issue is further developed in rabbinic texts which address the paradoxes inherent to God's relationship with the world.

Some rabbinic texts attempt to resolve the paradox of transcendence and immanence. Thus *Midrash Psalms* on 24:1 suggests that unlike a human king who is limited to staying in one room at a time, God is able to be in more than one place, filling both the upper worlds (transcendence) and the lower world (immanence). Some of these texts suggest a further transformation of the model of sacred space. Due to God's omnipresence, God is equally present in all places at all times. *Genesis Rabbah* 1:18, for example, suggests that God is the place of the world, the world (and any particular place in it) is not God's place.

Many texts address the paradox created by God's distinctive presence in the Temple and the possibility of God's being present in other parts of the world as well. *Numbers Rabbah*, Naso, 12:4, examines this issue both in respect of the Tabernacle and the Temple.

> It is written, 'And Moses was not able to enter the tent of meeting, because the glory of the Eternal filled the sanctuary' (Exodus 40:35). Rabbi Joshua of Sikhnin said in the name of Rabbi Levi: The matter is like a cave which lies by the sea shore; the tide rises and fills the cave with water, but the sea is still as full. So the sanctuary and the tent of meeting were filled with the radiance of the Shekhinah,[24] but the world was no less filled with God's glory.[25]

This text provides a transition between the centralized and the decentralized models. The uniqueness of the Temple, as the place where God is specially manifest, is preserved while still allowing for God, or God *Shekhinah* to be present throughout the rest of the world as well.

The concept of the *Shekhinah* is a significant factor in the development of rabbinic theology and its application to decentralized sacred space. As stated above, the rabbis distinguished between two aspects of relations to God. The essential essence of God is fundamentally transcendent. It is this aspect which is (in some texts) uniquely associated with the Temple. The *Shekhinah*, which comes from the Hebrew root שכן meaning either dwelling or indwelling, is immanent and present both throughout the world and in the Temple.[26] The concept of the *Shekhinah* is perhaps more closely associated with the people rather than to a specific place.[27] This is suggested in *Lamentations Rabbah* (1:33) which describes God's presence as going into exile with the people.[28]

Many texts reflect the need to justify or explain the nature of decentralized sacred spaces, and to demonstrate God's presence in them. Thus, *Deuteronomy Rabbah*, Ki Tavo, 7:2 states: 'God says: "Who has ever come into a synagogue, and not found my glory there?" Rabbi Abahu adds, "not only that, if you are in my synagogue, God stands by you."' Other texts describe God as metaphorically leaping from one synagogue to the next.[29] Thus like the Temple, God is present in each synagogue, yet unlike centralized space, that presence is, by definition, nonexclusive.

The presence of the *Shekhinah* in decentralized sacred space is closely related to the nature of the sacred space. Sacred space was defined by use and dynamic.[30] A building was only a synagogue if it were used as such. Similarly the presence of the *Shekhinah* does not seem to have been intrinsic; many texts suggest that it was related to presence of the community (as suggested in the text from *Deuteronomy Rabbah*), or to the performance of commandments.

Several different texts associate the presence of the *Shekhinah* to a variety of different situations and activities. Thus *Avot* 3:2 states in the name of Rabbi Hananiah b. Teradion that if two men sit together discussing the Torah, then God's *Shekhinah* is with them. *B. Berakhot* 6a ties the presence of the *Shekhinah* to sitting in judgment.[31] Thus God's presence, like sacred space, is conditional. When a synagogue is used for the purposes of study or *halakhah* it becomes a sacred space, a place where God is present.

Avot 3:6 is particularly significant in this respect. It lists a variety of different groupings of people and associates the presence of the *Shekhinah* with each.

> Rabbi Halafta b. Dosa of Kefar Hanania said: If ten men sit together and occupy themselves with the Law, the divine presence rests among them, for it is written, 'God stands in the congregation of God' (Psalm 82:1). And how do we know this of five? Because it is written, 'and has founded his group on the earth' (Amos 9:6). And from where three? Because it is written, 'God judges among the judges' (Psalm 82:1). And from where even two? Because it is written, 'Then those who feared the Eternal spoke with one another and the Eternal paid heed to them, and heard' (Malachi 3:16). And from where even one? Because it is written, 'In every place where I record my name I will come to you and bless you' (Exodus 20:24).

This text begins by establishing a direct connection between the *Shekhinah* and the community. Ten men, the *minyan*, represented the smallest possible number of men needed for a viable community. The last section emphasizes the ubiquitousness of the *Shekhinah*: it can appear in any place which God chooses.

The presence of the *Shekhinah* in decentralized space is also different from that in centralized space in respect to purity. As discussed above, in the centralized model the presence of God was directly associated with purity, and thus only the absolutely pure, the High Priest, could come into direct contact with the most holy objects, and perhaps the divine. Many texts suggest that this relationship was not significant in respect of decentralized sacred space. Thus *Sifre Numbers*, Naso, 1, 1b states: 'Beloved are the Israelites to God, because even when they are unclean, the *Shekhinah* dwells among them.' *Yoma* 56b makes a similar point, emphasizing that the Temple (and the purification process associated with it) is no longer necessary for direct contact with God. This transformation in respect of purity is related to that of intrinsic to extrinsic holiness. Texts, which discuss the absence or removal of the *Shekhinah*, associate it with extrinsic, or moral failings (that is failings which are due to choice rather than inherent failings). *Sifra*, Kedoshim, 89a states that injustice causes the *Shekhinah* to depart from Israel. *Deuteronomy Rabbah*, Ki Tetze, 6:14 states that God removes the *Shekhinah* from Israel due to slander. Other texts add bloodshed and incest.[32] These texts suggest the following set of relations:

God (Transcendent)/Intrinsic Holiness/Centralized Space/Unique Connection to the Divine/Intrinsic Purity (impurity);

Shekhinah (Immanent)/Conditional (actional) Holiness/Decentralized Space/ Universal Connection/Extrinsic (moral qualities).

The Home

The synagogue, however, was only part of the transformation of sacred space, and the replacement of the Temple. The home also takes on aspects of the Temple and becomes a locus of sacred space. The home, as the smallest noncommunal level of segmentation, is the logical partner of the *minyan*, the smallest communal level of segmentation. One of the strongest associations of the home with the Temple occurs on Pesach. During the *Seder* the leader takes on many aspects of the priestly ritual. The leader, for example, ritually washes his hands in symbolic association with the priests, linking the *Seder* with the offering of the Paschal sacrifice. The Pesach *Seder* table symbolically is transformed into the altar and the house into the Temple. Other connections with the Temple are found in the Shabbat candles and table which in part represent the Menorah and the altar of the Temple. The home is also directly associated with the Temple through the term מקדש מעט 'small temple,' which is commonly used to describe the home. The term suggests that like the synagogue the home replaces some aspects of the Temple.

Many of the texts which discuss the presence or the absence of the *Shekhinah* also refer to the home. Thus its presence is associated with meals and with husbands and wives. *B. Sota* 17a states, for example, 'When husband and wife are worthy, the *Shekhinah* abides among them.' Thus God's presence is linked to the home as well as the synagogue.

If the home is examined in the context of the main element of decentralized sacred space its significance is clarified. Decentralized sacred space, and the presence of the *Shekhinah* is particularly associated with the performance of commandments. The home, as a locus of *halakhah*, is probably second only to the synagogue. The home as a particular sacred space may be tied to this legal (or actional) concentration.

The home as a sacred space fits within the structural pattern of decentralized sacred space. It is the logical noncommunal extension of structural, segmentary opposition, which is ultimately based on the smallest unit in the system. In transforming the house into a sacred space two aspects of the system, the social and the ritual, are united, and create a system of mutual justification. The home and the family are supported by the theological and the ritual, and equally the theological and the ritual are supported by the home.

Decentralized Sacred Space: A (not) B

In order to clarify the way in which the underlying structure is exemplified in both variants of decentralized sacred space, it is necessary to focus on the nature of the oppositions involved. On the widest level the opposition between Israel (the people) and the nations is strongly maintained. As the rabbinic period progressed the external boundary ceased to be problematic, both regarding endogamy or direct positive cultural influence. Thus the structural equation at the macro-level was strongly emphasized, without the need for strong opposition from the internal conceptual models. The internal opposition no longer needed to recapitulate the external opposition directly in order to justify it.

The focus of opposition on the micro-level shifts. The external boundary allowed the structural opposition move to the smallest possible units, on both the communal and family level. This refocusing was, in part, related to the extension of endogamy – a variation of the underlying structure at the level of social organization – which logically emphasizes the smallest possible circle of relations. Endogamy, logically, pulls inward. Thus, each unit is set in opposition to other similar internal units, all on the same structural level, creating a micro A (not) B model.

One significant feature of this variant of the segmentary model is the equality of all units. The hierarchical possibilities of the segmentary system which are emphasized in the biblical model, as part of the validation of the external boundary, are not found in the rabbinic model. This aspect is reflected in the transformation in access to sacred space: all male Israelites have actual or potential access to all sacred spaces, and to all positions within the community. The role of rabbi is therefore not a structural category, as was the role of the priest, that is, as a qualitatively distinct caste. It is merely one role that any male within the community could potentially take on.

This understanding of the role of the rabbi is emphasized in many rabbinic texts. These texts describe the origins of different sages. The texts suggest that rabbis could come from any part of society. Thus, *b. Yoma* describes the origins of two important sages. It focuses on the poverty of Hillel's origins and the wealth of those of Rabbi Elazar. Other rabbis were said to have come from priestly origins, and one, Resh Lakish, was said to be a highwayman before becoming a rabbi. On a more general level, the equality of Israel before God is also frequently stated in rabbinic texts.

This transformation in focus is mirrored in the transformations in myth between the biblical and the rabbinic period. Biblical myths – in order to resolve the problem of endogamy created by weak external boundaries, and thus strengthen those boundaries – emphasized narratively actual incest and therefore the need to marry as closely as possible. Transformation of the people as a whole, through divine rebirth, is symbolic and occurs in each generation culminating in the origins of the *Cohanim*. It therefore suggests that although all Israel is qualitatively, symbolically reborn, the *Cohanim* are closer to this and therefore qualitatively distinct from the rest of the Israelites. Rabbinic narrative myths shift the symbolic and actual elements. They de-emphasize the incestuous elements, perhaps because endogamy no longer needed to be internally enforced, thus transforming the actual incest into symbolic incest.[33] The rebirth is both transformed in the opposite direction and refocused almost completely on Isaac. Many midrashic texts suggest that Isaac, reinterpreting Genesis 22, was actually sacrificed and reborn.[34] The focus on Isaac as an actually reborn figure emphasizes the equality of all Israelites. It suggests that as all are descended from a divinely reborn figure, all are qualitatively equal before God.

Domus Dei, Domus Ecclesiae

One influential analysis of sacred space which is relevant to the discussion here is that of H. Turner (1979). He examines models of sacred space (and the Temple and synagogue specifically) and their transformation. His analysis focuses on the phenomenology of sacred spaces on a broad cross-cultural basis, and in several important respects is indebted to Eliade.[35] He discusses the relationship between two types of sacred spaces, *domus dei* and *domus ecclesiae*, which are in many respects applicable to the Temple and the synagogue respectively.

Some of the key features which Turner suggests distinguish the two types of sacred spaces are the nature of God's presence and the character of the access to the sacred space. The *domus dei* is understood as being (at least in part) the particular residence of the divine. The divine is associated with the location and it is the point in which the human and the divine can interact. Because of this association, the *domus dei* is typically built on a grand scale. Another significant feature is the restriction in respect of access. The *domus dei* typically is restricted to a particular class or caste.[36] The *domus ecclesiae*, of which, he suggests, the synagogue is a good example, is essentially dynamic. It is not the residence of God, but rather a place where God can be met. It is also a democratic institution, emphasizing the community rather than a priestly caste. Ultimately, the presence of God is tied to the community rather than divine sanction or presence.[37]

Although these aspects of Turner's analysis are consonant with that suggested here, there are several issues of contention. Turner's analysis has a clearly theological bias. It views the *domus ecclesiae* as being spiritually superior to the *domus dei*. In effect, he suggests that the original model used by the Israelites, the Tent of Meeting, was essentially a *domus ecclesiae*, a place which emphasized individual spirituality, which is associated with the prophetic rather than the priestly form of spirituality.[38] With the settlement of the land, the Israelites created temples essentially using a Canaanite model.[39] He argues that the *domus dei* model is essentially flawed, particularly because of its static nature and due to the theological problem of immanence and transcendence, and that these problems are only resolved with the return to the *domus ecclesiae* model. His argument as a whole is directed toward the establishment of Christianity in which this process reaches its logical conclusion (Turner, H., 1979: 104). It is perhaps unsurprising that he suggests that the sacred space exemplified by the *domus ecclesiae* is particularly found in the three monotheistic traditions, Judaism, Christianity, and Islam.

Turner does touch on the process of transformation between the various models. The motivating factor in the transformation to a *domus dei* model appears to be growth and expansion. The movements back to the purer *domus ecclesiae* derive from revival or reformation movements that seek to recover the original spiritual forms. There is, however, no clear association of this theological transformation with any broader sociological phenomena. Although Turner examines the movements between models (which he ethnocentrically labels 'Advances and Retreats,'[40]) the book is a polemical argument in favor of abandoning the *domus dei* form or radically transforming it, due to the situation of the real world, into some new form which combines the two. In spite of this grudging recognition it is clear that Turner regards the *domus ecclesiae* as the positive Christian norm.[41]

This bias led Turner in his discussion of the history of the synagogue to view all developments which he perceives as returning to the Temple form to be problematic. This is illustrated in his discussion of the Ark in the synagogue in which he suggests that the elaboration of the Ark is associated with a partial return to a *domus dei* model (Turner, 1979: 290). He implicitly criticizes an American rabbi for stating that the presence of the Ark transforms a room into a synagogue (Turner, 1979: 292).

His focus on the Ark as the only significant holy space, although in part true, ignores the significance of the *bimah*. Indeed, Turner suggests that in spite of the progressive elaboration of the *bimah*, mirroring that of the Ark, this is 'entirely appropriate' and does not in any way transform the synagogue from a *domus ecclesiae* to a *domus dei*. His argument ignores the sacred aspects of the *bimah* and its equivalence respecting access to both the Ark and the *bimah*. As discussed above, access to the *bimah* had a limiting factor. Although all (male) members of the community could in principle go up to the *bimah*, they were only allowed to do so if invited. This same type of exclusion is found in respect to the Ark. In spite of this limitation, there was equal access to both the Ark and *bimah*, with no exclusive group being given sole access. His methodology leads him to draw this false distinction. If one is focusing on the question of the presence of God, then clearly the Ark and its elaboration must be more significant than a raised reading desk. Yet, ironically, from a rabbinic perspective, it is the *bimah* and the activities which occur there that cause God to be present rather than the Ark or its contents.

A further problem lies in the nature of the relationship or experience of God within sacred space. At times Turner seems to imply that the Tent of Meeting and the *domus ecclesiae* model emphasize the transcendent aspect of the divinity rather than the immanent.[42] He argues that the transformation from residence to appearance is based on this theological point. Although this understanding of transcendence and immanence may be appropriate to Christian theology, it does not fit with the Jewish understanding of the relationship with God as exemplified in the synagogue. As suggested above, the essential factor in creating dynamic sacred space is precisely the presence of God. This presence, the *Shekhinah*, although associated with the people and their performance of commandments, represents the immanent aspect of the divine. Although it does not dwell in the synagogue, the texts cited above clearly demonstrate that its presence was an essential component.

The objections to Turner's approach can be summed up in one overall criticism. Turner's analysis is based on a particular Christian theological position regarding sacred space – the interrelationship between incarnation and the church (that is, the people) as the true meeting place with God. Perhaps unconsciously, Turner's arguments use this model as the ideal type against which all other expressions are judged. This is true even in respect of specific architectural forms. It is questionable whether such a culture-specific model can be usefully applied on a cross-cultural (or even historical) basis.

Conclusions

During the rabbinic period there is a transformation in the model of sacred space from a centralized to a decentralized model. Sacred space in this period is moved from the Temple to the synagogue and the home. Both the biblical and the rabbinic models are expressions of the underlying structural equation of A (not) B.

The biblical, centralized model reflects the macro-level of the equation; the strong central focus emphasizes the boundary between Israel and the nations. The rabbinic, decentralized model reflects the micro- , segmentary level. It de-emphasizes the external boundary and allows a high degree of internal segmentation into communities, exemplified by synagogues, and families, exemplified by homes. Because the external boundary does not need to be maintained, the internal relation between segments does not have to recapitulate the structure of the external opposition. This allows the high degree of internal segmentation at the lowest levels, with opposition only between units of similar quality. At the lowest level, and with the removal of internal qualitative differentiations, there is no intrinsic difference between any of the segments.

It is likely that this transformation is in part related to Israel's sociological situation. During the biblical period, or more precisely the period in which the biblical text was being edited, external boundaries were not strongly defined. One significant aspect of the boundary is perhaps associated with the question or problem of endogamy, an issue which is increasingly important during the postexilic period. During that period endogamy needed to be internally maintained in the face of a culturally mixed society. Similarly, Israelite culture was open to a wide range of influences from other cultures. The increasingly centralized model is in part a response to this sociological situation creating and emphasizing external boundaries.

During the rabbinic period, however, especially as it moves into the Middle Ages, there is a progressive tightening of external boundaries. This tightening is due to external rather than internal forces. With this transformation in social context, endogamy was in effect enforced externally. This led to a transformation in emphasis in the equation to the micro-level. Without the need for strong external boundaries internal segmentation could occur. This led to a transformation in the model of sacred space. The synagogue and the home, both of which represented the smallest level of segmentation, became the dominant sacred places.

Although the macro-model is not emphasized during the rabbinic period, several aspects of it are still found in Jewish sacred spaces. These function on an ideological level, and create a connection with both the Temple, the past, and the messianic age, the future. Functional sacred space is essentially historical and diachronic and stands between these two ahistorical points.

Notes

1. See Leviticus 23:10–17.
2. See Deuteronomy 26:1–16.
3. See Leviticus 23:17.
4. Jastrow defines the term זבים as 'men afflicted with gonorrhea'. See Jastrow, M. (1971) *Dictionary of the Talmud*, New York: Judaica Press, p. 377.
5. See page 23.
6. The *Mishnah* was edited around CE 200. The Temple in Jerusalem was destroyed in 70 CE and Jewish occupation of Jerusalem was ended in CE 130.
7. For a similar approach from a different theoretical perspective see Maier, E. (1975) 'Torah as Movable Territory' in *Annals of the Association of American Geographers* **65**, 18–32.
8. The first datable place of worship equivalent to a synagogue is found in an Egyptian inscription from the second century BCE. The inscription is a dedication of a Jewish *proseuche* (a term used for an institution similar to the synagogue) to the Ptolemaic king and queen. See Elbogen, I. (1993) *Jewish Liturgy: A Comprehensive History* (translated R. Scheindlin), New York: JTSA, p. 338.
9. This principle is stated in *m. Gittin* 5:9. It suggests that although the rabbis believed that the *Cohanim* did not have an intrinsic right to receive this honor, due to the respect which the *Cohanim* believed that they deserved the rabbis gave them the honor, to preserve communal harmony. They also may have wanted to recognize the biblical institution while minimizing its power and role.

10. See Elbogen, 1993: 139; and *m. Megillah* 4:6, *b. Megillah* 23a.
11. See chapter 6 for a discussion of women's access to sacred space in early synagogues.
12. See Elbogen, 1993: 343–7 (especially Scheindlin's additions on the basis of more recent archeological findings, p. 346).
13. See for example *b. Shabbat* 11a.
14. Elbogen, 1993: 352. Elbogen reports that this practice was followed in seventeenth century Poland by adding an extra beam to the roof of the synagogue.
15. See for example, *Midrash Psalms* on 5:4. Other texts suggest that other elements available to all Jews also replace sacrifice, for example *Abot D'Rabbi Natan* 11a, in which good deeds are said to replace sacrifice as a means of atonement.
16. A *mezuzah* is a box placed on the doors of Jewish buildings, particularly homes. It contains two passages from Deuteronomy 6:4–9 and 11: 13–21. It is fastened to the right-hand doorpost.
17. That is, the form which predominated from the Middle Ages to the mid-nineteenth century. It is also the form which is, for the most part, retained in Orthodox synagogues today.
18. Maimonides states that it is an obligation to place the *Bimah* (also called the *Almemor*) in the center of the synagogue (*Mishne Torah*, Laws of Prayer, 11:3). Although Karo in the *Shulchan Aruch* does not follow Maimonides, Isserlis does. Elbogen states that this pattern was universally followed in Germany and Poland (Elbogen, 1993: 361).
19. *T. Megillah* 4:21.
20. *T Megillah* 4:21.
21. Interestingly this same term is used by Zionists to describe the process of Immigrating to the State of Israel. This usage emphasizes the conceptualization of the State of Israel as modern sacred space – many of the immigrants are secular rather than religious Jews.
22. The Ark was often elevated so that it had to be approached by steps. See Elbogen, 1993: 359.
23. The symbolic power of the west is retained in some rabbinic texts. E. Urbach cites a text which attempts to distinguish between Jewish prayer and Christian prayer (which was also oriented toward Jerusalem), suggesting that prayer should be toward the west 'because the *Shekhinah* is in the west.' Urbach also indicates that many early synagogues were built with a westward orientation. See Urbach, E.E. (1979) *The Sages*, Cambridge: Harvard University Press, pp. 62–3.
24. The *Shekhinah* is the rabbinic term for the immanent aspect of the divine. It should be seen in experiential terms, when God is experienced as close, God is called the *Shekhinah Genesis Rabbah*, in Bereshit, 4:4, emphasizes this point. It suggests that although God remains the same, one's image or experience of God changes. See also *Numbers Rabbah*, Naso, 12:3. For a detailed discussion of the development of the concept see Urbach, 1979: 37–65.
25. For detailed discussion of this text see: Urbach, 1979: 46.
26. It should be noted, however, that there are texts in which the presence of the *Shekhinah* is limited to the land of Israel. Thus, *Sifre Zuta*, Naso, states: 'The land of Canaan is fit to contain the House of the *Shekhinah*, but TransJordan is not fit for the House of the *Shekhinah*.' A similar concept is also found in the *Mekilta* 1b which examines the question of Jonah fleeing from God. These texts may reflect a middle position in the transformation of the model of sacred space.
27. Urbach suggests a transformation in the use of the term. In texts written in (or

describing) the period prior to the destruction of the Temple, the *Shekhinah* was used to describe the experience of God at a particular place. After the destruction, however, it was more closely connected with the people (Urbach, 1979: 43). This transformation is in keeping with that suggested here respecting centralized and decentralized sacred space.

28. This concept is also found in *Sifre Numbers*, Be'haalotekha, 84, 22b, which states that the *Shekhinah* goes into Exile with Israel and will return when Israel returns. This is also emphasized in *Sifre Numbers*, Masse'e, 161, 62b–63a which also emphasizes that the *Shekhinah* is with Israel even in its impurity.

29. See for example *Numbers Rabbah*, Naso, 11:2.

30. C. Primus takes a similar position to that suggested here. He argues that in the rabbinic period sacred space becomes associated with the performance of commandments; it is actionally defined rather than intrinsically defined. See Primus, C. (1986) 'The Borders of Judaism: The Land of Israel in Early Rabbinic Judaism' in Hoffman, L. (ed.) *The Land of Israel: Jewish Perspectives*, Notre Dame: University of Notre Dame Press, p. 106.

31. It also includes material parallel to that found in *Avot* 3:6. It begins with a statement that men's prayers are only heard in the synagogue and then proves (using the same proof as *Avot*) that God is found in the synagogue, and in the presence of ten men. The text then works through other combinations, three men, two and one, and proves in each case that God is in their midst provided they are engaged in particular activities.

32. See for example *Sifre Numbers*, Masai, 161; *Sifre Deuteronomy*, Shoftim, 148, Ki Tetze, 254.

33. See for example the rabbinic reinterpretations of Abraham's and Sarah's relationship in regard to Genesis 20 in *Lekakh Tov* on Genesis 11:29 and 20:12. These texts argue that Sarah was not Abraham's sister as stated in Genesis 20 but rather his niece.

34. See for example *Genesis Rabbah* 56:19 and *Pirke de Rabbi Eliezer* 31. These and related texts are analyzed in detail in Kunin, 1996: 226–30, 249–52, Spiegel, S. (1979) *The Last Trial*, New York: Behrman House.

35. See for example his discussion of the significant characteristics of sacred spaces. Turner, H., 1979: 15–33.

36. One other aspect of the *domus dei* model needs to be addressed – the issue of microcosm. Turner, following Eliade's lead argues that temples (and the Temple in Jerusalem) function as a microcosm, representing the cosmic abode. Although Turner recognizes that this is a contentious position quoting R. De Vaux's ([1961] *Ancient Israel*, New York: McGraw-Hill) opposition to it, he ultimately accepts this view. The examples he uses in support, however, do not support the concept of microcosm. The only significant elements they support are, God's dwelling in the Temple (Turner, H., 1979: 57), a preordained plan for it (1979: 58), and a cosmological reference based on its geographic orientation (1979: 59). Turner takes this position because he wishes there to be an almost literal understanding of God's dwelling in the Temple and in *domus dei* in general. The only texts which support his view are postbiblical.

37. See Turner, H., 1979: 100.

38. See Turner, H., 1979: 88–96. Turner can only make this argument by emphasizing the distinction between the Tent of Meeting, described in Exodus 35–50, and the elaborate Tabernacle described in Exodus 25–33. Following Haran he suggests that while the elaborate Tabernacle may be an idealization, the simple Tent of Meeting may reflect the actual practice during the Mosaic period.

Due to the history of the composition and editing of the text, as well as the historical questions which might be raised about the Mosaic period, it is questionable as to whether either one of the models has any great historic depth or indeed historical priority. It may be that they are contemporary variations reflecting the two different models of sacred space that are found throughout the text, that is, a centralized model focusing on the Temple and a segmentary model focusing on multiple sacred centers.

Turner's arguments about the nature of the Tent of Meeting and his identification of it as a *domus ecclesiae* are also questionable. His arguments concerning the presence of the Ark or some similar cultic item seem to be special pleading and only exclude the Ark on the basis of it being of Canaanite origin – an assertion which is not universally accepted – and thus not existing in the time of Moses. If the text is placed in its historical and editorial context, then even if the Ark was not of Semitic origin it would have already existed. Turner also points to the use of a simple tent shrine among contemporary Muslim communities. It is questionable whether this usage which emerges from actual nomadic communities and from a fully developed monotheistic religious theology are applicable to Israel during the period of the creation of the texts.

39. Turner is not necessarily suggesting that the Israelites copied the Canaanites, rather the Temple is seen as an exemplar of a universal form of sacred space.
40. See for example Turner, 1979: 227–59.
41. See for example Turner, 1979: 341.
42. See for example Turner, 1979: 92.

4 Pilgrimage

Pilgrimage is a significant complex often associated with sacred space. Throughout different periods of Jewish history pilgrimage has been of greater or lesser significance and played a variety of different roles. This chapter examines these different roles and their relationship to different models of sacred space. It also places the discussion into the wider context of anthropological analysis. Much of the anthropological groundwork for its analysis has been laid by Victor Turner.[1] Although his work broadly focuses on Christian pilgrimages, it suggests that the model developed can be applied to Jewish and Islamic pilgrimages as well (1978: 1). The case of Jewish pilgrimage, however, appears to have several significant differences and suggests the necessity of refining the general model. The role of liminality and the related aspects of the pilgrimage complex are culture specific, and thus should not be emphasized as the significant characteristics of pilgrimage in a cross-cultural context.

Turner observes that pilgrimages share several features with *rites de passage*, translated as 'rites of transition,' as analyzed by Arnold van Gennep (Turner, V. and Turner E., 1978: 2). Pilgrimages, like rites of transition, are characterized by three phases: the separation phase, the liminal phase, and the reintegration phase. Turner suggests that pilgrimages are also transformative. They allow people to transform their individual status whether in the eyes of society or in respect to salvation. The liminal phase is that which allows the individual to move to a new status or state, which is concretized in the reintegration phase.

Turner's analysis focuses on the intermediate or liminal phase. During this phase the individual is in a condition of transition, often between one status and another. He is a mediator containing elements of both his previous state and his new state. The liminal is ambiguous and often outside of the usual societal restraints. In pilgrimages this ambiguity is often expressed in the removal of hierarchy. All pilgrims are equal regardless of their actual social position.

Turner suggests that the term liminoid may be more correct than liminal regarding pilgrimage. The difference in terminology relates in part to the aspect of obligation. In societies with formal *rites de passage*, these rituals are usually obligatory. All men, for example, must move from the status of boy to adult. Thus, liminality includes this element. Pilgrimage, although transformative and mediatory, however, is usually not (Turner suggests never) truly obligatory. Thus it is not properly liminal. Liminoid is used to describe phenomena that have some, but not all, characteristics of the liminal (1978: 253).

His analysis suggests that the liminoid phase is connected with the act of pilgrimage rather than the performance of rituals at the conclusion of it. Christian pilgrimage is seen as having an initiatory role. Like ceremonies of initiation (in many societies), pilgrimages have aspects of trial and tribulation, obstacles that prepare the pilgrim for his transformation through exposure to religious sacra at the conclusion of the pilgrimage. To an extent, in Christian pilgrimage it is the journey and the trials along the way that are significant rather than the conclusion of the pilgrimage at the sacred site.[2] He suggests that pilgrimages of the 'historical religions' (presumably Judaism, Christianity, Islam, and perhaps Buddhism) lead to transformation of the individual in respect to his moral state, perhaps to prepare him for the afterlife (1978: 8). It may also include a transformation in social status, which is usually secondary.

As mentioned above, Turner observes, however, that there is a significant difference between pilgrimages and rites of transition. He argues that unlike rites of transition which tend to be obligatory, pilgrimages are voluntary. Turner emphasizes the aspect of freedom of choice. He contrasts the freedom expressed by the pilgrimage with the obligatory nature of hierarchical social structure. He suggests that even in respect to the *Hajj*, which is in principle obligatory, the possible extenuating circumstances render it also a free rather than an obligated choice.

In this respect, as in many others, pilgrimages are seen as being antistructure. They are a means, for at least a short period, of moving outside of hierarchical relationships and the orthodox modes of religious observance. He suggests that for these reasons pilgrimages are usually regarded with suspicion by the organized religious authorities. Pilgrimages are moves toward the periphery away from the cultural center which refocus the individual toward a spiritual rather than a temporal religious or secular center.

The antistructural aspect of pilgrimage is enhanced by the liminal aspects of the journey and culminates in the united throng at the conclusion. These elements create or enhance a feeling (or experience) of *communitas* which by its very nature implies a dissolving of barriers and social distinctions. Turner describes this experience as being 'undifferentiated, egalitarian, direct, extant, nonrational, existential, I-thou' (1978: 250). He suggests that *communitas* and structure are 'indisseverably related.' Emphasis on one side of the equation leads to a complementary strengthening of the other side. The *communitas* created by pilgrimage is the natural reaction to the highly structured nature of society (Turner, V. and Turner, E., 1978: 252).

Pilgrimages are roughly divided into four ideal types: prototypical, archaic, medieval, and modern. Pilgrimages, however, may in practice include elements of more than one type (1978: 21). Turner argues, however, that one model – deriving from the pilgrimage's historical origins – will predominate.

Prototypical pilgrimages are those which were inaugurated by an early (or significant) leader of the religion. Unlike archaic pilgrimages which include syncretistic elements, this type owes its origins to the actions of the founder or founders rather than the previous sanctity of the place.[3] In structuralist terms, they emerge from the indigenous structural pattern. This type of pilgrimage, Turner suggests, is characteristic of historical religions.

Archaic pilgrimages are also found in historical religions. They, however, emerge from earlier religious beliefs and symbols. Although the archaic shrines and symbols are transformed to fit into the new religious framework, they retain certain aspects of the earlier tradition. From a structuralist perspective it is likely that the syncretistic elements have been significantly transformed to fit into their new cultural context, as cultural elements or symbols are not artifacts or survivals – they are part of a contemporary (to their usage) structural complex. Biblical and medieval Jewish pilgrimages share characteristics of both the prototypical and archaic models.

Medieval pilgrimages are more culturally circumscribed. They refer to the pilgrimages of medieval Christianity in Europe. Although these pilgrimages tend to emerge from a patriotic context, due to their theological orthodoxy they develop into a more universal focus of pilgrimage (by universal we mean in respect to medieval Christianity). In many cases these pilgrimages are focused on sites of apparitions or the miraculous (Turner, V. and Turner, E., 1978: 172).

The final form suggested by Turner is modern pilgrimage. This form tends to further focus on the individual (a factor already present, albeit to a lesser degree, in the other forms). It is characterized by a strong devotional, pietistic element. Turner suggests that it is part of a system of apologetics responding to the secular modern world. This type of pilgrimage forms part of a complex variation including archaic and medieval elements found among the Ultraorthodox Jewish community and the Sefardic community, especially those from Islamic countries. The mainstream of Judaism has found various forms of accommodation to the secular modern world.

Three different models of pilgrimage are found during the course of Jewish history. These models are associated with a different model of sacred space and only partially conform to the ideal types suggested by Turner. A strong emphasis on pilgrimage to Jerusalem is found in both the biblical text and those rabbinic texts dealing with the period prior to the destruction of the Temple.

As mentioned above, this type of pilgrimage shares elements of both the prototypical and the archaic ideal types. During the period after the destruction until the modern era, although we find a weaker focus on pilgrimage in general, there is also the development of a wider range of pilgrimage sites. Pilgrimage to some of these sites continues into the modern period. It has elements of the archaic, medieval, and modern ideal types.

During the modern period, pilgrimage for the wider Jewish community is focused on the State of Israel. It is argued that this pilgrimage is a return to the prototypical model. While for the Hasidic and Sefardic communities pilgrimage is refocused onto the individual saint.

In the case of the Hasidic community pilgrimage is focused on the person of the Tzadik and his court and contains significant aspects of the modern pilgrimage ideal type. Sefardic pilgrimage, for example, Moroccan Jews, refocus pilgrimage onto tombs of saints. Although, as discussed below, both Sefardic and Hasidic pilgrimage contain elements of the archaic and medieval types, it is also characterized by a strong individualistic element similar to the modern type.

Prototypical Pilgrimage

Pilgrimage to Jerusalem during the First and Second Temple periods is phenomenologically similar to the pilgrimages which Turner defines as prototypical. The typology of pilgrimage is, however, problematic. As stated above, Turner's model includes two significant characteristics: prototypical pilgrimage is specifically not syncretistic, and the pilgrimage is inaugurated by an early leader and may retrace his steps (for example, those of Jesus or Mohammed). Pilgrimage to Jerusalem (and to the other early pilgrimage sites) appears to conform to neither of these elements.

Jerusalem and the other holy places were not culturally specific to the Israelites. The biblical texts indicate that many of these sites were Canaanite holy places before they were taken over by the Israelites. Thus there is a strong syncretistic element to the sanctity of Jerusalem itself. Jerusalem is also not clearly associated with an early religious leader. Moses, for example, never arrived in Jerusalem. There are, however, several connections which are associated mythologically and liturgically with early leaders. David is closely associated with Jerusalem both as a political and religious center. Abraham (and Isaac) are associated mythologically with Jerusalem. The rabbis identified Jerusalem as the site of the 'Sacrifice of Isaac.'

Liturgically, however, the three pilgrimage festivals (the significant times of pilgrimage to Jerusalem) are closely associated with the exodus from Egypt. Each festival commemorates a different part of the exodus. Thus the pilgrimages reenact, physically and spiritually, the exodus. It is for this reason, and due to the centrality of this form of pilgrimage, that we feel comfortable in identifying it as fitting into the prototypical model.

In both the biblical and the rabbinic texts dealing with the period of the Second Temple, pilgrimage to Jerusalem is presented as a commandment incumbent on all Israelite men. Exodus 23:17, for example, states: 'Three times in the year all your males shall appear before the Lord.' The three times referred to in this verse are the festivals of Passover, Shavuot, and Sukkot. These festivals are called in Hebrew the רגלים. The root of this word, i.e. רגל comes from the Hebrew word meaning foot, emphasizing the pilgrimage aspect of these particular festivals.

Although this text does not specifically define the locus of pilgrimage (appearing before the lord is locationally ambiguous), it is likely that, by the time of the editing of the texts, Jerusalem, and more specifically the Temple was understood to be the chosen sacred space.[4] This is supported by verses 26–33 of 1 Kings in which Jeroboam causes two new Holy Sites, Dan and Beth El, to be (re)developed in order to divert people from continuing to make pilgrimages to Jerusalem. The biblical texts include indications that other sites had been sacred, and been the locus of pilgrimage, for example, Shiloh, but by the exilic period Jerusalem was seen as the sole acceptable site for pilgrimage and sacrifice.

Prior (narratively) to the conquest of Jerusalem, the biblical text focuses on other earlier sacred places. These places, especially Shiloh are phenomenologically similar to Jerusalem and the Temple in as much as the presence of the Ark of the Covenant is one of their significant features. Pilgrimage to Shiloh is described in the first chapter of 1 Samuel. Although the text does not indicate which festival (if any) the pilgrimage is connected with, it does include three significant elements. First, the pilgrimage is performed on a yearly basis (see verse 3). Second, the pilgrimage is for the purpose of sacrifice. The sacrificial element probably has a covenantal aspect, in that it is eaten by Elkanah and his family in what may be a covenantal feast, mirroring the eating of the Paschal sacrifice. The third significant element is that the entire family participates in the pilgrimage.[5] The only exception to this is found in verse 22, in which Hannah chooses not to participate in the yearly pilgrimage until Samuel is weaned. The reason given in the text is that she waits until she can fulfill her promise and give Samuel into the service of the Lord.

It is likely that the story of Samuel's birth is tied to the pilgrimage in order to emphasize the transformative aspects of the events, and therefore the covenantal aspects as well. His birth occurs through divine intervention and is mythologically similar to births described in Genesis many of which require similar intervention. In Genesis this type of birth is mythologically associated with rebirth and transformation. The factor common to the births in Genesis is an emphasis on chosenness and covenant. The rabbis emphasize this link by liturgically associating this text with Genesis 22, suggesting perhaps that Hannah's actions were the appropriate means of transforming her child and entering him into God's service. It is also likely that by linking this myth of divine birth to pilgrimage the transformative aspect of pilgrimage itself is mythologically validated and supported. This transformation, however, does not occur in the individual pilgrim. It is intrinsic to Israel as a whole. The pilgrimage merely validates the qualitative distinction between categories.

As discussed above, Victor Turner interprets pilgrimage as a liminoid phenomena. Pilgrimage in some way transforms the pilgrim into a new status or role. First Samuel supports this analysis by merging two mythological/ritual elements, i.e. divine birth and pilgrimage. The divine birth of Samuel highlights the qualitative transformation already found within the individual Israelite (and the Israelite community as a whole), which is reenacted or reconsecrated by the sacrifice which is the culmination of the pilgrimage. Pilgrimage is thus liminoid to the extent that it reflects this intrinsic transformation or distinction between Israel and the nations.

The transformation effected by biblical and rabbinic prototypical pilgrimage (as well as the other types of Jewish pilgrimage), however, is of a different class to that discussed by Turner. He compares the transformation to that found in rites of transition. As such these changes are both significant and permanent. In order to change one's status, a person need only perform the ritual or go on the pilgrimage once (as in the case of the *Hajj*). Biblical pilgrimage, however, is in principle maximally performed three times per year or minimally (as in 1 Samuel) once per year. Thus the transformation lacks the permanence of rites of transition.

The transformation itself is also of a different class. It works primarily on the mythological or structural level. Pilgrimage was the obligation of all Israelite men (and as suggested was also often a family affair). The transformation cannot refer to a significant internal change in status.

One text in the Jerusalem Talmud (*Sukkot*, Perek 5, Halakhah 1) suggests that pilgrimage ideally effected a transformation in spiritual status or at least religious observance. The text suggests that the pilgrimage stimulated those who performed it to study the Torah (upon their return). This, however, is not a new obligation; it is one which is already obligatory. The text also states that the spirit of the Lord poured out from the Temple. There is no suggestion, however, that this meant a spiritual elevation for the pilgrim. It is just as likely that it refers to the role of the Temple in bringing God's presence into the world.

Thus the transformation must work at a wider level. All Israelites are in principle at the same level of status as they all are equally responsible to go to the Temple. The change in status – which is relative and oppositional – therefore must be in regard to those who do not (and who are not obligated to) make the pilgrimage, that is, non-Israelites. This is supported in Josephus' discussion of the pilgrimage. He describes the pilgrimage as encompassing Israelites/Jews from throughout the diaspora, emphasizing that it strengthened a sense of national and religious identity (that is, in opposition to those outside of that identity).

This higher level of opposition is in keeping with the mythological associations developed by 1 Samuel. The narrative is structurally related to the Death/Rebirth mytheme and the divine (virgin) birth mythemes found in Genesis. Those mythemes were, at least in part, associated with the sociological phenomena of endogamy, and the opposition of Israel to the nations.[6] Thus pilgrimage functions on a structural level to emphasize and develop the opposition between two mutually exclusive categories. It reflects the underlying structural equation of A (not) B.

If these three elements, that is the aspect of obligation, repetition, and of relative status are brought together it is apparent that the effect of biblical and rabbinic prototypical pilgrimage is not actually transformative. Rather, it serves to emphasize and revalidate. The distinction between Israel and the nations developed in the pilgrimage is not an actual transformation. That distinction is intrinsic to the Israelite understanding of self and the other. Pilgrimage revalidates – on a yearly basis – what is essentially a dialectical opposition between the two categories, that is between Israel and the Nations.

Thus this category of pilgrimage is fundamentally different from that studied by Turner. Rather than transforming the individual in opposition to other members of his own culture, this form of pilgrimage works on a societal level. No actual individual transformation occurs. If we can speak of transformation at all, it is only in respect of a revalidation of the Israelite identity as a whole. The aspect of significant liminality in respect of transformation is thus absent. In this respect biblical and rabbinic pilgrimage is not antistructural. It does not serve as a means by which the individual can move out of his cultural sphere.

It is likely that this transformation is also related to the location of biblical and rabbinic sacred space, unlike that studied by Turner which is, at least notionally, on the periphery. The Temple was in the center of the Israelite nation. Jerusalem served as both the spiritual and political center. Thus pilgrimage rather than weakening political social bonds actually emphasized and strengthened them. It focused on the cohesion of the people as opposed to the other nations round about.

The aspect of revalidation is further developed in the covenantal aspect of the three pilgrimage festivals. Although the festivals were originally tied to the agricultural cycle, by the time of the editorial present of the text they were also given historical associations. Passover was tied to the exodus from Egypt. Shavuot was associated with the giving of the commandments on Mount Sinai. Sukkot was tied to the 40 years of wandering in the wilderness. All three celebrations were thus associated to the events surrounding the acceptance of the covenant by Israel, and thus its birth as a nation apart. Mythologically and ritually the three festivals should be seen as yearly restating and reaccepting the covenantal relationship with God. As in the case of the opposition between Israel and the nations which is seen to be intrinsic, the covenant was understood to be permanent, that is, at Sinai it was accepted for both those present and those not present. In spite of this, periodic restatement of the covenant strengthens both the concept of covenant and the opposition to those not bound by that relationship.

The covenantal aspect of pilgrimage and the three pilgrimage festivals is highlighted in 2 Chronicles 29 and 30. These texts describe the reconsecration of the Temple by Hezekiah and the national celebration of Passover following the reconsecration. The description is prefaced by a verse in which Hezekiah professes the wish to reestablish the covenant with God (29:10). It concludes with the Israelite people, as a whole, reestablishing their covenantal relationship with God through the destruction of shrines, altars, and sacred pillars throughout the land (31:1). Pilgrimage is thus closely associated with the covenant and the ongoing relationship of Israel to its God.

Associated with this initial difference of Israelite prototypical pilgrimage from Turner's model, there are several other departures, the most significant of which is the place of liminality. In Turner's model liminality is found in two primary areas. First, in the transformation of status of the pilgrim there is an intermediate period in which the individual is moved to an ambiguous state between statuses. This is associated with the anti-hierarchical aspect of pilgrimage. Second, the act of pilgrimage itself is liminoid in as much as the pilgrimage is a journey between two places, and is characterized by ambiguity and danger. Thus the physical/geographic liminality mirrors the individual's personal liminality.

It is already noted that the transformational aspect of pilgrimage is significantly modified. It serves a validatory role, reconsecrating a status which is intrinsic to the pilgrim. The pilgrim, therefore, does not pass through a liminal or intermediate position in respect of status.

There are similar developments in respect of the understanding of the liminal aspects of the journey element of pilgrimage. Unlike the pilgrimages described by Turner, Israelite prototypical pilgrimage seems to pay little regard to the journey, that is to the physical expression of liminality. None of the biblical or rabbinic texts which discuss pilgrimage emphasize the journey.[7] In 1 Samuel, for example the narrative begins at Shiloh, the holy place; no mention is made of the journey to Shiloh. Similarly other texts only focus on what is to be done at the Temple. Thus in 2 Chronicles 30, the text jumps immediately from the messengers of Hezekiah calling people to come to Jerusalem, and their arrival there. The text emphasizes the act of sacrifice, that is the rituals at the sacred place, rather than the journey. In rabbinic texts, we similarly find discussions centering on what is done in Jerusalem.[8]

Lamentations Rabbah is often cited to supported the use of the recitation of psalms during the pilgrimage to Jerusalem. The text mentions several psalms and the particular occasions for their recitation. It states, for example that Psalm 122 is recited in the ways (בדרכים) (*Lamentations Rabbah* 1 no. 52).[9] This text, however, is not conclusive. The term 'the ways' is by no means clear. In the context of the midrash it could mean roads in Jerusalem leading up to the Temple. The other locations mentioned are all in the Temple itself. The historical authority of the midrash can also be questioned. *Lamentations Rabbah* is probably a fifth-century CE text and thus was written around 400 years after the destruction of the Temple.[10] It is also possible that the text describes practices current at the time of its composition rather than those of an earlier period.

If, however, it is accepted that psalms were recited, this does not minimize the distinction in significance attributed to the ritual rites in the Temple in comparison to those of the journey. The journey is still of little spiritual significance and can, at most, be seen as a preparation for the significant events in Jerusalem. The recitation of psalms, therefore, does not support Turner's model of liminality.

Texts from *m. Bikkurim* add further details to the description of the pilgrimage process in respect of the festival of Sukkot. They state that the people living in a particular vicinity would gather together, sleeping on the roads rather than in homes.[11] The text also includes a quotation from Jeremiah (31:6) 'Come, let us go up to Zion, to the Lord our God,' which was recited upon preparing to go up (3:2). The procession into Jerusalem is headed by an ox with gilded horns and a flute player (3:3). The majority of the text, however, focuses on the rituals in and around Jerusalem.

Thus, the process of pilgrimage appears to be insignificant. The significance is entirely focused on the end point at which the sacrifice is performed. The liminality of the pilgrimage is therefore not in the act of pilgrimage but rather in the end point of the pilgrimage. The Temple is the liminal space between God and man, and the liminal space in which the covenantal relationship can be reaffirmed.

As discussed above, the Israelite model of space contains within it two opposite types of liminal space. Mountains and raised places are positive liminal space. Pits and graves are negative liminal space. The liminality of the spaces, however, is structurally problematic and thus it is transformed by strengthening the positive or negative modalities. Similarly, the status of the Temple (and other sacred spaces centered on the Ark) are in this type of positively transformed liminal space. This Temple is liminal in both a physical and spiritual respect. It is notionally on a hill and several texts associate Jerusalem with the mountains. It is also the place where two structurally opposed categories meet, that is man and God.

A further significant difference between the pilgrimages found in biblical and rabbinic texts and those discussed by Turner is found in respect of obligation. Turner emphasizes the voluntary nature of pilgrimage. He suggests that even in the case of the *Hajj* which is, in principle, obligatory, there is a strong voluntary element (1978: 8). As mentioned above, biblical pilgrimage is in principle obligatory.[12] This is restated in M. Hagigah 1:1. This text lists those who are exempt from pilgrimage to Jerusalem. It suggests that all able-bodied men were so obligated. Texts in the Talmud indicate a transformation in the understanding of obligation. *B. Hagigah* 6a transforms the obligation into a meritorious act,[13] thereby changing it into a voluntary act. It is likely that this reflects the historical circumstances of the Babylonian Talmud which was edited during a period in which the Temple no longer stood, and was historically and geographically distant.[14]

Pilgrimage can only be understood as voluntary if the transformation effected by it is extrinsic. If, however, as in the case of Israelite prototypical pilgrimage the transformation (or status) is intrinsic, then pilgrimage must be in principle obligatory, even if not everyone actually participates in it.

There is one area, however, which accords with Turner's model. Like the pilgrimages described by Turner, Jewish prototypical pilgrimage includes a strong element of *communitas*. Many of the rituals connected with the three pilgrimage festivals emphasize the cultural and ideal equality of all Israelites. This concept is developed in an interesting text in *m. Bikkurim* 3:7. This text describes an attempt to reduce a social and ritual distinction between those who are literate and those who are not. It deals with the obligation to recite the words of Deuteronomy 26:5–10. The *Mishnah* decides that the priest read the prayer with the lay person repeating it after so that there be no distinction between people. Thus the ritual reduces or removes the distinction in social (educational) hierarchy. This reduction of social hierarchy may also be indicated by *m. Bikkurim* 3:4. The text states that all carried the baskets containing the first fruits, even King Agrippa.

Communitas is also emphasized in the descriptions of the pilgrimage in Josephus. In *Antiquities* he emphasizes that pilgrimage created or strengthened social cohesion (4: 203–4). Other texts speak of the large numbers of people who came to Jerusalem and suggest that they came from throughout the diaspora.[15] *m. Bikkurim* 3:2 speaks of people who came from both near and far away from Jerusalem, and indicates that the offerings brought differed depending on the origin of the pilgrims. *B Taanit* 19b also emphasizes the large numbers of pilgrims by focusing on the problems of providing water for them. Thus pilgrimage provided a focus of social cohesion, bringing together Jews from both Judea and the diaspora, with *communitas* serving a significant unifying mechanism.[16]

As a social phenomena pilgrimage is nonhierarchical (rather than anti-hierarchical). All Israelites are equal in the performance of the commandments. The offerings of the poor are equivalent to those of the rich (see *m. Bikkurim* 3:8), though each will give in his own way. Pilgrimage, as a creator of *communitas*, emphasizes the structural unity of Israel which fits in with the structural model of Israelite thought. All Israelites are by definition in the same category in opposition to the nations. It is suggested above (regarding the Tabernacle and Temple) that the types of oppositions (and thus hierarchical categories employed) are relative, depending on the level of opposition. Jewish prototypical pilgrimage emphasizes the opposition between Israel and the nations on the macro-level, thus internal oppositions and hierarchies are irrelevant.

The differences in model highlighted here in respect of biblical and early rabbinic prototypical pilgrimage to Jerusalem are also evident in prototypical pilgrimage to Jerusalem in the centuries following the destruction of the Temple.[17] After the destruction in 70 CE, sacrifices were no longer performed in Jerusalem and the obligatory aspect of pilgrimage was no longer binding. Pilgrimage to the site of the Temple, however, continued.[18] Although this form of pilgrimage was not obligatory, it does not seem to have given those who went on it any change in social or spiritual status.

The differences between Hebrew prototypical pilgrimage and that discussed by Turner ultimately derive from aspects of Hebrew underlying structure. The equation A (not) B has implications in respect of both liminality and *communitas*. Liminality implies the possibility of mediation. The indeterminate, mediatory status during the pilgrimage identified by Turner is not possible within the Hebrew structural model. Mediation diminishes the qualitative distinction between categories by suggesting that categories can be bridged and are thus not mutually exclusive. In an A (not) B system, mediators or liminal states must be removed or transformed to reduce their ambiguity. This explains the absence of a significant liminal aspect of Hebrew prototypical pilgrimage. The two complementary levels of liminality, that is the physical and the spiritual, are absent.

On a wider level Hebrew prototypical pilgrimage does not function, in a strict sense, as a rite of transition. Rites of transition, especially the liminoid forms, create internal structural oppositions, through highlighting individual permanent transformation (in opposition to those within the culture who have not been so transformed). The transformation effected by Hebrew prototypical pilgrimage does not create internal opposition. It functions to revalidate an intrinsic aspect of the Hebrew understanding of self. Although some internal divisions are developed in Hebrew culture on the micro-level, prototypical pilgrimage works, by definition, on the macro-level. Thus pilgrimage to Jerusalem, as an expression of underlying structure, strengthened the qualitative boundaries and distinctions between Israel (the pilgrims) and the nations (non-pilgrims).

Communitas is also extended to fit Hebrew structural needs. It is not antistructural in a strong sense. Although it may challenge internal hierarchical distinctions, this is in keeping with the wider understanding of the unity of Israel as a kingdom of priests. The internal unity is in direct opposition to the external world. The *communitas* created by pilgrimage strengthens this element of social cohesion and thus is in keeping with underlying structure. It is for this reason that we also find a difference in the locus of pilgrimage. If pilgrimage functions to emphasize and strengthen internal social cohesion, then the place of pilgrimage should be central rather than peripheral which is the case with Jerusalem.

Archaic/Medieval Pilgrimage[19]

Neither archaic nor medieval pilgrimage is found in a pure form in Jewish culture. Variations on the two, however, appear in several manifestations in Jewish culture. Many of these, although originating in pre-modern communities, persist into the modern period. Two such phenomena, one in the Sefardic and one in the Ashkinazic community, are the veneration of graves of saints among the Moroccan Jews and that of living *Tzaddikim* or religious leaders among the Hasidim.[20]

Moroccan pilgrimage was centered around the veneration of the graves of particular local saints. Initially the pilgrimages were localized, focusing on saints connected to one's particular community. Veneration of certain saints beyond the local community, however, was also often more widespread within the larger Moroccan community (Ben-Ami, 1981: 288).

Pilgrimage in Morocco served very different explicit purposes than the primary pilgrimages to the Temple in Jerusalem.[21] It was performed to fulfill vows, as a response to dreams, and to place particular requests before the saint (Ben-Ami, 1981: 290). There were, however, also annual festivities which attracted large numbers which probably served to strengthen communal identity (Ben-Ami, 1981: 290).

Like biblical and rabbinic prototypical pilgrimage, Moroccan pilgrimage lacked a significant liminal element. Ben-Ami presents the details of a large number of folk tales concerning the saints and the pilgrimages. None of these tales focus on the journey; all deal with either the reasons for the pilgrimage or events at the tomb. Similarly the pilgrimage does not seem to relate to a liminoid transformation of the individual. Like the pilgrimage to Jerusalem, Moroccan pilgrimage contains a repetitive element. The pilgrim's status is not transformed or enhanced by the pilgrimage. The only liminal aspect is the Tomb (or saint) itself, which effects a connection between human beings and the divine world. In this respect the tomb shares characteristics of the Temple.[22]

The Moroccan pilgrimage sites share other elements in common with the Temple. One folk tale recounts problems encountered on a particular pilgrimage due to the presence of a menstruating woman. Like the Temple the holy sites needed to be free of impurity.

Hasidic pilgrimage also centers around saintly figures, that is the *Tzaddikim (or Rebbes)*. The *Tzaddikim*, however, are for the most part living figures. The one main exception is Nahman of Bratslav, a Hasidic leader of the eighteenth and nineteenth centuries, whose followers did not choose a successor upon his death and still venerate him.[23]

Hasidim minimally make annual pilgrimages to their *Rebbe's* court. Many Hasidic leaders stressed the importance of visiting the *Rebbe* frequently.[24] Mintz adds that it was customary to visit the *Rebbe* prior to the holidays, perhaps mirroring the visits to the Temple.[25] Sacred space and therefore pilgrimage is centered on the Tzadik who symbolically takes the place of the Temple.[26] This new form of sacred space, like that of Moroccan Jews, is multiple; it is also, however, dynamic rather than static.

Visiting the *Rebbe's* court was seen as a means of spiritual development – the *Rebbe* was the conduit to the divine. Like the pilgrimages discussed above, pilgrimage to the court does not include a significant liminal element. Being at the court is the essence; the journey is not. The fact of pilgrimage, similarly, does not effect a permanent transformation. It expresses one's spiritual obligations and connection to a particular community.

Hasidic pilgrimage reflects a similar structural model of space to that found in the Temple and Hebrew sacred space. The *Rebbe/Tzadik* is the spiritual center and conduit to God. He is surrounded by his court and Hasidim, who, in their turn, are surrounded by the Jewish people as a whole. The Jewish people are in structural opposition to the rest of the world.

This structural pattern is illustrated by the recent activities of the Habad Hasidic community. The *Rebbe* essentially addressed his own Hasidim and they in turn reached out to the Jewish community at large (in what was essentially an effort to bring the messiah). The level of extent of their reaching out or proselytization is indicative. Unlike most other missionizing groups they did not reach out beyond the borders of their own religion, rather their mission was to other Jews to bring them into the center. Those outside the boundary of the Jewish people are structurally (and mystically) irrelevant.[27]

Moroccan pilgrimage is the closest of the two to the archaic form. It contains many syncretistic elements. In many respects it is identical to the pilgrimages of the local Moroccan Muslim community.[28] Pilgrimages of the two communities share not only similarity in form but also in pilgrimage sites. Many of the saints, either Muslim or Jewish, are shared by the two communities.[29]

The Hasidic community's pilgrimage to visit *Tzaddikim*, however, does not share this direct similarity. *Tzaddikim*, as mentioned above, are living saints (though there is also some pilgrimage to the graves of dead *Tzaddikim*), thus pilgrimage is no longer to specific sites. It is mobile and dynamic. The spiritual origins of the Hasidic community and the role of the *Tzadik*, however, are related to the developments within the Eastern European community as a whole (and thus is to some extent syncretistic).

Both of these phenomena share significant elements characteristic of medieval pilgrimage. Both are culturally circumscribed. The pilgrimage to the graves of Moroccan saints is generally restricted to the Moroccan Jewish community. However, the veneration of Hasidic leaders is generally restricted to the circle of their own followers, which was often based on the geographic locus of origin of the Hasidic community.[30] These forms of pilgrimage, however, have not extended to a more universal purview.[31]

Moroccan pilgrimage has to some extent moved beyond its original cultural and geographic boundaries. With the move of the Moroccan Jewish community to the State of Israel after 1948, many of their saints were brought with them. Rather than going to holy sites back in Morocco, feasts were held in Israel. Veneration was also transferred to local saints. Tombs of ancient rabbis, for example, are now visited in the place of more recent Moroccan saints (Ben-Ami, 1981: 302).

These feasts include elements which are both locally and more nationally patriotic. Ben-Ami suggests that the Hillula, feasts connected with the veneration of saints, revolve in three concentric circles. Minimally they focus on the home or local synagogue and thus involve a limited number of people. The outermost circle is national involving much of the Moroccan community in Israel (1981: 303). If the different levels are placed in a dyadic segmentary model, the structural relations exemplified by the Hillula are identical to those developed by more general models of biblical and rabbinic sacred space (see the discussions of Hebrew sacred space in chapters 2 and 3).

As indicated, Hasidic pilgrimage is by definition dynamic; it follows the location of the *Tzadik* rather than a set holy site. Thus when the majority of the Hasidic community left Eastern Europe (for the most part for the USA) there was no significant transformation in the model of pilgrimage. More recently, however, among one group of Hasidim, the Habad, there has been a move to broaden the base of veneration for the *Tzadik*. The leader of the Habad community (also called the *Rebbe*) intentionally reached out to the broader Jewish community, as mentioned above, for Messianic reasons. Many people outside of his particular community, in return, recognized him as a significant holy figure and participated in pilgrimages to his religious court in New York. This universalization was further enhanced by the hope and expectation of many of his followers that he be the messiah.

Among both the Hasidic community and the Sefardic community (including the Moroccan community) there is an additional set of pilgrimages which share the elements of archaic, medieval, and modern pilgrimages. These pilgrimages are similar to those specifically of the Moroccan community described above. They focus on various tombs of sages and biblical figures in Israel. The sites of tombs of the biblical figures contain a strong syncretistic element and may derive from earlier or non-Jewish holy places; they are shared with the local Muslim and sometimes Christian populations. Those of more recent origin are also usually shared. Many, like the Tomb of David, a site venerated since the Middle Ages, have little or no connection with the biblical figures. The pilgrimage sites in respect of biblical figures include the tombs of David, the Patriarchs, Rachel, Joseph, Samuel, and Jethro.[32]

The tomb of Rachel is of special interest. Records of pilgrimage to this site go back into the Middle Ages. Benjamin of Tudela describes the site of the tomb in the twelfth century as a pillar made up of eleven stones, and a cupola with four columns. The only rite which he connects with this site is that the passing Jews would carve their names onto the pillar (1983: 86). In 1615 a *firman* was given by the Pasha of Egypt, presenting the Jews with exclusive rights to use the tomb for prayer.[33] Today, it is a pilgrimage site particularly associated with women, who pray there for fertility and other issues connected with child birth.

Several tombs thought to be of rabbinic sages are also sites of pilgrimage. The most significant of these sites is the town of Meron in the north of Israel.[34] Although evidence of pilgrimage to Meron has taken place from the Middle Ages, as evidenced by Benjamin of Tudela (1983: 89),[35] the focus of pilgrimage has changed. While Benjamin mentions several rabbinic figures as particularly significant, including Hillel, Shammai, Rabbi Benjamin ben Japheth, and Rabbi Jehudah ben Bathera (1983: 89), the significant figure of pilgrimage since the fifteenth century, Rabbi Shimon Bar Yochai, is not specifically mentioned by Benjamin of Tudela. This refocusing on to Rabbi Shimon Bar Yochai is due to the publication of the Zohar in the latter half of the thirteenth century.[36] The Zohar is attributed to Shimon Bar Yochai, who is said to be buried in Meron. Thus pilgrimage to Meron becomes essentially a mystical pilgrimage, and is primarily performed by the Hasidim and other Jewish mystical sects.[37] Pilgrimages by Hasidim to other rabbinic tombs also have mystical implications.

Pilgrimage to Meron is performed on the festival of Log B'Omer, which falls between Passover and Shavuot. Pilgrims meet in Safed, a city within close proximity to Meron which also has significant mystical connections.[38] After dancing and singing in Safed the pilgrims, carrying a decorated Torah, ride to Meron where they dance and sing around the tomb of Rabbi Shimon Bar Yochai. Bonfires are lit during the night. In an interesting association, young boys have the hair from their first haircut thrown into the bonfire, perhaps structurally mirroring their inclusion into the community symbolically delineated by the pilgrimage.

Like the pilgrimages discussed above, there is little or no liminal element found. Although the journey between Safed and Meron is ritualized, the journey itself is not significant save that it joins together two locations of mystical significance. The only significant transformative aspect of the pilgrimage is in respect of the young boys' hair. Yet even this element is indirect. The haircut does not take place on the pilgrimage and thus the burning is only confirmation of the transformation rather than a transformation itself.[39] There may, however, be an underlying symbolic association with the story of Samuel (or perhaps that of Isaac, Genesis 22) and its association with pilgrimage and therefore with sacrifice and rebirth.

The examples of Jewish archaic and medieval pilgrimage examined here are structurally similar to biblical and rabbinic prototypical pilgrimage. They are not strongly liminoid, either in respect of geography or spiritual status. They also are by definition repeatable rather than once in a lifetime events. There are, however, also some important differences. As suggested by Turner, medieval pilgrimage works, at least initially, with a more narrow focus, for example, one particular community or country. All of the pilgrimages in this section have this as a defining characteristic. Structurally they strengthen or confirm an inner boundary rather than the external boundaries strengthened by prototypical pilgrimage.

This transformation in focus and boundary maintenance is closely related to more general models of sacred space detailed in chapters 2 and 3. As discussed, during the biblical and early rabbinic periods sacred space is unitary and centralized, creating strong external boundaries. The centralized, unitary form of pilgrimage fits in with this model, emphasizing the boundary between corporate Israel (who go on the pilgrimage) and the nations (who do not). During the period until the nineteenth century, strong external boundaries are created externally, often both geographically and socially. During this period sacred space is fragmented, emphasizing internal rather than external groupings. The pilgrimages which flourished are similarly fragmented. They primarily emphasize, therefore, structural boundaries between individuals, internal communities. The extension in respect of the extension of Habad Hasidic and Moroccan pilgrimages to wider elements of the Jewish community is also closely related to transformations in the model of sacred space. With the loss of external boundaries characteristic of the modern period, Jewish sacred space has transformed to recreate external boundaries. The relative universalization of these archaic and medieval pilgrimages is part of this process of transformation. The change is also found in the final form of pilgrimage, modern secular pilgrimage, discussed below.

Modern Secular Pilgrimage

Modern Jewish pilgrimage is exemplified by organized pilgrimages of young Jews to Israel. Before this form of pilgrimage is analyzed, however, it is necessary to discuss the relationship of pilgrimage and tourism, as it might be contended that organized trips to Israel do not fit into the conceptual category of pilgrimage. Many of the significant issues regarding the relationship between pilgrimage and tourism are addressed by Eric Cohen.[40] Interestingly Cohen's initial distinction between tourism and pilgrimage focuses on the concept of sacred center.[41] He suggests that tourism is characterized by movement to the periphery. It emphasizes a movement outside of one's cultural boundaries and expectations (Cohen, 1992: 52). Pilgrimage, on the other hand, is a movement to a center. This centrality is not necessarily geographic but is rather spiritual.[42] Cohen, however, does not limit the sacred center to traditional sources of spirituality, for example, religion. He also suggests that modern cultural monuments can also be sacred centers and thus pilgrimage sites, for example, the Lincoln Memorial in the United States or Mount Herzl in Israel. Both of these sites are associated with national rather than religious ideals (Cohen, 1992: 52).

The essential difference between pilgrims and tourists primarily lies not in the location of the journey, any site can serve for both, but in the nature of the experience. There is an existential quality found in pilgrimage (perhaps characterized as rapture) which is not generally found in tourism which is often characterized as recreational or diversionary (Cohen, 1992: 54). The pilgrim views the center as a subject while the tourist views it as an object.

In respect of these characterizations, the trips to Israel can be seen as pilgrimages rather than tourism. Although Israel is geographically peripheral, it is perceived as being central in several respects. It is historically central, being perceived as the site of the beginnings of Jewish history and that of its formative period. It is spiritually central, containing the holiest sites shared by the Jewish community as a whole. It is perceived as being culturally central. Israel is often depicted as the cultural well from which Jews in the diaspora draw their inspiration. It is also politically central, especially in respect of the role which Zionism plays in the wider Jewish community.

The nature of the pilgrimage and Israel as a sacred center is based on all of these different foundations. The pilgrimages, as discussed below, are only partially religious or conventionally spiritual; they are also and perhaps essentially aimed at an existential experience of secular aspects of Israel as a sacred center. The experience of the pilgrims is not meant to be one of visiting a museum.[43] All of the activities and elements of the pilgrimage emphasize the active and the experiential – for example, working on a kibbutz or training in an army camp. The pilgrim is meant to almost become part of Israel rather than an observer of it.

During the modern period, especially, though not exclusively, after 1948 (the founding of the modern State of Israel) a new form of pilgrimage which is essentially prototypical has developed. Young Jews from all parts of the Jewish community spend an extended period, on average two months, in the State of Israel. This new form is essentially secular. Although it might include some religious elements, these are not primary to its purposes or structural role. This pilgrimage does not fit into Turner's typology of modern pilgrimage.

Unlike modern pilgrimage, as defined by Turner, which tends to be individualistic, Jewish modern secular pilgrimage is strongly communal and group oriented. Most of the young people will travel with groups from their own religious, political, or social movements. The American Reform Movement, for example, sponsors a large number of trips to Israel primarily for their own youth. The pilgrimage itself also strongly emphasizes the group, with many activities to develop group identity.[44] This emphasis is illustrated by a particular group which failed to develop this feeling of identity or *communitas*. Due primarily to this lack, the group was considered by both its own leaders and the rabbis working for the movement in Israel to be a failure.

The pietistic element of many modern pilgrimages is also absent. Although many of these pilgrimages are sponsored by religious movements, the pilgrimages themselves are not specially or differentially religious. The religious observance found will typically be the same as found in either congregations in the originating country or in the youth movements. Many of the groups, however, are sponsored by secular Jewish organizations and will include relatively little religious content.

The focus of pilgrimage is also not particularly religious. The 'holy' sites visited include both religious and secular locations, with perhaps the majority being associated with recent events in Israeli (and modern Jewish) history. There is a strong emphasis on modern Israeli culture. Many groups spend time working on a kibbutz, often on kibbutzim which are antireligious.

The United Synagogue Youth's (USY) pilgrimage to Israel, although sponsored by a religious movement, focuses primarily on secular and Zionist sites in Israel.[45] Of the forty days of the pilgrimage only five are specifically devoted to religious activities. The groups also spend four days on a youth military base doing activities connected with the Israeli army.[46]

Both the army and kibbutz experience utilized by the various programs also facilitate the development of *communitas*. *Communitas* or group identity is emphasized by many of these pilgrimages both on the macro- and micro-levels. It is focused on in educational programs, many of which are experiential. It is also developed in respect of religious practice. In the Reform pilgrimages, for example, most religious elements are created or led by members with little or no rabbinic or professional input. Thus Jewish religion is dehierarchized.[47]

The secularized focus is also indicated in the educational programming used in some of the pilgrimages. The American Reform Movement, for example, offered its groups programs on charity (with an emphasis on charitable activities in Israel) and on anti-Semitism. The ideological focus of the latter was the danger of being a Jew in the diaspora, and thus the importance of Israel and Zionism. The Conservative movement offers its youth similar educational programming, with the addition of a single program on spirituality.[48]

Distrust of modernity is also a significant element of Turner's model absent from Jewish modern secular pilgrimage. Most of the young people who go on these pilgrimages are fully integrated into the modern world. The pilgrimages are not a rejection of that world, but rather a celebration of the fact that the Jewish people, through the State of Israel, have become fully part of that world. Throughout the pilgrimage, guides point out the modern innovations of Israeli culture. If there is a rejection of modernity, it is tied to the relaxation of external boundaries and the resulting intermarriage. It is not unlikely that one agenda of the pilgrimages, on the part of the movements and families, is the hope that relationships be formed with other Jews (that is, that their children marry within the Jewish community). Thus modern secular pilgrimage is associated with the cultural issue of endogamy and the structural equation of A (not) B.

In several respects Jewish modern secular pilgrimage fits the typology of prototypical pilgrimage and is structurally similar to biblical and rabbinic prototypical pilgrimage. The pilgrimages often focus on the Israeli War of Independence, visiting sites of significant battles,[49] in a sense retracing the steps leading to the founding of the State.

The State of Israel, as a whole, becomes the sacred space. It is placed in structural opposition to both the diaspora, which in Zionist ideology is artificial and impermanent, and more importantly, to the nations of the world. The pilgrimage, with its focus on history and culture, becomes a means of strengthening or creating the external boundaries between Israel, the people and nation, and the world.

The aspect of liminality is more ambiguous in respect to the modern secular form of Jewish pilgrimage. Unlike the other forms of Jewish pilgrimage, it seems to place a stronger emphasis on the act of pilgrimage (as opposed to rituals at the conclusion of pilgrimage). All of the pilgrimages to Israel include a significant element of travel around Israel to different sacred spaces. This may be analogous to the geographic liminality highlighted by Turner. If, however, the State of Israel, as a whole, is sacred space, then the significant travel is within sacred space, not to sacred space, and thus is not liminal.

The aspect of transformation and thus spiritual (or cultural) liminality is also absent. The pilgrims are not transformed in any significant respect. Like the other forms of Jewish pilgrimage, pilgrimages (or trips) to Israel are not meant to be once in a lifetime. Modern Jewish secular pilgrimage focuses on building permanent ongoing ties to the State of Israel, and also contains a strong emphasis on *Aliyah*, immigration to Israel.[50]

As in biblical prototypical pilgrimage, pilgrimage is to the center rather than the periphery. Interestingly, however, the centrality of Israel contains ambiguities. On the one hand, Israel is certainly peripheral to the interests and political aspirations of many of the pilgrims who have no plans to remain in Israel after the pilgrimage, and are involved in and committed to their nations of origin. On the other, many of them retain a strong commitment to Israel and a desire to support it politically and monetarily. To many of these Jews, Israel represents a religious center – despite the fact that the pilgrimages themselves tend to focus on the secular rather than the religious.

In respect of culture, however, Israel is increasingly understood by many elements within the Jewish community as being the center and source for the worldwide Jewish community. The transformation is reflected in the move from a bipolar model of cultural creativity to a single-center model. This reflects the more general trend of transformation of Jewish identity and sacred space. The bipolar or multipolar model reflects the structural segmentation characteristic of the rabbinic and premodern period. The overall structural equation of A (not) B was not culturally problematic as it was validated and supported by external relations. Israel (the people) was qualitatively distinct from the nations round about. The single-center model is a response to the modern fluidity of boundaries and its cognitive conflict with the structural equation. The boundaries between A and B appear to become fluid. Focus and emphasis on a single center strengthens cultural (communal) unity in opposition to both all things external from that center and the divisions within the community itself. A single center, therefore, validates the structural equation and reemphasizes the cultural distinction between Israel and the nations.[51]

There are, however, interesting differences between modern secular prototypical pilgrimage and biblical prototypical pilgrimage. While biblical pilgrimage was at least ideologically obligatory, modern secular pilgrimage is voluntary. This difference may be due in part to the transformation from religious to secular. The secular or cultural does not have the commanding authority of the religious.[52]

The transformation from religious to secular sacred space in part reflects the heterogeneous nature of the modern Jewish religious community. Since the nineteenth century the Jewish community has been segmented on rigid self-defined theological lines. Various movements have developed which define both the theological nature of Judaism, the role of *Halakhah* (Jewish Law), and the very definition of Jewishness (that is, who is a Jew and how does a person become a Jew) in very different ways. Increasingly, the religious aspect of Jewish culture does not play a unifying role. Thus religious sacred space cannot serve to emphasize cultural unity and distinctiveness. Secular sacred space, however, because it is equally shared by all Jewish communities and movements, with the exception of certain Hasidic groups who reject the secular state, can serve as a new means of creating and emphasizing cultural and structural boundaries.

Conclusions

This chapter has focused on the significant differences between Jewish pilgrimage and the model proposed by Turner. The most significant difference is found in respect of liminality. Turner's analysis focuses on the role of liminality as the significant aspect of pilgrimage. As discussed, however, liminality is essentially absent from Jewish pilgrimage. This absence is related to the underlying structure of Jewish (Hebrew) culture. In a structure based on the A (not) B equation, liminality or liminal categories would be structurally problematic. They suggest that the two categories, A and B, are bridgeable, that they are actually not mutually distinct. Thus Jewish rituals, including pilgrimage, do not contain a liminal(oid) aspect.

The analysis of Hebrew material suggests the need to modify general models which focus on particular characteristics of pilgrimage, for example the liminoid, which suggest a direct association with rites of transition. They appear not to be intrinsic aspects of pilgrimage, and thus there is no direct analogy with rites of transition. Liminality is a marker connected with level of transformation effected by the pilgrimage. If the pilgrimage is tied to individual transformation, then liminality may be emphasized. If, however, it is associated with group or cultural transformation, then liminality may be de-emphasized.

Liminality is also a reflection of underlying structure. In the Hebrew model of A (not) B, the liminal would be structurally problematic. Thus it is not an essential aspect of Hebrew ritual either in respect of pilgrimage or rites of transition. Most of the pilgrimages analyzed by Turner (as well as Crumrine and Morinis) arise from different Christian cultures. One aspect of Christian underlying structure (as reflected in the New Testament) is positive mediation, giving the equation A (and) B. Thus it is not surprising that liminality or mediation is a characteristic element of both Christian pilgrimage and ritual.

A similar problem is found in respect of the general approach to pilgrimage suggested by Crumrine and Morinis. Their analysis, while also based on the model proposed by Van Genip, focuses on the aspect of transformation rather than liminality (which can be seen as two sides of the same coin) (1991: 11).[53] They present a sophisticated structuralist argument focusing on the role of the pilgrimage site as a mediating category which facilitates the transformation of the pilgrim from profane to sacred. Although their use of structuralist models may be appropriate in respect of the Latin American pilgrimages analyzed (that is in societies which allow movement and mediation between categories), their models are not universally applicable. As suggested above, transformation of the pilgrim is not a significant or necessary aspect of Hebrew pilgrimage, and, mediation between categories is structurally problematic in Hebrew underlying structure.

Their application of Lévi-Strauss's equation:

$$A_{(x)}: B_{(y)} :: B_{(x)}: Y_{(A^{-1})}$$

illustrates some of the problems with the application of their model to Hebrew material. All three terms, that is A, B, and Y, represent the stages of development (or transformation) within the pilgrim. A, for example, is the profane state of the pilgrim prior to separation stage of pilgrimage. While Y represents the sacred state of the pilgrim after incorporation. The functions

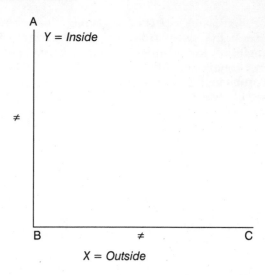

Figure 4.1 Structural Oppositions of Hebrew Pilgrimage

x, y and A^{-1} represent the qualitative states of the three terms. It is through term B, representing both the transition stage and the pilgrimage site that A is transformed into Y (1991: 13).

As indicated this presents two problems in respect of the Hebrew material. First, as Hebrew structure does not allow movement between categories, it is structurally impossible for A to be transformed into Y. Second, the mediatory role of B is similarly structurally untenable because it suggests that the categories can be bridged.

Lévi-Strauss's equation, however, is applicable to Hebrew pilgrimage if the value of the terms and functions are changed. The level of structural oppositions is the first area which must be reexamined. If transformation is not internal and each element must be only in one exclusive category, opposition cannot be found within the pilgrim. Rather, the pilgrim (who in this case represents Israel) must be in structural opposition to other categories. The significant oppositions are illustrated in Figure 4.1. In this diagram, A represents the sacred space, which in turn is symbolic of the divine. B represents the Israelite pilgrim both before and after pilgrimage, as there is no qualitative transformation. The opposition between A and B is ultimately between the divine and the human, which in Israelite terms is unbridgeable.

The second opposition is between B and C, with C representing the nations. B, however, is not transformed. Rather, the opposition is contextual. In respect of A, B is profane, while in respect of C, B is sacred. Thus the relationship suggested by the equation is one of analogy rather than transformation. The relationship of the two oppositions is illustrated in the following equation:

$$(B \neq A) \neq C$$

This equation illustrates the relationship of B and A in opposition to C.

If Lévi-Strauss's equation is now reexamined, the initial opposition, that is $A:B$, therefore must be changed from internal to external categories, one representing the pilgrim and the other representing the pilgrimage site or the divine. Thus this opposition reflects the absolute distinction between man (including Israel) and God.[54] The functions y and x are respectively sacred and profane. The first half of the equation is thus:

$$A_{(y)}:B_{(x)}$$

$$\textit{God (Sacred Space)}_{(sacred/inside)}:\textit{Israel (Humanity)}_{(profane/outside)}$$

which illustrates the logical opposition between the divine and human.

The second half of the equation repeats term B. It is now modified (or defined) by function y. On this side of the equation Israel, who go on pilgrimages, are opposed to those who do not. In the diagram this second term of the opposition is clearly stated, that is C, the nations. The equation, however, uses terms (and functions) already given to define C. This is expressed by the equation:

$$X_{(a^{-1})} = C$$

which defines C as being equal to the function of B in the first half of the equation, that is X, which is transformed into a term. The term X is modified by a function which is defined as the inversion of the initial term, that is A. The second half of the equation is thus:

$$B_{(y)}:X_{(A^{-1})}$$

$$\textit{Israel}_{(inside)}:\textit{Outside}_{(non\text{-}god)}$$

which examines and defines the term which is in logical opposition to Israel. The complete equation,

$$A_{(y)}:B_{(x)}::B_{(y)}:X_{(A^{-1})}$$

$$\textit{God}_{(inside)}:\textit{Israel (humanity)}_{(outside)}::\textit{Israel}_{(inside)}:\textit{Outside}_{(non\text{-}god)}$$

states the analogy between the relationships expressed by the two halves. It allows the definition of C, the nations, as outside/non-Divine. The equation expresses a relationship of macro- to micro-levels. The opposition of God to Israel/Humanity, the macro-level, is mirrored in that between Israel and the nations, the micro-level. It does not illustrate any aspect of transformation or transition.

The role of *communitas* as a universal characteristic of pilgrimage has also been questioned. Although it is found in most (if not all) Hebrew pilgrimage, scholars have identified pilgrimages where it is absent or its presence is overemphasized. Bowman, citing the work of Sallnow, suggests that the emphasis on *communitas* may be created by the religious hierarchy associated with the pilgrimage rather than something which the pilgrims themselves either aspire to or achieve (1985: 6).[55] He argues that it is unlikely or difficult to prove that *communitas* or Durkheim's effervescence is the significant characteristic of pilgrimage (1985: 6).

Thus the various elements highlighted by Turner and other scholars, that is, liminality, *communitas*, obligatory/voluntary, centrality or peripherality, cannot be seen as fixed elements of all pilgrimages. Each element will be differentially significant depending on the underlying structural context out of which the pilgrimage arises. The presence or absence of each element will be indicative of the culture specific underlying structural relations.

Notes

1. See for example Turner, V. and Turner, E. (1978). Turner's work has been criticized and expanded in opposing ways by Sallnow and Morinis. Sallnow emphasizes the social and communal aspects of pilgrimage (see for example Eade, J. and Sallnow, M. (1991) *Contesting the Sacred: The Anthropology of Christian Pilgrimage*, London: Routledge) while Morinis emphasizes the role of pilgrimage in individual transformation (see for example Morinis, A. (ed.) (1992) *Sacred Journeys: The Anthropology of Pilgrimage*, Westport: Greenwood Press). See also Pechilis' discussion which highlights both the changes in Turner's approach, and emphasizes the notion of negotiation, a feature also discussed by Eade and Sallnow, as a significant feature of both pilgrimage and ritual (Pechilis, K. (1992) 'To Pilgrimage It' in *Journal of Ritual Studies* **6.2**, 59–91).
2. Good examples of this emphasis are found in literature, for example *Canterbury Tales* or *A Pilgrim's Progress*.
3. It might be thought that prototypical pilgrimage is an example of ontogeny recapitulating cosmogony (see for example, Eliade, 1954: 22; and Eilberg-Schwartz, H. (1987) 'Creation and Classification in Judaism: From Priestly to Rabbinic Conceptions' in *History of Religions* **26**, n. 4, 357–8). Although in respect of Jewish pilgrimage this may play a part, a much more significant aspect of prototypical pilgrimage in particular and all Jewish pilgrimage in general is the process of using history to create or emphasize societal cohesion. In no case do the pilgrimage events need to 'exactly repeat' those of the past – a fact illustrated by the location of pilgrimage, Jerusalem rather than Mount Sinai – they allude to those events and therefore the historical link which binds the community on both the human and divine levels.
4. It is likely that the texts are ambiguous in order to avoid anachronism.
5. In the rabbinic texts women are not obligated to perform the commandment of pilgrimage (*m. Hagigah* 1:1). Several texts, however, suggest that women did so, with and without their husbands. See for example *b. Eruvin* 96a and *b. Nedarim* 23a.
6. For a detailed discussion of this association see Kunin, 1995.
7. It might be argued that the Exodus and the Sinai narratives are an example of the significance of the journey in pilgrimage. While it is true that the Exodus and the 40 years in the wilderness were a liminal and transformative period, this does not support the existence of this element in pilgrimage. The movement between

Egypt and Canaan, with the wilderness mediating the two opposite poles, was not a pilgrimage itself, nor did it need to be actually reenacted. The transformation which occurred is described in the text as permanent. Each subsequent generation is already part of the covenant. The narrative is only relevant if we accept that it reflects an actual ritual process, that is, actual pilgrimages in the wilderness for which the text provides a liturgical basis. Much of the argument supporting such pilgrimages rests on an understanding of myth, that is, that myth derives from ritual, which is no longer generally accepted.

8. Some scholars interpret some of the psalms as being used during the pilgrimage to Jerusalem. There is, however, no authoritative direct evidence to support this. The assumption might ultimately rest on an imposition of Christian models of pilgrimage on the Israelite material.

9. Other psalms mentioned in the text include Psalms 42, 80 and 150. *M. Bikkurim* also includes Psalm 40. The Jerusalem Talmud states that Psalms 120–134 were recited on the way up the Temple Mount, but does not indicate whether psalms were recited during the journey.

10. See Strack, H. L. and Stemberger, G. (1991) *Introduction to the Talmud and Midrash*, Edinburgh: T. & T. Clark, pp. 308–12.

11. This is interpreted as a means of avoiding impurity (from the dead) which they might encounter in a home. See Albeck, H. (1959) *Shesh Sidre Mishnah, Seder Zeraim* (The Six Orders of the *Mishnah*, Seder Zeraim), Jerusalem: Mosad Byalik, p. 318. Thus its liminal aspects are minimized.

12. There is some dispute about the nature of the obligation. In principle, however, all Israelite men were so obligated.

13. See also *b. Pesachim* 8b and *b. Hagigah* 7b.

14. The *Mishnah* was also edited after the destruction of the Temple. It may, however, include material which was contemporary with the existence of the Temple. Even if later composition is assumed, the text often reflects an idealization of Temple practice. It was also written in Judea and thus may reflect the greater ease of pilgrimage than in the case of the Babylonian Talmud.

15. This is also suggested by the laws concerning the Second Passover. In certain circumstances one could celebrate Passover a month late. One of these was distance away from Jerusalem. See for example: *b. Pesachim* 6b, 67a, and 93a. Alon, G. ((1984) *The Jews in Their Land in the Talmudic Age*, Jerusalem: Magnes Press) demonstrates the participation of diaspora communities in pilgrimage (346).

16. The aspect of *communitas* and the significance of the pilgrimage in creating and strengthening national identity is highlighted by Alon (1984: 47). He suggests that 'the Jews of the diaspora went on the pilgrimage to Jerusalem at least once,' and that it served to bind them to their fellow Jews. Alon states that 'the Temple was enormously significant as a cementing factor for the nation and its culture' (1984: 47). He also mentions the significance of the half-shekel (paid by all Jews to support the Temple) in creating a broad national identity.

17. Although Jews were apparently not allowed during the period following the destruction of the Temple into Jerusalem for most of the year, they were allowed to pray at the Western Wall on the 9th of Av (the day commemorating the destruction of the Temple). Jerome describes this event in the fourth century. See Peters, F. E. (1986) *Jerusalem and Mecca: The Typology of the Holy City*, New York: New York University Press, pp. 52–3, in which he quotes *In Sophoniam* **1**, 15–16.

18. Some discussion of this continued pilgrimage is found in a fascinating docu-

ment put together by the Commission for the Wailing Wall in *The Rights and Claims of Muslims and Jews in Connection with the Wailing Wall at Jerusalem* (Beirut, 1968). See, for example, page 19 where such pilgrimages are documented from the third century to the twentieth century.

19. The pilgrimages discussed here also include aspects of Turner's modern form of pilgrimage. They include a stronger focus on individual piety than is found in prototypical pilgrimage. They are also performed by communities which reject different aspects of the modern world. All of the pilgrimages examined in this section continue into the modern period.

20. For a complete discussion of the veneration of saints in Morocco see Ben-Ami, I. (1981) 'Folk Veneration of Saints among the Moroccan Jews,' in Morag, S., Ben-Ami, I. and Stillman, N. (eds) *Studies in Judaism and Islam*, New York: Magnes Press.

21. Individual pilgrimages to Jerusalem were performed in order to fulfill vows or offer individual sacrifices. Like the communal, the individual pilgrimages focused on the rites at the Temple and did not involve a significant transformation in status.

22. It is interesting that the tomb as a sacred space is an inversion of the sacred space represented by the Temple. The Temple was on a mountain and the preserve of the priesthood, while the tomb is symbolically lowered space and is forbidden to the priesthood (who were not allowed to come into contact with dead human bodies).

23. Reb Nahman of Bratslav's life and relations to his followers is analyzed in Green, A. (1979) *Tormented Master: A Life of Rabbi Nahman of Bratslav*, New York: University of Alabama Press.

24. See for example Rabinowicz, H. (1988) *Hasidism: The Movement and its Masters*, Northvale: J. Aronson, p. 321.

25. Mintz, J. (1968) *Legends of the Hasidim*, Chicago: University of Chicago Press, p. 103.

26. This is stated explicitly in Heschel, A. J. (1985) *The Circle of the Baal Shem Tov*, Chicago: University of Chicago Press, pp. xxxvii–xxxviii.

27. This structural pattern and the qualitative opposition between Israel and the nations is stated specifically in the primary mystical/philosophical text of the Habad movement, the *Likkutei Amarim – Tanya* of Rabbi Schneur Zalman of Liadi (New York: Habad, 1984). He makes a qualitative distinction between the souls of Israel and that of the nations. In his discussion of the part of the soul which is the source of both good and evil inclinations, he suggests that that of Israel comes from a source which contains both good and evil. It originates from the 'esoteric "Tree of Knowledge of Good and Evil,"' reflecting the ability of Israel to choose between good and evil. The souls of the nations, on the other hand, come from absolutely unclean sources with no elements of good at all. All apparently good deeds done by the nations are done for evil reasons (1984:6). This emphasizes that although there may be qualitative distinctions of good within Israel, Israel as a whole is absolutely in qualitative opposition to the nations.

28. See also Gellner, E. (1969) *Saints of the Atlas*, London: Weidenfeld & Nicolson; and Crapanzano, V. (1973) *The Hamadsha: A Study in Moroccan Ethnopsychiatry*, Berkeley: University of California Press. See also Dwyer, D. (1978) *Images and Self-Images: Male and Female in Morocco*, New York, Columbia University Press (especially p. 50).

29. This phenomena is discussed in detail in Ben-Ami (1981: 283).

30. The significant exception to this narrow cultural penetration was the Lubavitcher Rebbe. Due in part to his own efforts to speak to a wider Jewish community, to his political influence, and to the wide respect for his scholarship and spirituality, he was widely venerated even beyond the borders of his own community. This may be relate to the pattern of universalizing that Turner highlights in respect of medieval pilgrimage.
31. The difference between Jewish and Christian medieval pilgrimage in respect of universality may be related to a difference of attitude toward homogeneity. The Jewish community in respect of dogma and practice is ideally heterogeneous. Thus there is no need for localized saints to be universally venerated.
32. Benjamin of Tudela, for example, describes a visit to David's Tomb in the late twelfth century (Benjamin of Tudela (1983) *The Itinerary of Benjamin of Tudela*, Malibu: J. Simon, p. 84). He describes the site as being discovered some fifteen years prior to his visit, with the sanctity of the tomb being confirmed by a miraculous vision (1983: 85).

    He also describes the Tombs of the Patriarchs and Matriarchs in Hebron. At the time of the visit the site was clearly holy to both Jews and Muslims (Benjamin of Tudela, 1983: 86). He indicates that the site was venerated by Jews who made pilgrimages to it, and that they used it as a special burial site (1983: 87).
33. See Hollis, C. and Brownrigg, R. (1969) *Holy Places*, New York: Praeger, p. 16.
34. For a more detailed discussion of Pilgrimage to Meron see Myerhoff, B. (1993) 'Pilgrimage to Meron: Inner and Outer Peregrinations' in Lavie, S., Narayan, K. and Rosaldo, R. (eds) *Creativity/Anthropology*, Ithaca: Cornell University Press, pp. 211–22; and, Turner, E. (1993) 'Bar Yohai, Mystic: The Creative Persona and his Pilgrimage' in Lavie, S., Narayan, K. and Rosaldo, R. (eds) *Creativity/Anthropology*, Ithaca: Cornell University Press, pp. 225–52.
35. Isaac Ben Joseph, a Kabbalist from Spain mentions that large numbers of people came from 'far and wide' on pilgrimages to the tombs of rabbinic sages outside of Tiberias. He mentions particularly sepulchres of the disciples of Rabbi Akiva (who was thought to be a mystic) and of Johanan ben Zakkai (Peters, 1986: 14).
36. See Scholem, G. (1974) *Kabbalah*, New York: New York Times Books, p. 232.
37. G. Scholem mentions that Isaac Luria (a mystic born in 1534) may have participated in the pilgrimage to Meron prior to his settling in Safed in 1569 (1974: 421).
38. Meron is six miles from Safed.
39. In some cases the hair is actually cut in Meron, especially for Hasidim who live in Israel. Edith Turner describes this event (1993: 246). She describes it as an immediate transformation of the child from the world of the women to that of the men. There is, however, no liminal period. Whether the hair cutting takes place in Meron or elsewhere, the transformation is immediate.
40. The relationship between pilgrimage and tourism is discussed by Eric Cohen in 'Pilgrimage and Tourism: Convergence and Divergence' in Morinis, A. (ed.) (1992) *Sacred Journeys: The Anthropology of Pilgrimage*, Westport: Greenwood Press, pp. 47–61. It should be noted that Turner touched on this question, indicating that a 'tourist was half a pilgrim' (Turner, 1978: 20). This question is also addressed in Reader, I. and Walter, T. (eds) (1993) *Pilgrimage in Popular Culture*, London: Macmillan. They argue that both popularly and phenomenologically secular pilgrimages, for example the Liverpool football ground at Anfield, or Graceland, are similar to religious pilgrimages (Reader and Walter,

1993: 2–10). Their discussion about the relationship between pilgrimage and tourism highlights the existential elements discussed on p. 79. It emphasizes the need to distinguish between the experience and attitude of the pilgrim or tourist as opposed to the site visited. See for example Lockwood, Allison (1981) *Passionate Pilgrims: The American Traveller in Great Britain 1800–1914*, New York: Cornwall Books, p. 65. This point is emphasized in Walter's discussion of visits to war graves. He distinguishes between those who visit as pilgrims, with a subject relation to the site, and those who visit as tourists, who treat it as an object (for example of curiosity) (see Walter, T. (1993) 'War Grave Pilgrimage,' Reader, I. and Walter, T. (eds) *Pilgrimage in Popular Culture*, London: Macmillan, p. 63.

Reader and Walter emphasize the relationship between pilgrimage and death. They associate this, to some extent, with notions of rebirth and transformation (1993: 18). They also suggest that saints, through their mediatory position between the human and the divine, were able to give access to the divine. They argue that secular heroes or war dead act in a similar way. It is likely, however, that in making this association they are confusing categories. Saints are visited because they stand in a liminal position in respect of the divine. The heroes are precisely not liminal. Even in the case mentioned (Reader and Walter, 1993: 21) the grave of the rock star (or the dead relative) is visited for its own sake rather than its liminality. The two examples of secular pilgrimage might better be characterized as prototypical. The connection with the hero is a connection and association with the past, emphasizing the individual's connection with it rather than their individual spiritual/secular transformation.

41. In this respect Cohen's understanding of pilgrimage is closer to that suggested here than to many of the other models which suggest a movement to the periphery.
42. Cohen bases this model on Eliade's concept of a sacred center which unites heaven and earth (Cohen, 1992: 51).
43. Though it must be noted that the existential aspect is not experienced by all who go on the Israel pilgrimages (nor perhaps on any particular pilgrimage). Nonetheless, that is the essential goal of the pilgrimage.
44. Information about the American Reform pilgrimages is derived from participant observation.
45. Of the main youth trips to Israel, only the USY calls the trip a pilgrimage.
46. The material published by USY specifically advertising the Israel Pilgrimage mentions no religious aspects of the pilgrimage. It lists the 'highlights' as being: 'Archaeology Dig, Hiking Ein Gedi, Climbing Masada, Snorkeling in Eilat, Exploring Jerusalem, 5-day Gadna Option (simulated military field training).' The more general literature, however, does indicate that the participants will live as observant Jews. The information used here is from a pamphlet published by USY for the 1996 summer programs, as well as a sample itinerary for the Israel Pilgrimage.
47. This is an inversion of the cultural transformations in modern Judaism, in which the rabbi is given an increasingly central position in ritual practice.
48. This program appears to be directly connected with the concept of pilgrimage. It is a simulation connected with Meron.
49. The USY itinerary indicates that on at least eleven days, sites connected with Israel's foundation and wars are visited.
50. In the view of Zionists *Aliyah* is a significant transformation. *Aliyah* is the opposite of pilgrimage, which usually includes a return to one's original place.

This view of transformation is not entirely shared by communities outside of Israel.

51. The role of the State of Israel in validating the structural unity of Israel (the people) is illustrated in the Law of Return. This law gives all Jews, as defined by any segment of the community, the automatic right to become Israeli citizens. Thus the Law stands in opposition to the segmentation of the community, and creates a distinction between Jews who have this right and non-Jews who do not.

    It is precisely this fact that has led to a battle over this law. Certain Ultra-orthodox leaders have attempted to redefine who this law relates to and therefore to redefine who is a Jew. This has recently (April 1997) come to the fore with a vote in the Israeli parliament giving the Orthodox establishment the right to determine which diaspora conversions will be acceptable in regard to the right of return.

52. The cultural or nationalistic is also weakened by the conflict in patriotisms. American Jews, for example, must resolve the internal conflict between American identity and patriotism, and their ties to Jewish culture and Israeli nationalism (Zionism).

53. It is not unlikely that both their focus on liminality and transformation, and their version of the equation arise from their emphasis on the individual experience of pilgrimage, as opposed to the group or social dimensions.

54. For the purposes of the analysis given here, the roles of A and B have been reversed from that found in Crumrine and Morinis (1991: 13). This is due to analogy rather than transformational use of the equation. If the divine (which in Hebrew terms can never be profane) was on both sides of the equation, both sides would express exactly the same thing, that is, the opposition between man and God.

    In order to fit with the diagrammatic placement of God on the higher vertical plane, the functions of the equation are also reversed. Since, however, the changes are consistent on both sides of the equation, it is still valid.

55. Bowman's discussion is found in Makhan Jha (ed.) (1985) *Dimensions of Pilgrimage*, New Delhi: Inter-India Publications, pp. 1–9. M. Sallnow's discussion of *communitas* is found in (1981) 'Communitas Reconsidered: The Sociology of Andean Pilgrimage,' *Man* **16**, 163–82. See also M. Sallnow (1987) *Pilgrims of the Andes: Regional Cults in Cusco*, Washington: Smithsonian Institution Press.

5 Toward Centralization: Modern Jewish Sacred Space

Ethnographic analysis and comparison of the use of functional sacred space in modern Jewish communities reveal many of the significant features of sacred space. This chapter presents the findings of ethnographic fieldwork in Reform, Liberal, and Orthodox synagogues in the United Kingdom. This research was conducted over several years. It includes both participant observation and interviews in four synagogues (two Reform, one Liberal, and one Orthodox) and a survey of practice in all Reform and Liberal congregations.[1] Observations and interviews have also been conducted in American Reform and Conservative congregations.[2] The analysis of this research suggests that there are patterns of transformation between (and within) the movements.[3] These patterns are found in four areas: the restriction of access to sacred space, the role of the rabbi, the formality of the service, and the associated sanctity of the synagogue as a sacred space.

The Movements

The Orthodox community in Britain is the largest of the three. It can be roughly divided into several subgroupings including the United Synagogue, the Federation, and other Ultraorthodox and Hasidic communities. All of the observations were conducted in synagogues belonging to the United Synagogue. The United Synagogue is the largest Orthodox grouping (and the largest Jewish community in general) and in many respects is perceived as the official Jewish community. The Chief Rabbi, for example, is the rabbinic head of the United Synagogue.[4] There is very little synagogue autonomy and rabbis are under the authority of the Chief Rabbi and the London *Beit Din* (or other regional religious courts in Manchester and Glasgow).[5]

The United Synagogue is the most centrist of the Orthodox communities. This is indicated both within the service by a relatively formal structure and the use of English in some non-*halakhic* prayers (for example, the prayer for the country). The United Synagogue and its members also participate in aspects of the wider British community. Its members work in a wide range of areas of employment and participate fully in modern British culture, for example, music and art. The movement sometimes involves itself in political and moral issues regarding the wider community.[6]

In respect of Jewish law and tradition, the United Synagogue can be characterized as traditionally *halakhic*. They accept the view that the Torah, both written and oral, were given by God to Moses on Mount Sinai. They generally have the ideology that *halakha* does not change and that modern ideas or approaches are not relevant for religious decision-making. Such change as there is, occurs very slowly. In respect of their religious structures and services they follow the traditional forms and structures deriving from the medieval codes with very few changes or additions. The only significant modern additions are the prayers for the country (both Britain and the State of Israel) which are recited in English (the prayer for the State of Israel is also recited in Hebrew).[7]

The Reform Movement (RSGB) is the largest of the non-Orthodox communities in Britain. Although the movement is currently (1997) led by a rabbi, Rabbi A. Bayfield, it is much less hierarchically organized than the United Synagogue.[8] Each synagogue has a strong degree of independence with respect to most aspects of its religious practice. This independence is indicated by the variation in practice in respect of the roles of women in ritual. While many synagogues allow their women equal opportunity to participate in ritual, in line with the stated position of the movement, others limit women's participation and some will not allow women trained as rabbis by the movement's rabbinical school (the Leo Baeck College) to lead services.

In respect of participation and relation to modern culture the Reform community is more highly integrated than the Orthodox. Its members are fully involved in all aspects of modern British culture, regarding employment, education, and recreation. While Orthodox children are likely to go to schools with an Orthodox religious orientation, most children from the Reform Movement will attend secular educational institutions. The movement itself is also shaped by modern culture. Aspects of its ritual practice have been altered to fit into the modern world, and modern sensibilities. Thus for example, the religious services are much shorter than those found in Orthodox communities and most mentions of sacrifice (which offends modern taste) have been removed from the *siddur* (prayer book). On a wider level the Reform movement has also changed in response to modern ideas, especially in its stated position toward women. The movement now trains women as rabbis and generally allows them to participate in ritual.

Although the British Reform Movement is generally respectful of tradition and Jewish law, it also feels comfortable in making changes whether in ritual or nonritual Jewish practice. The movement since its origins in the mid-nineteenth century has always been of more conservative character than the Reform Movements in Germany or the United States.[9] This has led to the British Reform movement's liturgy and ritual practice retaining more similarities to the traditional forms than either the British Liberal Movement or the American Reform Movement. This conservativism is also reflected in the use of sacred place discussed below.[10]

The founders of the Reform Movement, however, shared with those of other Reform movements a hostility toward the Oral Law and what they saw as rabbinic innovations on a purer form of biblical or prophetic Judaism.[11] Although this antipathy is no longer a feature of British Reform Judaism, it has left its mark in many of the changes which have been made from more traditional modes of practice, for example the general removal of second days of festivals and repetition in liturgy. On a wider level this hostility has left its mark in respect of the decision-making process. Although Reform rabbis today consider traditional rabbinic positions and arguments, the process for making decisions is far removed from the traditional *halahkic* process.[12] Although precedents of Jewish law are generally given a voice in decisions, modern ideas, values, and sensibilities are generally the deciding factors.[13]

Liberal Judaism (ULPS) is the smallest movement in Britain. In many respects it is similar to the Reform Movement. Its members are equally integrated and assimilated into modern British society. The essential differences between the two movements lie in their attitude toward tradition. While British Reform Judaism is essentially conservative and pragmatic in relationship to tradition, the Liberal Movement is often ideologically motivated. It makes changes to traditional patterns in response to developments in theology and understanding. Thus for example, it has been far more consistent (in its recent prayer book) than the Reform Movement in removing noninclusive language.[14] This ideological basis has also led to a de-emphasis on ritual action with a corresponding emphasis on belief. This has also led the Liberal Movement to change its definition of Jewishness, based on either the mother or the father, with an emphasis on belief rather than genealogy. In this and other respects Liberal Judaism is closely related to the American Classical Reform model. In general, the Liberal Movement is more comfortable with changing tradition in response to the modern world.

The Order of Service

In order to highlight the differences between the different communities it is necessary to discuss briefly the key elements of a typical Shabbat *Shacharit* (Morning) service.[15] The service can be divided into five sections for the Reform and Liberal congregations and six sections for the Orthodox. These sections include: the introductory section; the Shema and its blessings; the Prayer section; the Torah Service; and the concluding prayers. The Orthodox service also includes a supplementary section called the *Musaf* or additional section.

The service begins with an introductory section, which is intended to prepare the individual and community for prayer. In the Orthodox (and Conservative) versions this is an extended section with texts which are taken both from the Bible and purely liturgical elements. Although there is a leader[16] for this part of the service, much of this section of the service is recited by the individual. This section can be subdivided into two subsections, morning benedictions and פסוקי דזמרה, morning psalms.[17] The morning benedictions center on blessings derived from *b. Ber.* 60b, with related study passages. The morning psalms comprise a selection of psalms, for example, Psalm 92, and conclude with a *hatzi-kaddish*.[18] Among both the Reform and Liberal communities this section of the service is particularly curtailed – more extensively in the Liberal service than the Reform. This part of the service will generally be recited in the same manner as the rest of the service with certain prayers read or sung by the leader, while others are read or sung in unison by the congregation.

The second section of the service centers on the *Shema*, which is comprised of three sections of the Torah: Deuteronomy 6:4–9; 11:13–21; and Numbers 15:37–41. The *Shema* is preceded by the call to prayer, the *barchu*, which officially begins the service, and two additional blessings. The first of these benedictions deals with creation and the second with God's love for Israel. A blessing concerning redemption follows the *Shema*. In all forms of the service the call to prayer is read by the leader with the congregation responding. In Orthodox congregations the blessings following the call to prayer are read individually with the leader reading aloud opening and closing verses. The first line of the *Shema* is read aloud with the remaining sections being read individually. In the Liberal and Reform congregations the blessings which follow the call to prayer are read either by the leader or aloud communally. The first two lines of the *Shema* and the first paragraph are usually read or chanted aloud.[19] In the Reform congregations the second two paragraphs are often read individually. Liberal congregations usually omit the second paragraph and much of the third. The benedictions that follow the *Shema* are often read by the leader with a few lines being sung in Hebrew.

The third section has a variety of names: the *Tifilah*, Prayer; the *Amidah*, Standing; and the *Shemona Esre*, the Eighteen. This is the part of the service that is traditionally the primary prayer section. In Orthodox synagogues[20] this section is repeated twice. The first time it is read individually and the second is led by the service leader. In all Liberal and most Reform congregations this section is only read once.[21] Sections of it may be sung and the other elements are read communally. The only individual element that is retained by the Liberal and Reform congregations is found in the conclusion of this section, namely a few minutes of silent prayer.

The service continues with the section in which a part of the Torah is read. During this the Torah is removed from the Ark. In all of the different congregations this is the most formal section of the service. A variety of people are invited up to the *bimah* to participate in various ways, for example: to recite blessings; to take the scroll from the Ark. The central part of this section is the reading from the Torah itself. In Orthodox and many Conservative synagogues the entire traditional Torah portion for the week, consisting of several chapters, is chanted. In Liberal and Reform congregations a much smaller portion is read (or occasionally chanted). In the Liberal and Reform congregations observed the Torah Portion averaged fifteen

verses. These usually, though not necessarily, were taken from the traditional Torah portion. After the Torah Scroll is read a traditional
supplementary reading taken from one of the prophets is read or chanted.
This section concludes with the Torah being returned to the Ark.

The Orthodox service continues with a *Musaf* or additional service which
commemorates the additional sacrifice which was offered on the Shabbat.
The service begins with a repetition (with some changes) of the *Amidah*
which is recited in the same fashion as in the earlier section of the service.
The *Musaf* then concludes with a prayer called the *Aleynu*[22] and a memorial
prayer. The *Musaf* service has been taken out of both the Reform and Liberal
Shabbat prayer books, and is not performed in Reform and Liberal congregations. The service concludes with the *Aleynu* and the Memorial
prayer.

Structure of Sacred Space

There are significant differences in structure and use of sacred space
between the Orthodox and non-Orthodox congregations. The architectural
plans for the Orthodox observed and non-Orthodox synagogues are illustrated in Figures 5.1 and 5.2.[23] In the Orthodox synagogues observed, there
were two foci. The primary focus, the Ark was placed on the eastern wall.[24]
It contains the scrolls of the Torah, and is seen as being the most sacred place
in the synagogue.

Most of the service including the reading of the scroll, however, takes
place on the *bimah*, a raised platform in the center of the synagogue. Chairs
surround the *bimah* on all sides. This placement of the *bimah* in the center of
the synagogue places it in the center of the community. It suggests that the
leader is one of the community rather than separate from it. In a similar
respect, the leader of the service faces the Ark rather than the community,
praying with the community.[25]

There is, however, a division in access within the community as a whole.
Women are not allowed to enter the main section of the sanctuary. In many
Orthodox synagogues (including those studied) the women's section is a
gallery above the main sanctuary. In others the women's section is separated from the sanctuary by some type of partition called a *Mehitzah*. Most
Orthodox synagogues in the United Kingdom are built according to these
plans.[26] However, some Orthodox synagogues in both the United Kingdom
and the United States are built according to the plan illustrated in Figure 5.2.
The significant difference between these synagogues (who use the non-
traditional model) and the non-Orthodox synagogues is found in respect of
the direction in which the leader stands. In Orthodox (and most Conservative) synagogues this will always be in the same direction as the
congregation, that is toward the Ark.

The structure and use of space in modern Orthodox synagogues retains
a strong tie to the segmentary, decentralized model of Jewish sacred
space. This is emphasized by the position of the *bimah* in relation to the

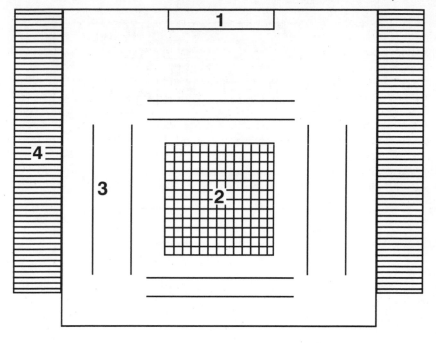

1 Ark
2 *Bimah*
3 Men's Section
4 Women's Gallery

Figure 5.1 Plan of Traditional Synagogue

congregational seats. The rabbi is not qualitatively distinguished from the congregants, he (and the other leaders of the service) face in the same direction, emphasizing the unity of the congregation and suggesting that sacred space is relative (in respect of use) rather than intrinsic.

The architectural plan of the non-Orthodox synagogues (including many Conservative synagogues) suggests a different understanding of sacred space and the role of leadership.[27] Like the Orthodox synagogues, the Ark is found on the eastern wall. The *bimah*, however, is placed next to the Ark, along the eastern wall, with the reading desk and lecterns (called *Amudim*) facing the congregation.[28] There is a clear demarcation in space and direction between the congregation and the *bimah*. This structure, and thus the placement of the leaders facing the congregation, suggests that the leader is praying for rather than praying with the congregation. There is, however, no division between men and women in most Reform and Liberal congregations.[29] Even in those British Reform and Liberal congregations which do not allow women complete equality there is no distinction between men and women in respect of seating.[30]

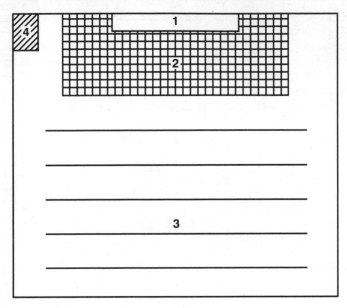

1 Ark
2 *Bimah*
3 Congregation (men and women)
4 Organ (in Reform and Liberal Temples)

Figure 5.2 Plan of non-Traditional Synagogue

In a survey of all Liberal and Reform synagogues in the United Kingdom only one synagogue consistently used a different seating arrangement. That synagogue places the reading desk on the west side of the synagogue facing the Ark with the seats on either side. This synagogue, however, is different from most other Reform synagogues in several respects, for example, more extensive use of Hebrew, and silent *Amidah*. It has also retained a stance of independence in respect of the central rabbinical institutions and movement and currently does not have a rabbi. Although several other synagogues reported occasionally trying other formations, none of these on an ongoing basis moved away from the more usual setup.

The architectural arrangements employed by the non-Orthodox movements can in part be traced to an attempt to conform to a Christian model. It is, however, also tied to structural transformations in modern Jewish culture. Modern functional sacred space, as discussed above, is moving toward a variation on the centralized model of sacred space. The synagogue or temple, the name used by American Reform Jews and also by many American Conservative Jews (in common conversation rather than officially) is increasingly becoming more closely associated with static or intrinsic sacred space. This is suggested by the use of the word temple, seeing the synagogue as an actual permanent replacement for the Temple in

Jerusalem.[31] The architecture reflects this transformation by creating an increasingly exclusive space, the *bimah*, and creating distance between the leader, usually a rabbi, and the congregation. Although the British Reform movement has moved in this direction architecturally, and to an extent in respect to the rabbinical role, the transformation is not as consciously expressed as in the other two. This type of transformation is highlighted below in respect of the role of the rabbi and the democratization of sacred space.

The Role of the Rabbi

The role of the rabbi in the synagogue reflects similar trends to that found in respect of architecture. In the Orthodox synagogues studied, one employed a rabbi and the second did not. In the first synagogue, although the rabbi was present at most of the services observed, he was not expected to lead all of the services.[32] On every occasion, the first section of the service was led by other members of the congregation. The rabbi led the Torah service, usually read the scroll, and led the *Musaf* service. In addition he also gave a sermon in English. The sermon is the only element of these roles which is usually restricted to the rabbi (when a synagogue has a rabbi). In the synagogue without a rabbi, all of these roles, including the sermon, were performed by lay people. In other Orthodox synagogues a *chazan* (cantor) or lay people will lead much of the service and read from the scroll. The rabbi might be expected to give only the sermon.

The role of the rabbi in Reform and Liberal congregations is different from that in Orthodox congregations. In both the congregations observed and those surveyed, the rabbis, when present, were expected to lead most elements of the service.[33] The only significant exception to this was in synagogues which had musical soloists or choirs who led the sung elements of the service. In respect of the synagogues studied, the rabbi also was expected to read from the Torah Scroll and give a sermon.[34] Many of the rabbis interviewed in the survey had never seen a service led by lay people in their own synagogues.

Thus the role of the rabbi in leading services is much stronger in the Reform and Liberal synagogues than it is in Orthodox synagogues. One reason for this, especially though not exclusively in respect of reading from the scroll, is the problem of skills. In many progressive synagogues the rabbi is (or is thought to be) the only person with the requisite skills. In one of the Liberal synagogues observed there was a small group of lay people who had some of the necessary skills and therefore occasionally led services, usually when the rabbi was away.[35] There is, however, a more fundamental reason for the difference – a move toward a new form of centralized sacred space which can also be seen in the architectural plans.

It is observed above in regard to synagogue architecture that the architectural plan of Reform and Liberal synagogues reflects a separation of significant sacred space from congregational space. The *bimah* is placed at one end of the synagogue facing the congregation. It is placed directly next to the ark, suggesting a structural association between the sanctity of the Ark and that of the *bimah*. The prominence of the rabbi in leading services is a further reflection of the transformation to a centralized model. Centralized Jewish sacred space, for example static and exclusive, was exemplified by the priesthood of pre-diaspora Judaism. Thus with the increasing centralization of modern Jewish culture, it is not surprising that the rabbinic role takes on aspects of the priestly role.[36] On the level of underlying structure it is expected that a transformation in one cultural sphere will be reflected in other cultural spheres.

The transformation in the rabbinic role toward the priesthood model is also seen in respect of the Priestly Benediction. In an Orthodox Shabbat Service there is no final benediction. It can be argued that the rabbi has no significant role in blessing the congregation; all equally ask God for blessing. The Priestly Benediction is read in the service as part of the *Amidah*. It is, however, introduced by a statement that these were the words which Aaron and his sons the *Cohanim* (the Priests), used to bless the people. Thus it makes a clear distinction in role between the priests and the rabbis. The only occasions in which this text is used as a benediction is when it is recited by the descendants of the *Cohanim* on the High Holy Days and the three pilgrimage festivals, that is, Sukkot, Pesach, and Shavuot.

In the Liberal and Reform synagogues it is customary to conclude the service with a final benediction. Although many different forms of benedictions are used, most rabbis interviewed (and most services observed) frequently used the Priestly Benediction. In cases where it was known, most rabbis reported that when lay people led the service, either other benedictions or variations on the Priestly Benediction were used. The most frequent variation was a change in the word 'you' to 'us,' for example, 'May God bless us and keep us,' rather than, 'May God bless you and keep you.' In other cases it was observed that lay people used no benediction when concluding the service. Interviews with lay people suggest that many see the Priestly Benediction as belonging to the rabbinic role. In one service observed, although the service was completely led by lay people, when it came to the Priestly Benediction at the conclusion, the leaders asked a rabbinic student who happened to be in the congregation to recite it, the implication being that the rabbinic student was the closest thing to a rabbi at the service.

This understanding of the Priestly Benediction as restricted to the rabbi, although found in both British movements, is more strongly associated with the Liberal movement. Both ethnographic observation and interviews confirm this distinction. Of those Reform rabbis who used the Priestly Benediction, none thought that lay people either should or would not use it when they led the service. Most of the Liberal rabbis who used it, however, thought that lay people would not use it when leading services.

There are two different forms of translation of this text.[37] The older form of translation, still used by the Reform Movement is:

May the Lord bless you and keep you.
May the light of the Lord's presence shine upon you and be gracious to you.
May the face of the Lord shine upon you and give you peace.

The version used in the Liberal prayer book, *Service of the Heart*, is:

The Lord bless you and keep you.
The face of the Lord shine upon you and be gracious to you.
The face of the Lord shine upon you and give you peace.

Although the difference is subtle, the removal of the word 'may' makes the action of conferring the benediction much stronger. It suggests that the rabbi is the special conduit of blessing rather than one of the congregation asking God for blessing. The difference in text suggests that the rabbis of the Liberal movement (as a movement) are closer to the priestly model than are those of the Reform Movement.

The priestly role is further exemplified in the practice found in some American Reform temples. These Reform temples have remained in the Classical Reform model. They reject many of the changes back toward a more traditional model recently taken by the Reform Movement as a whole. Their practice was probably the norm until the late sixties. In these temples, when reciting the Priestly Benediction many rabbis lifted their arms in imitation of the priests in the Temple. This makes a direct symbolic association between the rabbi and the priest, suggesting that just as the priests were the unique conduits of divine power, so too are the rabbis. One rabbi described feeling spiritual power going from his arms to the congregation. Lay people when leading services would never imitate this action.[38]

It is interesting that this ritual practice was found particularly in the United States as opposed to the United Kingdom. It is associated with, as mentioned above, a change in the designation of synagogue to temple. This suggests that the Reform Movement in the United States in certain respects was closer to the centralized model of sacred space than either of the progressive movements in the United Kingdom.

The mainstream of the Reform Movement in the United States today, however, appears to have moved away from this position. In many respects it has become increasingly traditional. This is exemplified by the Priestly Benediction. In many synagogues it is not used at all, and in those where it is used, very few rabbis continue to raise their arms. The translation found in the American Reform prayer book, *Gates of Prayer*, includes the word may.

It is suggested above that the move to a centralized model of sacred space, found in all modern Jewish communities is associated with relaxed external boundaries. The extreme form of centralized sacred space exemplified by the Classical Reform model may be tied to a time in modern American history in which there was a de-emphasis on ethnic (or religious) divisions in American society. The melting pot was the primary metaphor used. It is significant that this model was never used in respect of British society, suggesting a reason why the British progressive movements never moved as strongly toward the centralized model. The strong priestly element of the

American rabbinate was part of a cultural transformation responding to the weakening of boundaries.

It is possible that the other changes taking place in the American Reform Movement today are also related to the rediscovery of ethnic diversity in American society, recreating externally imposed boundaries between groups, thus reducing the pressure to move toward a strongly centralized model. One of these changes discussed below (page 108), which also includes a move toward more traditional models of worship, is the development of small segmented groupings within many Reform synagogues (especially those in areas of high Jewish population density) called prayer groups which conduct more traditional services separately from the main temple community.[39]

In spite of this weakening of the centralized model in American Reform Judaism, all modern Jewish movements have taken on aspects of the centralized model of sacred space. In all movements the role of the rabbi has priestly elements. Even the minimal role of the rabbi in Orthodox services is a significant increase from the role found before the twentieth century. For example, the weekly sermon is a relatively modern innovation, which first developed in the mid-nineteenth century.[40] And prior to the modern period the rabbi may have had little or no role in leading services.

There are two areas in which the Orthodox community includes a strong priestly element. It is significant, however, that these elements are not associated with the role of the rabbi. As mentioned above, the Priestly Benediction is recited five times a year by the descendants of the *Cohanim*. These five religious festivals and occasions are closely associated with the Temple and thus the use of this ritual creates a symbolic association between the Temple and current religious practice: Rosh Hashanah, Yom Kippur, Sukkot, Pesach, and Shavuot. The second area is in respect of the Torah service. The first two Torah blessings are reserved for descendants of the *Cohanim* and the *Levites* (Temple functionaries) respectively. The role of the two groups in the Torah service can be understood as symbolically opening the sacred to the rest of the community. Their role, however, is not ritually necessary because if there are no *Cohanim* or *Levites* present, the ritual may still be performed. They also have very little other significance in the community and are generally seen as part of the congregation. This priestly aspect is separate and distinct from the rabbinic role, and emphasizes the distinction between the rabbinic and the priestly.[41]

Ethnographic evidence, from Reform and Liberal congregations, suggests that the Liberal movement contains a strong priestly element, exemplified in the translation of the Priestly Benediction and its restricted usage. It is also found in the restricted access to sacred space and the formality of the service discussed below. The Reform movement, however, has a slightly weaker form.

One priestly element which is occasionally found in all the communities is the wearing of robes by the rabbi and cantor. In Britain robes are worn by many Reform, Liberal, and all Orthodox rabbis who are connected to the United Synagogue movement.[42] In the United States robes are most often worn in Reform synagogues.[43] This practice has been observed in the Reform, Liberal, and Orthodox synagogues in Britain and in Reform synagogues in the United States. The robe can be understood as a priestly element for two reasons. It indicates a formalization of the service in imitation of non-Jewish practice which places a strong emphasis on the role of the leader. It also creates a distinction between the rabbi and congregation.[44] Lawrence Hoffman suggests that the wearing of robes was instituted as part of a more generalized pattern of transformation in the European Reform Movement, associated with formalization and acceptance of European cultural norms (1987: 162).

It is likely that the difference between the British Reform and Liberal movements is related to their respective approaches to modern culture. Although both are ideologically in favor of full integration with modern western culture, there is a significant distinction in respect of its inclusion into religious services and religious practice. The Liberal movement has made many more accommodations to western culture. For example, there is much greater use of English as the language of prayer, and it has made many more changes in the liturgy based on modern values than has the Reform movement.[45] It is not therefore surprising that the Liberal Movement uses a more centralized model of sacred space than found in the Reform Movement.

As indicated in the discussion of robes, some aspects of the centralization associated with the priestly aspects of Judaism are also found in the Orthodox community, especially in Britain. This element is most strongly found in the United Synagogue, the largest and perhaps most centralized of Orthodox organizations in Britain. It is possible that the existence of the position of Chief Rabbi itself is also part of a centralizing trend.[46]

It is not unlikely that the United Synagogue and the community which it represents have, until recently, made a stronger emphasis on accommodation to British cultural norms than either other Orthodox communities in Britain or those in the United States and that this has led to a strong centralized model both in imitation and in order to create stronger external boundaries.[47] This supposition is supported by a statement from an interview in Glasgow. The informant stated that his parents had the choice of going to either a synagogue affiliated with the United Synagogue or an unaffiliated one. They chose the unaffiliated synagogue because it was considered to be more traditional. This was due to the inclusion of a prayer for the King (now the Queen) recited in English that was read only in synagogues affiliated with the United Synagogue. The synagogue was derogatorily called the 'May He' synagogue, taken from the first two words of the prayer.

Access to Sacred Space

One of the significant elements of the centralized model of sacred space exemplified by the Temple in Jerusalem was an exclusivity in respect of access to sacred space. As discussed above, the Temple and its precincts were progressively more exclusive, culminating in the Holy of Holies. The decentralized or macro-model of sacred space is exemplified by relatively freer access to sacred space.

On one level there is a clear democratization of sacred space within Orthodox synagogues. During the course of the service a wide range of men move between the various spaces. During a normal Sabbath service,[48] in addition to the men who lead various segments of the service, at least seven men are called up to the Torah. These men recite the blessings before and after the reading of the Torah. In one of the Orthodox synagogues observed these seven were supplemented by an additional number of men, not required by Jewish law or tradition, who were also called up to recite these blessings.[49] A number of other men also participated in other aspects of the Torah service, for example opening the Ark and taking the mantle off the scroll. On other occasions, as indicated above, men other than the rabbi would read from the scroll. An additional man recites the blessings and chants the weekly *Haftara*, that is, reading from the Prophets. Thus in the Orthodox service all men are eligible to lead and participate in the most significant elements of the service, and in each particular service a number of the men do so.

There is, however, one significant area in which the Orthodox community retains a restriction in respect of access to sacred space. Women are restricted to a particular section of the synagogue, either a gallery or an area partitioned off from the main sanctuary.[50] Women in the Orthodox community today are also not allowed to participate in the Torah service, or to lead any other parts of the service. These restrictions derive in part from the model of the Temple, with it's Women's Court, and perhaps even more from the patriarchal approach which has been characteristic of Jewish culture up to (and perhaps including) the modern period. This element is discussed in detail in chapter 6.

Although in principle Reform and Liberal communities make no distinction between members of the community, and thus support open access to sacred space, the practice of many Reform and most (if not all) Liberal synagogues reflect a much more restrictive approach. In both Liberal and Reform synagogues the number of people called to the Torah is much smaller than in Orthodox synagogues. The average number, based on a survey of rabbis and lay leaders, in the Reform synagogues was 2.5 and in the Liberal synagogues 1.[51] In many of the Liberal synagogues only the rabbi recites the blessings and reads from the scroll. In respect of the other roles in the Torah service the numbers are identical to that found in Orthodox synagogues.

In respect of women, however, the Reform and Liberal movements support full access and equality. All Progressive synagogues have mixed seating. In most Liberal synagogues (with one exception) men and women have equal access to sacred space and to participation in all aspects of the service. In many Reform synagogues this is also true. There are, however, a significant number of Reform synagogues, many of them large and centrally located, who restrict women's access to sacred space. In some cases women are not allowed to participate in the Torah service, in others women are forbidden from leading any aspect of the service as a whole.

Interviews were conducted with members of three Reform synagogues in which women were not allowed equal access to sacred space. In many of the interviews the primary explanation given for the restrictions was based on tradition, that is, it is against tradition to allow women to participate. When pressed to explain this response, the interviewees stated that women should not be allowed to touch the Torah because they might make it impure. This explanation is interesting in two respects. First, it is not an accurate statement of Jewish Law. The *Shulkhan Aruch*, the primary code of Jewish law, states that a Torah can never become impure, even if touched by a woman in *niddah* (a menstruant). Second, using purity as a determinant of access to sacred space makes an association with macro-structure, that is, the centralized sacred space exemplified by the Temple. Access to the Temple was specifically determined by purity or impurity (see below, chapter 6, for a detailed discussion of this issue).

Significant differential in access to sacred space is found in a second ritual element of the Torah Service. In Orthodox synagogues both prior to and after the reading of the Torah, the Torah is processed around the synagogue. During this procession all of the men touch the scroll with their *talitot* (prayer shawls). In the synagogues observed the atmosphere of the procession is very informal – for example, the rabbi greeted members of the congregation as did the other people participating in the procession.[52] The ritual emphasizes that the Torah, the most sacred ritual object, is part of the community and that each person has a direct and personal connection with it.[53]

These ritual processions have been minimized to a great extent in most Liberal and Reform congregations. Most Liberal congregations have removed the processions entirely from their services. The Torah is never taken down from the *bimah*. When there is a procession very few people touch the scroll and the atmosphere is very formal. Touching or bowing to the scroll is considered undignified or idolatry. Torah processions are found in most Reform synagogues. The atmosphere tends to be slightly less formal than that found in Liberal synagogues.

These examples suggest that in spite of the democratic principles which are central to Progressive ideologies, general access to sacred space is minimized in comparison to Orthodox synagogues, the only significant exception to this being the position of women. The difference in access is directly associated with the change in model found in the modern Jewish community from the micro- to a macro-model introduced above. In the micro-model, with a low level of differentiation between congregant and rabbi, access to sacred space is generalized. In the macro-model, with a progressively higher level of differentiation (that is, a move toward a priestly model), access to sacred space is relatively restricted. These differences are also supported and reflected in the respective architectural plans of the synagogues.

Forms of Prayer

The role of the individual is also developed in respect of the forms of prayer used by the different synagogues. The formality of the service is one means through which the individual can be emphasized or de-emphasized. In Orthodox services prayer tends to be relatively informal. Although the liturgy is fixed by Jewish law, much of the service is read individually, with the leader beginning and ending prayers or sections of the service to keep the community relatively together. The individual aspects of prayer are also emphasized by the movements made by the people praying. People sway back and forth and bow at various points of the service. The movements are done individually and emphasize that although the community is praying together, prayer is ultimately individual communication with God.

The informality of the service is carried over to the general atmosphere of the service. Orthodox services tend to be less decorous than non-Orthodox services (including Conservative). People talk with each other, often about things which have nothing to do with the service. There is a strongly social atmosphere with people greeting each other. There is also a constant movement into and out of the service, with people arriving throughout the service. The informality reinforces the focus on the individual, reflecting the view that people move in and out of prayer and have individual needs and pace of prayer.[54]

The atmosphere and approach to prayer are in keeping with the micro-model of sacred space. This model focuses on the individual, and individual access to sacred space. By moving the center of prayer to the individual, it emphasizes the essential equality of the community, and the view that prayer is direct individual connection with God with no intermediary.

The form of the Liberal and Reform services is much more formal in structure and atmosphere. The services observed in Liberal synagogues are very highly structured. The Liberal prayer book used during the study, *Service of the Heart*, includes rubrics for each liturgical element.[55] These indicate whether the text should be read by the leader, sung by the choir, or read by the congregation. These rubrics were taken seriously, to the extent that when they were not followed visible dissent was observed.

As indicated above, there was very little room for individual prayer. The conclusion of the *Amidah* was the only part of the service which included silent prayer and was usually allotted only a minute or two. The sections read by the congregation, in Hebrew or English, were read in unison. The survey of Liberal congregations indicates that most followed this formal structure of service.

The atmosphere of the services in the Liberal synagogues was similarly decorous. During the course of the service people would sit quietly, only speaking when called to do so by the service. People would generally arrive at the service on time, with those who frequently arrived late being remarked upon. This pattern of decorous behavior was also evident in respect of movement during prayer. Unlike the Orthodox synagogues in which there was a high degree of movement, for example swaying, the

Liberal synagogues were characterized by controlled behavior.[56] The congregation would sit and stand as a group with little or no individual variation.

The Reform services observed tended to be less formally structured than those found in Liberal synagogues. This was reflected by *Forms of Prayer*, the prayer book or *Siddur* used by Reform congregations. Unlike the Liberal prayer book, *Forms of Prayer* includes very few rubrics. Although there are certain sections which are read only by the leader, most other sections are read, in Hebrew or in English, by the congregation as a whole. Unlike the Orthodox service, however, this is not essentially individual reading as it tends to be read in unison.

Like the Liberal services, there is very little room for individual prayer or expression in British Reform services. Although in several synagogues the second two paragraphs of the *Shema* are recited silently, in many the only silent prayer is a few minutes at the conclusion of the *Amidah*. In two synagogues a silent *Amidah* was introduced by the rabbi. It was retained by one of the synagogues but dropped by the second when a new rabbi was hired. In both of these cases the rabbis who introduced the silent *Amidah* were on the traditional end of the Reform movement (at least in respect of practice).

In respect of atmosphere, the Reform synagogues observed a similar pattern of decorum to that found in Liberal congregations. There was little or no talking within the congregation during services. Most members would arrive at the beginning of the service, or wait till a pause in the service to enter. Individual behavior is also generally controlled, with only a few individuals swaying during prayer.

Professor Lawrence Hoffman discusses, from the perspective of liturgy, some of the defining characteristics of the early Reform movement, characteristics which shaped both of the English movements. He highlights the move from traditional modes of chanting to the style used for the singing of Christian hymns.[57] He argues that this and related transformations in vocabulary, for example an emphasis on transcendence, are part of a generalized pattern creating social distance between the congregation and the numinous and the functionaries connected with it. Hoffman ties together the behavior of the congregation in respect of formality and distance and the reserved status of the rabbi, in a priestly, separate status, emphasized by the wearing of robes and the distance of the congregants from the sancta. He suggests that these factors were connected in part to aspects of the cultural environment of post-Enlightenment Europe, with the non-Orthodox Jewish community, in part, consciously transforming itself to fit within the framework of both European propriety and philosophy (Hoffman, 1987: 161–3).

These examples of religious practice in Reform and Liberal congregations reveal several trends which are associated with the transformation of modern Jewish culture from the decentralized to the centralized model. The ethnographic analysis, supported by Professor Hoffman, suggests that these developments have occurred to different degrees in the movements discussed, with the greatest transformation being associated with the degree of openness and acceptance of modern western cultural forms.

As noted above (see pages 51 and 102), one area which indicates a move away from this centralizing trend is the prayer group movement within the Reform and Conservative communities in the United States. Within many Reform synagogues we find increasing segmentation and dissatisfaction with the centralized models. This has led to the development of small, self-selected, groups within the temples which conduct their own services and often engage in other ritual and social activities together. The services conducted are phenomenologically similar to those found in traditional models of Judaism. They usually have no formal leadership, thereby removing the priestly elements often associated with the role of rabbi in the Reform movement, and a high degree of participation and access to sacred space. The atmosphere of their services is informal. There is often an emphasis on Jewish education and development of skills. Many of the people involved in prayer groups see themselves as the most committed members of their communities. These groups allow their members to be fully involved in ritual action and to design forms of worship, usually more traditional than the norm in temples. It appears that this phenomenon is particularly associated with areas with strong Jewish ethnic identity. In those less Jewishly central areas, where the community is perhaps less self-confident, the prayer group movement is less pronounced.[58]

Conclusions

All of the factors discussed in this chapter are related to this transformation. The architectural plan of the synagogues reveals a movement of focus. The *bimah* is moved from the center of the congregation to separate it from and face the congregation. Sacred space is disengaged from the community in a similar way to its use in the Temple. The terminology used by American Reform synagogues, that is, temple rather than synagogue, emphasizes this transformation. The relatively restricted access to sacred space further emphasizes the changes in plan. Sacred space represented by the *bimah* and the Torah are increasingly separated from the community, with access given primarily to an almost priestly, professional caste, that is, rabbis, cantors, and sometimes specially trained lay people. The priestly aspects of the rabbinic role are also transformed. Certain roles in the service and particular prayers are increasingly restricted to the rabbi. The clergy is also often particularly distinguished from the congregation through the use of robes and other formal garments. The role of the individual is also correspondingly increasingly minimized. The Reform and Liberal movements place a much higher degree of emphasis on the community than on the individual. This transformation is in line with the move toward the centralized model which places a higher degree of emphasis on external, that is, group boundaries, than it does on internal, that is, individual boundaries. In each of these factors the Liberal movement (and segments of the American

Reform) tends to be the closest to the more highly centralized pole.

This analysis suggests that certain elements are associated with a centralized model of sacred space. The place itself, for example the temple, may be viewed as intrinsically or specially holy. This holiness is distinct from that created by the use of the space. Access to the more significant sacred spaces, for example the *bimah*, is restricted. The service as a whole or significant elements of it are reserved for the leader – perhaps with an emphasis on conferring blessing. The services themselves may also be highly formal in structure with an emphasis on the group rather than the individual. Within the Jewish framework, the move toward a centralized model is also associated with a centralization in group or movement structure. It is not surprising that the American Reform movement, which represents the strongest version of the centralized model, is also the most highly centralized movement as well.

Notes

1. Although there is a Conservative Movement in Britain, it is very small and not yet a significant element within the Jewish community. It is generally similar to the traditional end of the American Conservative Movement.
2. The developments in the synagogue in all three main American movements is analyzed in detail in Werthheimer, J. (1987) *The American Synagogue: A Sanctuary Transformed*, Cambridge: Cambridge University Press.
3. While there are significant differences between the non-Orthodox movements, which in many cases define these movements, there is also significant variation within movements. This variation is more pronounced in the American Reform and Conservative Movements than in the Reform and Liberal Movements of the UK. The two movements in the UK are together broadly equivalent to the American Reform Movement, representing the two main wings of that movement. In respect of the issues discussed in this chapter, there is relatively little variation in the Orthodox community as most of the issues are considered to be determined by Jewish Law.
4. Although the Chief Rabbi's official title is the Chief Rabbi of the United Synagogue of British Jewry, he is perceived by many within the wider Jewish community and the non-Jewish community as being the leader and spokesperson of all Jews of Britain.
5. The religious court with the final authority in respect of decisions in Jewish law.
6. To some extent the position of the United Synagogue in respect of British culture can be expressed in the words of a nineteenth-century Orthodox thinker, Samson Raphael Hirsch, *Torah im Derehk Eretz* (Torah and the way of the world), meaning on a limited level, study of Torah in association with modern knowledge, and on a wider level, the creative interrelationship between Torah, Jewish tradition, and modern culture, each working in its own sphere of competence. Although Hirsch's position has recently been criticized by Jonathan Sacks, the current Chief Rabbi, and is rejected by other Orthodox leaders, it remains a fair characterization of the behavior of United Synagogue and its members. See Sacks, J. (1990) *Tradition in an Untraditional Age: Essays on Modern Jewish Thought*, London: Vallentine, Mitchell, pp. 3–17.

7. The modern Orthodox movement in the United States is not phenomeno-logically dissimilar. The major difference lies in the role of the Chief Rabbi. The American movement is much less hierarchically organized and does not have a position with the same formal and informal authority.

8. The head of the RSGB before Rabbi Bayfield was not a rabbi. It is possible that the change in policy was in part motivated by the wish to give the movement both internally and externally a spokesperson with greater authority.

9. For discussion about the significant elements of the British Reform Movement see Marmur, D. (ed.) (1973) *Reform Judaism: Essays on Reform Judaism in Britain*, London: Reform Synagogues of Great Britain.

10. This conservative trend has led some people to suggest that the British Reform Movement is analogous to the American Conservative Movement rather than the American Reform Movement. This analogy, however, is only based on surface elements. The basic approach of the Reform movement in respect of *halakhah* is much closer to that of the American Reform Movement than to the Conservative Movement. Both British and American Reform do not generally use a traditional *halakhic* process in making decisions (see below). The Conservative Movement, however, bases its approach to Judaism precisely on an *halakhic* basis.

11. Leigh, M. (1973) 'Reform Judaism in Britain (1840–1970),' in Marmur, D. (ed.) (1973) *Reform Judaism: Essays on Reform Judaism in Britain*, London: Reform Synagogues of Great Britain, p. 12.

12. For a detailed analysis of the *halakhic* process see Roth, J. (1986) *The halakhic Process: A Systemic Analysis*, New York: Jewish Theological Seminary. Although it might be argued by some Orthodox thinkers that this book presents the *halakhic* process from a conservative view, the book convincingly demonstrates a methodology of decision-making which has been the basis of Jewish decision-making over the last one thousand five hundred years. This process is still followed within Conservative and Orthodox communities, but is generally not used in Reform or Liberal decision-making. Within the American Reform movement some attention has been given to the process, as indicated in a series of publications presenting *Responsa* on a wide variety of *halakhic* issues (see for example Freehof, S. (1980) *New Reform Responsa*, Cincinnati: Hebrew Union College Press; or Jacob, W. (1987) *Contemporary American Reform Responsa*, New York: CCAR). Although many of these discussions use the traditional *halakhic* form and style of argumentation they appear to be a reversal of the process, being written after the decisions have been made rather than being the basis for the decisions.

13. This is illustrated in the process observed which decided the content of the festival prayer book recently published by the RSGB. In the discussion several rabbis requested the addition of several prayers which would traditionally be found in festival services, in essence presenting the traditional position. Other rabbis suggested that with the addition of these elements the service would become too long for the congregants, i.e. representing modern conditions and sensibilities; ultimately this position was accepted and most of the additional prayers were not added into the *makhzor*. The significance of modern values vis-à-vis tradition is also reflected in the changed role of women in Reform synagogues and the recent changes in the language of prayer, that is, changing the language and liturgy to include women.

14. This refers to language about both human beings and God which is considered to be sexist, for example, man or Lord respectively.

15. Traditional Judaism has three times for services during the day: the morning (*Shacharit*), the afternoon (*Minchah*), and evening (*Maariv*). For a discussion of Jewish prayer with some anthropological insight, see Heilman, S. (1973) *Synagogue Life: A Study in Symbolic Interaction*, Chicago: University of Chicago Press, pp. 65–9.

16. The term 'leader' is used here rather than rabbi (or other official, e.g. a cantor) because in all the Jewish communities studied, this role could be fulfilled by any member of the community (male member among the Orthodox). In the Orthodox synagogues observed (and the Conservative synagogue), this section of the service was usually not led by the rabbi. In the Reform and Liberal congregations it was usually led by the rabbi when he or she was present.

17. For a discussion of the content and history of this section see Elbogen, 1993: 72–80.

18. The *hatzi-kaddish* is a form of the *kaddish* prayer which is written primarily in Aramaic. It is essentially a doxology. In part, it is used within the service to mark the separation between sections.

19. The first two lines of the *Shema*:

> Hear Israel, the Lord is our God, the Lord is one
> Blessed be God's glorious kingdom forever.

The first of these is viewed both by traditional, and by Progressive Jews as the key statement of Jewish faith. It is for this reason that it is read while standing in American Reform, many British Reform, and Liberal synagogues.

20. Conservative synagogues also follow the traditional practice.

21. A silent *Amidah* has been observed in two Reform congregations. In both cases this was introduced by rabbis who were more traditionally oriented. In one case when the rabbi left the congregation the practice was retained until a new rabbi was hired. In the second case the practice has been retained, perhaps because no new rabbi has taken up that position.

22. The *Aleynu* is a prayer which recognizes a Jew's obligation to worship God, and looks forward to the time when God will rule a transformed world.

23. Some aspects of the development of synagogue architecture are discussed in greater detail in chapter 3.

24. See above, pages 51–2, for a detailed discussion of the Ark, its place and significance.

25. The only point at which the leader, in this case the rabbi, was observed to face the congregation was during the sermon. The sermon is the only significant nonparticipatory segment of the traditional service.

26. All of the Orthodox synagogues discussed in Wolfe, G. and Fine, J. ((1978) *The Synagogues of New York's Lower East Side*, New York: New York University Press) place their *bamot* in the center of the synagogue. The only significant exception is Congregation Anshe Slonim, pp. 96–7, the sole Reform synagogue described.

27. The architecture of Reform synagogues is discussed by Rabbi Daniel Freelander in a short article in *Reform Judaism* ((1994) 'Why Temples Look the Way they Do', *Reform Judaism* **23.1**, 35–7). It suggests that there are three stages in the development of Reform synagogues. The first pattern, before World War II, is similar to that of Orthodox synagogues. It should be noted, however, that important synagogues in the USA and Europe were already built according to Freelander's stage 2 pattern (see for example Elbogen, 1993: 358). The second, postwar, pattern was essentially that presented in Figure 5.2. Reform synagogues built in

suburbia were characterized by being especially large. Freelander suggests that synagogues built since the 1970s are smaller and more personal reflecting new styles in worship. The *bimah*, however, is still along one wall facing the congregation, and is often smaller than it had been in the earlier patterns of reform synagogues. The new pattern of more intimate synagogue architecture is also discussed in Rosenfeld, E. (1994) 'The New Intimate Sanctuary', *Reform Judaism*, **23.1**, 38–42. This transformation in structure is parallel to a return to more traditional patterns of worship. It is also associated with a slight move away from the more centralized model. It is likely that with the Reform synagogue no longer being as strongly identified with the Temple the grandeur of the architecture is reduced.

28. A recent discussion of American Reform Jewish custom highlights the practice of the rabbi facing the congregation rather than the Ark. It indicates that in most Reform and some Conservative communities the rabbi faces the congregation. It suggests that this is in part due to the placement of the *bimah* close to the Ark and the size of congregations. It is interesting to note that one of the justifications given for the change in religious practice is that the *Cohanim* face the congregation when they bless them. A second justification is that the preacher also faces the congregation. Both of these are rituals in which there is no congregational participation, and both emphasize the priestly aspect. See Jacob, 1987: 192.

29. Although there are no Reform synagogues in which men and women have separate seating, there are several synagogues in which there are limitations on women's roles. In certain synagogues women are not allowed onto the *bimah* and in others they are forbidden from touching the Torah.

30. At the time of this study one Liberal congregation and at least six Reform congregations restricted the roles of women in the synagogue. These restrictions ranged from not allowing women any leadership roles in religious services to forbidding them from touching the Torah scrolls.

31. In one interview the respondent stated that a temple was more than a synagogue. For a discussion of the change in terminology see Jick, L. (1987) 'The Reforms Synagogue' in J. Werthheimer (ed.) *The American Synagogue: A Sanctuary Transformed*, Cambridge: Cambridge University Press, pp. 89–90.

32. In Traditional synagogues (Conservative and Orthodox) the leader of the service or שליחצבור is seen as speaker, rather than representative or intermediary. Knowledge and ability are the only essential prerequisites for the role, which in principle can be performed by any man in Orthodox communities, or man or woman in most Conservative congregations. In many Orthodox and Conservative communities in the United States this role is filled by a *chazan*. Although this role may be professional, it is often also informal being filled by any male over thirteen years of age who has the requisite ability (see Heilman, 1973: 87).

33. Clearly in those synagogues where there was no rabbi, lay people led the services. In regard to the other rabbinic functions, e.g. weddings and funerals (and sometimes Bar/Bat Mitzvah) rabbis from the outside were brought in to leed these services.

34. See the discussion of Lawrence Hoffman's arguments on p. 107. He suggests that exclusivity in respect of access to the sancta, that is, holding or reading from the scroll, is part of a larger pattern of transformation within early Reform Judaism.

35. The Liberal Movement has held courses in London to train lay people to lead services. In spite of this, all Liberal rabbis in London interviewed indicated that

they rarely or never attended services led by lay people in their own congregations.

36. It should be noted that in none of the modern Jewish movements have the rabbis taken on all aspects of the priestly function (as exemplified in the Jerusalem Temples). The rabbinic role and the priestly role should be seen as two ideal types, ends of a polar axis with all movements (including the Orthodox) falling at various points along it.

37. Both of the versions are reasonable translations of the original text. The first translates the verbs in the jussive while the second translates them in the imperfect.

38. The Priestly Benediction is also used by Reform rabbis in a variety of other liturgical situations relevant to this discussion, for example, baby blessings, weddings, and *bar mitzvah*. It is also traditionally used in weddings and *brit milah* (circumcision). Most Reform rabbis will recite the benediction with their hands placed on the head or over the heads, in an attitude of conferring blessing. This is not usually done by more traditional rabbis.

It is interesting to note that the priestly aspect, and use of the Priestly Benediction, are also found in the Ordination ceremonies of the various movements. In the Reform and Liberal movements both in the United States and Britain, the ordination is performed by a laying-on of hands and recitation of the Priestly Benediction. In the Conservative movement, however, this element is not present, and Ordination is simply a graduation ceremony.

39. Prayer groups share many similarities to an earlier phenomenon, the *Havurah* movement, which is found within both the Conservative and American Reform Movements. Although *havurot* met (meet) for similar purposes to the prayer groups and were phenomenologically similar in respect to formality, they often also served a broader set of social needs. For discussion of the differences between the *Havurah* and the synagogue, see Hoffman, L. (1979) 'The Synagogue, the Havurah and Liable Communities', *Response*, **38**, 37–41

40. Elbogen suggests that although the sermon was a significant element of the ancient synagogue service, it has only reasserted itself, in all forms of Jewish communities, in recent times (1993: 157).

41. The *Mishnah* indicates that the *Cohanim* were only given this distinction for the sake of maintaining peace in the community and not for any intrinsic quality, *m. Gitten*: 5.9.

42. The United Synagogue is the largest Orthodox movement in the UK. The Chief Rabbi is the religious leader of this organization and is often perceived as being the spokesman of all Jews in the UK.

43. This practice is mentioned by Rabbi Walter Jacob who indicates that it occurs in a large number of reform synagogues (Jacob, 1987: 193).

44. In all synagogues, except for many Liberal and American Reform congregations, participants do wear special garments during prayer, that is, the *tallit* and skullcap. These religious garments are also worn by the rabbi. If he/she wears a robe, the *tallit* is worn over the robe. It should be noted that the *tallit* worn by many Reform rabbis and cantors has been redesigned and looks similar to a surplice.

45. One example of this type of liturgical change is found in respect of the value of universality. *Oseh Shalom* (found at the conclusion of the *Amidah* and the *Kaddish*) is a prayer which has been changed to reflect this value. The traditional version, found in the Reform *Siddur*, is: 'May the one who causes peace to reign in the Heavens, let peace descend upon us and on Israel.' In the Liberal prayer

book, there is an addition, in both the English and Hebrew, of 'and all mankind.'

It should be noted, however, that like the American Reform Movement the Liberal Movement is in some respects moving toward a more traditional model. In the Prayer Book published in 1995 there is a change to more traditional forms of prayer, and a greater usage of Hebrew as the language of prayer.

46. When the position was instituted there were attempts to make it qualitatively distinct from other Orthodox rabbis in Britain, suggesting a similarity to the High Priest.

47. It is also possible that the very negative feelings which are exhibited between the Orthodox community in Britain and the non-Orthodox community is a reflection of this trend. The strong centralization model would necessitate a rejection of any institution or organization which would weaken external boundaries and deny the authority of the center.

48. As opposed to certain special Shabbatot when additional sections of the Torah are read.

49. According to Jewish Law a minimum of seven men must be called up to the Torah on the Shabbat. This, however, can be supplemented by an additional number of men on Shabbat and festivals (Elbogen, 1993: 139).

50. See Heilman, 1973: 69–74. Unlike the community studied by Heilman, however, in the United Synagogue the segregation between men and women outside of the service proper is less extreme. For example, the unconscious separation which he observed in the *kiddush* after services was not observed in any of the congregations in Britain, nor was their a significant separation at other types of social events (Heilman, 1973: 70). His point that the Orthodox synagogue is primarily for the men (in regard to services) remains true in both the United States and Britain, though there is a strong trend among Orthodox women in both countries to be more involved in prayer and synagogue services (Heilman, 1973: 73).

51. These averages were also confirmed by observation.

52. This informal and social element of the Torah procession has also been observed in American Conservative congregations.

53. This type of connection is best exemplified during the festival of *Simchat Torah* in which all the Torahs are taken from the ark and danced in procession around the synagogue. Every member (male) who wishes to is allowed to carry and dance with the scroll. Celebration of this festival in Reform and Liberal synagogues tends to be much more respectful and restrained.

54. See Heilman, 1973: 68, 73. Heilman also closely examines the different types of social interactions which occur during the service. He highlights several categories including gossip and joking. One might also add business and synagogue politics. All of these categories have also been observed in British communities.

55. Although the new Liberal prayer book includes fewer rubrics, in the services observed the patterns established by the previous prayer book were still essentially in force.

56. The attribute of decorum as a response to western cultural differences has, to some extent, also affected the mainstream of American Orthodoxy. Gurock, for example states, '... gone now was the "prayer club room" intimacy that had earlier characterised synagogue life. Decorum, always the first demand of acculturating groups in making their religious regimen more intelligible and respectable to the world around them, was strongly emphasised' (Gurock, J.

(1987) 'The Orthodox Synagogue' in Werthheimer, J. (ed.), *The American Synagogue: A Sanctuary Transformed*, Cambridge: Cambridge University Press, p. 49). It is not unlikely that similar forces have shaped aspects of behavior in Orthodox synagogues in Britain.

57. He indicates that sometimes actual hymns were used with the Christological elements removed. See Hoffman, L. (1987) *Beyond the Text: A Holistic Approach to Liturgy*, Bloomington: Indiana University Press, pp. 161–2. See also Elbogen, 1993: 385.

58. It is interesting to note that in spite of attempts by an American rabbi in Britain to start a similar movement, it has not yet achieved any significant success. It is not unlikely that this is due to the relationship of the Jewish community in Britain to the wider community. Britain has never emphasized ethnic diversity and thus this type of internal segmentation within the progressive movements has not occurred.

Gender has always been a significant marker in models of Jewish sacred space. Over the periods of time discussed in this chapter different aspects of gender, particularly female gender, were emphasized as reasons for exclusion from sacred space. The transformation in the definition or valuation of feminine gender is shown to be directly related to the model of space. As the model transforms, so too does the understanding of gender. This chapter examines both the specific details of Israelite (biblical period) and Jewish (postbiblical period) sacred space and the abstract models which emerge from these specific cases. The analysis is divided into three periods: the Temple period, the *halakhic* (legal) period, and the modern period. The Temple period focuses on the sacred space exemplified by the Temple and thus in the context of the discussion here, extends until the destruction of the Second Temple in CE 70. The *halakhic* period covers the extensive period between CE 70 and the nineteenth century. Although during this period there are transformations in culture and ideology, it is unified by a process and approach to Jewish tradition and legal structure. There appears to be a relative continuity of structural transformation during this period, especially with respect to the role and perception of women, which justifies treating it as a single entity.[1] It is with the modern period, however, that there is a significant challenge to this approach and a transformation in both the understanding of gender and sacred space.

Biblical Sacred Space

As discussed in chapter 2, two versions of centralized sacred space are developed in the biblical text.[2] The first, found primarily in Exodus and Leviticus, is a dynamic version centered on the Israelite camp and ultimately on the Tent of Meeting and the Ark of the Covenant. This version should be considered an ideal model, that is, one which probably never existed in practice, but served as an idealization of the Temple and its structure. The second version is the Temple of Solomon itself. In many respects this model is also an idealization as the texts describing it were, at the very least, edited after its destruction. There is, however, an archeological basis for the existence of the structure. Both of these models as well as that of the Second Temple found in rabbinic texts have a similar understanding of the feminine and its exclusion from sacred precincts.

Exodus 25 initiates the description of the Ark and works outwards to the Tent of Meeting and the Tabernacle. The description suggests a model of apparently progressively more sacred concentric circles, with the Ark being the middle and thus most sacred. The camp (not specifically mentioned in this section of Exodus) is the final extent of these concentric circles, with the world outside being defined as profane. The pattern of decreasing holiness ends with the boundary of the camp. The widest boundary of the model suggests that the model is one of structurally opposed domains. The camp is in opposition to the world, the enclosure to the camp, and ultimately the Ark to the Tent of Meeting. Each level is a microcosm of the system. Each level is organized by the same underlying structural pattern.

Although the texts in Exodus 25–30 do not specifically exclude women from the sacred precincts, only men are mentioned. Chapter 28 discusses the clothing worn by the priests, specifically stating that they are for Aaron and his sons.[3] All texts describing the activities of the priests – their service in the Temple or the Tabernacle – are limited to Aaron and his male descendants.

Women of priestly descent are distinguished from the Israelites in general in one significant respect. While they live in their parental home they are entitled to eat the Trumah and tithed foods. These foods are forbidden to other Israelites. They retain this entitlement only so long as they are unmarried and without children (if they are divorced or widowed and have no children they can return to their parental home and eat foods tithed or given to the priests). It is likely, however, that this is due to the economic situation of the priests who had no land of their own and thus depended on these sanctified foods for their livelihood.[4]

The focus on male gender in the priesthood is developed in several other respects. The rules which distinguish the priests from the rest of the Israelites are specifically enjoined on the men. Thus Leviticus 10:8–11 discusses the distinctions between sacred and profane, the priests and the children of Israel in general. Verse 9 states: 'Drink no wine or strong drink, neither you, nor your sons with you, when you go into the Tent of Meeting.' This text is limited to men and suggests that women were not bound by the rule and were excluded from the Tent of Meeting.

The distinction of male and female in respect of sacred space is also developed in the texts concerning redemption of the first born (see for example, Numbers 3). The text describes a process through which the Israelites other than the Tribe of Levi paid a sum to free their firstborn sons from service in the sanctuary. The firstborn sons must be redeemed from service in the temple as opposed to firstborn children.[5] This suggests that the daughters were not seen as even being potentially eligible to come into contact with sacred space.

With respect to their exclusion from the Tent of Meeting women (descendants from Aaron) are similar to the other non-priests, male and female. All

Israelites of non-priestly descent were also excluded from the Tent of Meeting. The texts suggest the following structural equations: just as the Israelites in general are profane in comparison to the priests and thus are excluded from access to the most sacred spaces, women of priestly descent are profane in respect of the male priests and are thus excluded from access to the most sacred spaces. Both the Israelites (other than the priests) and women in particular may enter the Tabernacle and offer a sacrifice at the door of the Tent of Meeting, but only the male priests may actually perform the sacrifice and enter the Tent of Meeting itself.

The equation indicates that there must be a relationship or at least an analogy between the two classes, Israelite non-priests, and women of priestly descent and perhaps women in general.[6] Leviticus 12 suggests a significant area in respect of the understanding of women which may elucidate this analogy. It discusses the rules applying to a woman who has given birth to either a son or a daughter. In both cases she is unclean for a set period of time. For a son she is unclean for seven days, as well as an additional 33 days; for a daughter she is unclean for fourteen days plus an additional 66 days. In both cases she is forbidden to touch any hallowed object during the period of her impurity.

The text has several significant elements. The birth of a daughter leads to a longer period of impurity than that of a son, suggesting that daughters are intrinsically more impure than sons. The text also makes a direct analogy between the birth and menstruation. Both are periods of impurity when the woman is forbidden from access to hallowed objects. Other texts indicate that during menstruation a woman was an active source of impurity and could cause objects she touched (including other people) to become impure (see Leviticus 15). During the period in which she is impure the woman seems to be excluded from any type of social contact in which she might pass on her impurity.[7] The final element, and most significant for our purposes, is the exclusion from the sacred. Exclusion is based on ritual purity.

Thus if the aspect of purity is added to the original equation the following set of relations is suggested:

Women of Priestly Descent (and Women in General): Priests:: Israelites: Priests:: Unclean: Clean.

The priests are thus understood as being in some sense of purer descent than the Israelite non-priests and thus of greater ritual purity.[8] Women by their physical nature (regardless of their descent) and the Israelites by their descent are relatively more impure and thus excluded from direct access to sacred space.

The relative impurity of women, however, appears to be somewhat greater than that of the Israelites in general. The texts which deal with the impurity created by childbirth are juxtaposed with those about leprosy. Leprosy was the most significant form of ritual impurity and could lead to exclusion from the camp, the widest boundary of sacred space. The land outside of the camp was associated with the nations. It was understood to be the place of the nations as opposed to the camp which was the place of

Israel. Thus this suggests the following equation: leprosy = impurity = the nations. The impurity of the woman is perhaps only one level below that of leprosy. The structure of the Second Temple, discussed below, suggests that the analogy between the impurity of women and that of leprosy may be even stronger.

The association of women and menstruation with impurity is illustrated by the Hebrew word נדה, meaning impurity with the implications of being 'abhorrent and shunned' (BDB, 622).[9] This term is used widely in the biblical text to describe different types of impurity. These range from the defilement caused by a corpse to that caused by an incestuous relationship. In several texts, however, the term is used particularly to refer to the impurity caused by menstruation. In Ezekiel 18:6, for example, the text uses נדה as synonymous with menstrual impurity, that is, אשה נדה. It is likely that the semantic association between נדה and menstruation or feminine impurity is already very strong. By the Rabbinic period the word is used primarily to mean uncleanliness caused by menstruation.[10]

This model and associated understanding of gender is also found respecting static sacred space, that is, the Temple. Like the Tent of Meeting access to the sacred precincts is directly related to ritual purity – with women excluded on the grounds of being, at least to some degree, inherently unclean. The structure of the Second Temple, however, creates clearer markers in respect of access to sacred space.[11]

Solomon's Temple (described in 1 Kings 6 and 7) appears to be a static version of the Tent of Meeting and the enclosure. Its uses of space and restrictions in terms of access are probably similar. Only the priests would enter the Temple proper and only the High Priest the Holy of Holies. There is not found any particular restriction on the access of women. They appear to have been treated in the same way as Israelites in general; the only distinction is their periodic times of impurity. As in the case of the dynamic sacred space, however, women of priestly descent were barred from the priesthood.

The Second Temple

The Temple of Herod (as described in rabbinic texts and in Josephus[12]) presents a much more structured model of sacred space.[13] It had two main courts, the inner court which surrounded the Temple proper, and a second court built along the side and perhaps raised above the inner court.[16] This second court was called the *Ezrat Nashim* and was the extent of women's access to the sacred precincts.[15] Much of the area surrounding these two courts was the Gentiles' Court, beyond which only Israelites were allowed to pass.[16] Male Israelites were allowed to enter the inner court called *Ezrat Yisrael*, that is, Israel's court. The remaining segments of the Temple were progressively exclusive culminating in the Holy of Holies which was the special preserve of the High Priest – each section corresponding to a progressively more exclusive view of purity. The *Mishnah* specifically states that the Court of Women was raised above that of the Israelites, and that it served to prevent the men and women from mingling (*m. Middot* 2:5).

The Women's Court contained four chambers: of wines and oils; of wood; of Nazarites; and of Lepers. The latter of these chambers supports the association between the relative impurity of women and that of the leper. Like the woman the leper is allowed no further into the sacred precincts. The Nazarite is an interesting subcategory. Although the Nazarite was in a high state of purity, he also was outside of society and therefore for the period of his vow separate from Israel, in effect part of nature (symbolized by the growth of his hair). He is thus analogous to the nations who are excluded from contact with the sacred.

The woman and the leper are excluded from the sacred due to their impure status. The names of the courts suggest that women were structurally equivalent to the nations, that is, non-Israelites. Israelites were allowed into the inner court, Israelite women into the Women's Court, non-Israelites, specifically impure women, and men who were ritually impure, however, were permitted only into the Gentiles' court.

Mishnah Kelim (1:8) discusses the different degrees of holiness within the Temple. The description is much more complex than any of the previous models. Each section of the Temple, starting with access to the Temple Mount, is distinguished by degrees of purity. In this variation women who are menstruant or after childbirth[17] may enter the mount; gentiles are forbidden from entering the next level, that is, the rampart. The final significant element of this text in regard to the understanding of women relates to access to the Court of the Women. Even men who are not absolutely ritually clean are not permitted to go beyond it. The text by analogy supports the suggestion that women are never absolutely ritually pure and thus can never go beyond the Outer Court. As suggested in chapter 3, the categories of access to Jewish macro-space (the Temple) each level of space is related to a category of intrinsic purity or impurity.

The relationship between purity and contact with the sacred can best be illustrated in a somewhat later mystical text from *Perkei Heikhalot* (Chapter 20 Mishnayot 1–2). This text describes an attempt to bring a mystical sage out of his trance. The means of removing him from the presence of the divine is through bringing him into contact with a ritually impure object. Thus this supports the view that ritual purity is a significant marker. The object is the most minimally impure possible:

> Go and lay this cloth beside a woman who immersed herself and yet has not become pure, and let her immerse herself ... there will be one (Rabbi) who forbids (her to her husband) and the majority will permit. Say to that woman: Touch this cloth with the end of the middle finger of your hand ...[18]

The specific woman in the text is considered ritually clean by most of the rabbis, and thus permitted to her husband, yet she retains sufficient impurity to draw the mystic from his vision. The text supports the view that women, even after purification, retain an aspect of impurity which separates them from the divine.

The connection of ritual purity and access to the sacred in Jewish culture is found primarily in relation to centralized sacred space, whether the static form found in the Temple or the dynamic form found in the Tent of Meeting. Both forms share one key element. God's presence is more concentrated in the particular space than in any other. Both versions of the model are based on a unitary understanding of God's presence. God can only be manifest in this concentrated form in one place at a particular moment. In the dynamic form, the place is movable. It is, however, defined by the presence of the Ark of the Covenant. In the static form, sacred space is restricted. It too is defined by the presence of the Ark.

As these spaces become sacred through God's particular manifestation, purity becomes a significant element. As indicated in the mystical text, impurity is antithetical to God's presence. Some biblical texts suggest that impurity is also dangerous when in contact with the sacred. Thus any potential impurity must be avoided, and women who contain this potential or more likely inherent impurity must be separated from sacred space.

The position of women in regard to centralized sacred space, as suggested above, is part of a more general model of structural categorization. Women and impurity are used as markers in a logical system which distinguishes between mutually exclusive categories based on the structural equation A (not) B. Any element in category A cannot be in category B. On its broadest level this structure is used to distinguish between Israel (A) and the Nations (B). In the same way, women are thus logically opposed to men as pure is opposed to impure. Logically women are thus structurally equated with the nations. A structural equation which is illustrated in the structure of the Temple, that is, a distinction between the Court of the Israelites and the Women's Court.

Rabbinic Sacred Space

The Temple and the model of sacred space it exemplifies is primarily centralized and unique. God manifests in one space either uniquely or primarily. By the time the *Mishnah* was edited (CE 200), however, due to the destruction of the Temple by the Romans in CE 70, sacred space had been transformed into the decentralized form which characterizes the Jewish understanding of sacred space through the rabbinic and medieval periods until recently. The decentralized model of sacred space must, by definition, have a different understanding of the nature of sacred space as it is no longer the unique location of God's presence. It also develops a different understanding of the role and nature of women and a different explanation for their exclusion from the decentralized sacred spaces.[19]

This transformation of model is evident in all the rabbinic discussions of sacred space. Even when they are discussing the nature of God's presence in the Temple, they allow for God's presence elsewhere as well. This is indicated in a rabbinic text which makes an analogy between the Temple and a cave by the sea. The cave can be full of sea water without reducing the sea, so too can the Temple be full of God's presence without reducing its possibility of being elsewhere (or indeed everywhere) at the same time.

God's presence is no longer tied to a specific location or type of location. *Mishnah Avot* 3:2 indicates that God's presence is due to human action. It states that God's *Shekhina* (God's indwelling presence) manifests itself wherever two men study the Torah together. Other texts tie God's presence to the performance of other commandments, that is, reciting the blessing after the meal. The texts share two key elements: a communal element, and the performance of commandments.[20] These texts suggest that sacred space is thus redefined as the locus of commandment and community. Sacred space is therefore transformed into being both dynamic and multiple.[21]

Due to this transformation the nature of feminine exclusion is equally transformed. Sacred space is no longer tied absolutely to specific locations. Rather, it is tied to specific times and occasions (perhaps though not necessarily in specific locations). Although particular buildings, synagogues, are set aside for communal prayer, any building or location can become a locus of sacred space. All it requires (in the case of prayer) is that a minimum of ten men gather together. A synagogue, therefore, functions as a sacred space when it is used for communal worship.[22] At other times its sacredness is either in abeyance or nonexclusive. It is only at times of prayer that women are excluded from direct access to sacred space.

The Synagogue

Although the origins of the synagogue are obscure, by the first century (and certainly after the destruction of the Second Temple which is the concern of this section) it was firmly established as a communal institution.[23] Its structure and existence are taken for granted by both the *Mishnah* and the Talmud.[24] One early description of the synagogue found in the *Tosefta* (roughly contemporary with the *Mishnah*) states only that the doors of the synagogue should face the east, and indicates that the Ark may have been mobile rather than permanent (*t Megillah* 3:14). The *Tosefta*, however, does not give any information concerning the access of women.[25] Unfortunately, there is also very little textual evidence, in either the Talmud or *Mishnah*, for the way synagogue space was used.[26] It is unclear, for example, whether women were confined to a particular area, as is the case from the Middle Ages until today (in Orthodox synagogues).[27] Although some have interpreted the archaeological evidence to support the existence of such divisions there is little or no direct textual evidence to uphold their arguments.[28] Other scholars suggest that in late antiquity women were not specifically segregated.[29]

At least from the Middle Ages women were excluded from praying together with the men. In fourteenth-century synagogues in Provence, for example, women sat in the basement of the synagogue. This form of exclusion is supported by slightly earlier textual evidence. *Perkei D'Rabbi Eliezer* (an eighth-century text) states that when the Israelites stood on

Mount Sinai the men and women stood separately, suggesting that this was a practice in ritual occasions (Perek 40, section 1).[30] *Yalkut Shemone* (a thirteenth-century collection) commenting on Deuteronomy 23:14 states that men should not sit with women and attributes this to sexual attraction.

Thus by the early Middle Ages (and probably earlier) the synagogue was divided into sacred spaces of varying degrees of sanctity. The building was divided into two sections, one for the men and the second smaller area for the women. The male domain was subdivided into the area where the congregation sat and the *bimah* or raised platform, upon which the Torah was read, and finally the Ark, the most sacred space, where the Torah was kept. Although the degree of sanctity represented by these areas varied from less to more sacred, access to these areas did not vary. In principle all men had equal access to all areas of the synagogue. The only distinction in access was that the elders and respected members of the community were seated next to the Ark.[31]

The exclusion of women from the type of sacred space exemplified by the synagogue worked(s) on several levels. The first level relates to obligation. The rabbis considered that women were not obliged to fulfill the majority of commandments connected with the synagogue. This was based on the principle that women were not obligated by positive time-bound commandments (that is, commandments which had to be performed at a specific time).[32] Most rabbis throughout the period argue that although women are required to pray, this refers to private prayer rather than public.[33] This meant that women were not required to pray at specific times and thus did not have to attend synagogue services. This is not to suggest that women did not by definition attend synagogue services. Rather, it reflects a distinction between men and women in regard to their connection with the synagogue and its significance in their lives. There are, however, some texts from this period which strongly suggest that women not attend communal prayer.[34]

The distinction between men and women in respect of prayer highlights the association of men with public or communal aspects of culture and women with the private or home oriented aspects.[35] Only men were able to form the group which represented the minimum required for a community. Ten men or a *minyan* were required for any of the communal prayers to be recited. Ten women were not regarded as a group and were treated in Jewish law as ten individuals.[36]

Two areas related to prayer in the synagogue are the recitation of the Torah (on Monday, Thursday, and Saturday) and that of the Book of Esther (on the festival of Purim). The law treats these two areas differently. Women are exempt from the obligation to hear the Torah being read. As this was done three times a week, it suggests that women were not expected to attend these services.

Women are obligated by the *Mishnah*, however, to hear the Book of Esther. This suggests that although women were not generally expected or required to attend services in the synagogue during the early rabbinic period, at the very least on Purim they were obligated to do so. Thus to some extent they were permitted access to sacred space, though whether this was segregated or not is difficult to determine. In the *Mishnah* the text relating to the obligation to read the Book of Esther (*Megillah* 2:4) suggests that women were permitted to read the Book of Esther (probably in public). It states: 'All are eligible to read the Scroll excepting one that is deaf or an imbecile or a minor. Rabbi Judah declares a minor eligible.' The significance of this text is that, in general, when this type of list of people prohibited from some activity is given, women are usually included. This is clarified in the Talmud (*b Megillah* 4a) in which R. Joshua b. Levi states that women are obligated to read from the Megillah. Thus this further supports the possibility that women were granted limited access to sacred space at least in respect of Purim.[37]

Distinctions between men and women were also made in respect of the ritual garments worn during prayer. Women were not obligated to wear tefilin, ritual objects which would have been worn by men during weekday morning services (*b. Kedushin* 34a). Many rabbinic commentators forbid a woman from wearing tefilin on the grounds that they are a male garment. Women were prohibited from wearing clothing appertaining to men in Deuteronomy 22:5.[38] This distinction was more significant in respect of the tallit or prayer shawl which is worn during all morning services. As in the case of tefilin women were also not obligated to wear a tallit.[39] The fact that women did not wear these garments marginalized them in respect of the male community and may in fact have limited their access to certain sacred spaces – it was eventually the custom for men to be required to wear a tallit when approaching the Ark.

Women were also excluded from halakhic sacred space in a more significant respect. Based on the fact that they were not obligated to perform the significant commandments connected with the synagogue, they were also not permitted to lead the community in fulfilling these commandments. This was based on the general rule that only people who are obligated to do something can fulfill it for someone else.[40]

It is in respect of being called up to the Torah, that is, being summoned to sacred space, that we find both a range of opinion and an emphasis on the sexuality of women. The rabbis from the earliest period on are divided in respect of whether a woman can perform this commandment. *B Megillah* 23a states for example: 'Anyone may ascend for the seven honours, even a minor, even a woman, but the sages have said that a woman shall not read in public due to *k'vod hatzibbur*.' This text implies that there is no intrinsic reason (that is, purity) which prevents a woman from being given this honor. Rather, it is that her actions reflect in some way on the dignity of the community. The phrase *k'vod hatzibbur* is difficult to define exactly. It occurs only six times in the Talmud.[41] Each of the examples focuses on acts which were considered disrespectful to the community.[42] They do not, however, explain why a woman would infringe on that dignity.

Meiselman suggests that infringement is due to a woman's sexual nature: she would distract the community's mind from the text of the Torah

(Meiselman, 1978: 142). This argument would suggest that the exclusion of women is based on an intrinsic quality, that is, their inherent seductiveness.[43] *Halakhic* sources from the Middle Ages, however, support the argument that a woman is not prohibited from participation due to some intrinsic quality. Thus for example, a responsum by Maharam of Rothenburg (thirteenth century) clearly states that women, in one particular circumstance, may be allowed to read from the Torah (in public) and indicates that *k'vod hatzibbur* is related to shaming the community rather than a specific quality of the women.[44] These texts indicate that the women's sexuality is not the significant feature in their exclusion from sacred space during this period.

The Home

As indicated (see chapter 3), the synagogue is not the only significant locus of rabbinic (and modern) sacred space. The home is an equally significant location.[45] Many symbolic aspects of the Temple are developed in the home rather than the synagogue. On Friday night (the beginning of the Sabbath) two loaves of special bread (challah) are used, representing in part the shewbread from the Temple ritual. On Passover – a festival whose celebration was focused on the Temple and the Passover sacrifice – the main elements of the ritual are replaced by a ceremony in the home. The leader of the service is specifically associated in the ritual (through symbolically washing his hands) with the priests of the Temple and the table used in the ceremonial meal is associated with the altar. Thus the home, like the synagogue, is a replacement for the Temple and a locus of God's presence.

Women are not excluded from the home or from any of the rituals which normally occur in the home. Thus women are excluded from one type of sacred space, represented by the synagogue, and included in the second, represented by the home. The significant difference between these two sacred spaces appears to be the domain of cultural action. The synagogue represents public sacred space while the home represents the private.

If the basis of this differentiation is perceived to be due to an aspect of a woman's sexuality (as it is in many texts), the ethnographic material suggests that the model must be based on the woman's perceived seductiveness to men other than her husband. In private, where there is no fear of seduction, she is given normal access to sacred space.[46] In public, however, where she can be seen by other men and thus distract them, access is forbidden. This may be analogous to the current practice of very orthodox women concerning hair. A woman's hair is perceived to be seductive. Thus a married woman must always have her hair covered in public. In private, however, her husband is allowed to see her hair. Thus covering hair in public due to the danger of sexual attraction (and the danger of adultery) is equivalent to the avoiding of seduction which is the basis of the separation of men and women in prayer.[47]

Due to this differential treatment in respect of access to sacred space it is apparent that the reasons for exclusion must be transformed from that of the biblical and early rabbinic periods. Ritual purity can no longer be the determining factor, as it would be significant in both domains, the public and the private. The transformation is also evident in respect of the divergent *halakhic* opinions concerning the possible activity of women. This is best seen in respect of reading from the Torah. The Talmud implies that, in principle, women are permitted to perform this commandment and thus permitted to enter the most significant area of sacred space in the synagogue. The only reason given for not extending this privilege is a relative one, that is, the dignity of the congregation. Thus this exclusion is not based on elements intrinsic to women as was that of the Temple.

The model of sacred space also reveals a similar transformation. As suggested above, sacred space itself is no longer intrinsic. It is no longer tied to a specific location. It is relative to the activity and presence of a community. The prohibition of access to women is not based on the nature of the space. Rather, it is based on the needs and dignity of the community.

During the *halakhic* period issues of seduction and distraction are a constant explanation for the exclusion of the women. This explanation works on a very different level from that regarding purity as developed during the Temple period. It works on a micro-level while purity works on the macro-level. The problem of purity is part of a wider model distinguishing Israel from the nations. Israel is pure while the nations are impure. The exclusion of women from sacred space supports the model and thus strengthens external boundaries. The issue of seduction, however, has no relation to external boundaries. It is tied more specifically to the maintenance of internal family structures.

The two different models for sacred space and women are tied to their cultural and historical contexts. During the Temple period the model emphasizes the problem of endogamy and the need to emphasize external boundaries. During the *halakhic* period, in which the community becomes increasingly marginalized and culturally isolated (with strong externally created boundaries), there is a progressively stronger trend to emphasize and maintain internal structures.

The transformations discussed here fit into a broader model of transformation of emphasis in Jewish structure. The macro-model of A (not) B is emphasized when the openness of external boundaries clouds the distinction. The micro-model, focusing on the smallest possible unit, is emphasized when external boundaries are strong, making it unnecessary to strengthen the A (not) B model because the distinction between the two is unambiguous. In the modern period in which external boundaries are progressively weakening it is suggested that there is transformation in model which reemphasizes the external boundaries.[48] Due to modern cultural pressures the role of women in some variations of the new model include greater freedom of access to all aspects of sacred space.

The Modern Period

The role of gender in access to sacred space during the modern period is especially complex due to the fragmentation of the community in respect of ritual practice and theology. As indicated in chapter 5, the modern Jewish community is subdivided into at least four main subdivisions (excluding the secular community).[49] Each one of these communities has a different attitude in respect of the access of women to sacred space. The nature of the function of gender, however, has been transformed. It has become a marker of perceived authenticity between the various movements (and within movements). While in the two previous periods the conceptualization of gender was directly related to the nature of sacred space, which in turn was a function of boundaries, internal and external, in the modern period gender is only partially defined by sacred space (and only essentially within the Orthodox community). It is more directly related to the problem and nature of boundaries.

To a great extent the practice of the Orthodox communities is identical to that of the rabbinic period. Although in respect of practice there is little significant difference, the theological or legal justification for the practice is transformed. As discussed above, during the rabbinic period the exclusion was based on relative rather than intrinsic quality. It was due to the honor of the community rather than intrinsic impurity of women. During the modern period an additional element based on intrinsic quality has been added. This element is highlighted by the term קול אשה (a woman's voice). Many of the rabbinic texts explaining the limitations on women's roles and access written after the beginning of the nineteenth century, use this term (which is interestingly not often found in earlier discussions).[50] The use suggests that a woman's voice is perceived as being intrinsically seductive (in and of itself) and an obstacle to men's concentration in prayer.

Thus the impurity or danger posed by women is, as in the case of centralized sacred space, intrinsic. As suggested above (see chapter 5) one of the significant factors in shaping modern Jewish culture is the opening of external boundaries. This has led to a weakening of the conceptual boundaries essential for the maintenance of the A (not) B micro-model. It seems likely that the transformation in understanding of women to intrinsic exclusion is a return to a variation on the macro-model, which emphasizes the external boundaries. As in the case of the Temple Model the definition of women as intrinsically sexually provocative is associated with a logical pattern which creates a dialectical opposition between Israel and the nations which is based on intrinsic qualities.

The Orthodox communities both in the United States and Britain have, however, like the non-Orthodox, been influenced by western models. Orthodox women have begun to look for ways to express their spirituality and participate more actively in ritual. One of the ways that this trend is expressed is through the formation of women's prayer groups.[51] These groups meet on a regular basis for the purpose of religious services, with the reading of the Torah featuring in many of them. There are two main differences between these services and those performed by the community at large. First, because a full service (with all communal prayers) requires a minyan, a minimum of ten men, these prayers are omitted. Second, the services are only performed if no men are present. It is considered contrary to the *halakhah* for women to lead any part of the service in a man's presence. This trend, which may ultimately culminate in women taking more active roles in some Jewish communities, is similar to transformations in the non-Orthodox communities.[52] It is part of a transformation within the wider Jewish community in which women, as a symbolic constituent of a conceptual model, are no longer significant markers in respect of the structural role of sacred space. Paradoxically, however, due perhaps to its retention of other aspects of the micro (segmentary)-model of sacred space, in spite of the weakening of external boundaries, woman *qua* symbol is also moving toward the intrinsic purity model (of exclusion and inclusion) which characterized the macro (centralized)-model.

Interestingly, a similar paradox is found in some Progressive communities. Since the nineteenth century in the USA and the early part of the twentieth century in Britain there has been a progressive opening up of access to sacred space in Progressive communities. The process began with the end of separate seating and has culminated in the 1970s with the ordination of women rabbis. From its beginnings, leaders of the Reform movements addressed the question of the equality of women in respect of Jewish ritual life. In 1846, for example, a committee at the Breslau Conference averred the equality of men and women in respect of the commandments, obligation of women to receive religious instruction and to participate in public worship, and that they be counted as part of the *minyan*.[53] These developments were further expanded in the late nineteenth century in the United States, with the change to mixed seating and the participation of women in public ritual.[54] Although as early as 1922 the Central Conference of American Rabbis accepted the possibility of the ordination of women as rabbis, the first women were ordained by Hebrew Union College in 1972.[55]

Thus women have to a great degree been given complete access to sacred space. These transformations, however, unlike those between the Temple and rabbinic periods, which were essentially a structural response to transformation in boundary and self-definition, have arisen in dialogue, and as a reflection of the opening out of boundaries to the modern world. To some extent they may be said to be an attempt to conform to external models rather than to stand in opposition to them.[56]

Within the British Reform Movement, however, gender access works on a second related level. It creates internal boundaries which to some extent derive from notions of authenticity. In spite of the movement's public stand on gender equality, a significant number of synagogues chose to restrict women's access to sacred space in a variety of ways. In some, women are not permitted to read or touch the Torah; in others, women are not permitted to lead different aspects of the service. These restrictions are often perceived or justified on the basis of tradition and authenticity.

In many of these synagogues, the primary explanation for the exclusion given by the lay leaders and members is one of purity. In one synagogue in Manchester in which women are not allowed to touch the Torah, many congregants explained this on the basis of making the Torah impure.[57] This exclusion extended not only to women who were currently menstruating but to all women regardless of their condition. Thus we find a return to intrinsic impurity as the perceived basis of exclusion.[58]

As in the case of the model used by the Orthodox, the Progressive movements (especially in Britain) have transformed the conceptualization of women in two opposing ways. For the most part they have removed women as a significant marker, defining the nature of sacred space, in response to the western cultures in which they reside. To some degree, however, the nature of access and exclusion has returned to a Temple model with the reemphasis on intrinsic impurity.

It is likely that this second aspect of transformation is related to the opening of boundaries which is expressed by the first. During the nineteenth and twentieth centuries all Jewish movements and communities have perforce responded and been in dialog with modern culture. The boundaries which had been maintained through external forces have substantially been removed. This has led (as discussed in chapter 5) to the breakdown of the micro-, segmentary model, and the redevelopment, especially in those movements more open to external influences, of the centralized model. The use of intrinsic impurity may be a reflection of this wider cultural transformation.

This element is even more significant in the American Conservative movement, in which the transformation in gender access – with the association between tradition and authenticity – has led to the division of the movement into two separate movements. Throughout its recent history the Conservative movement has included wide variation in practice in respect of women's access to sacred space. One of the early and widely followed changes was the transformation to mixed seating. In 1955 the issue of participation in public ritual was first discussed. In 1973 the Committee on Law and Standards allowed Conservative congregations to count women within a *minyan*. This process culminated in 1983 with the ordination of women as Conservative rabbis.[59] All of these changes in respect of status are options within the movement with each synagogue choosing its own position within the broader framework. The final stage, however, led to a split within the movement and to the formation of a smaller movement which rejected the transformation in status.

Gender and gender access are also significant in creating boundaries on a second level, between and within Jewish religious movements. Whether a movement or community allows men and women to sit together, allows women to lead different elements of the service, or ordains women rabbis, have become markers both in self-definition (within movements) in respect of tradition, and between movements in regard to authenticity. In Britain and the United States those movements which reject this accommodation with modern culture have used the position and status of women as a means for demonstrating their level of traditional observance and their rejection of western cultural standards.

Conclusions

In the first two periods analyzed, the model used for the conceptual categorization of women was closely related to the nature of sacred space. During the Temple period in which sacred space was highly centralized, and the model emphasized the macro-level of opposition, creating clear and intrinsic boundaries between Israel and the nations, the conceptualization within the structure validated the macro-model by recapitulating it on the micro-level. Thus just as the opposition between Israel and the nations was intrinsic, the opposition between men and women, and therefore women's exclusion from sacred space, was also based on intrinsic qualities.

During the rabbinic period a segmentary variation of the structural model is employed. The macro-boundary was externally maintained and emphasized, thus the internal segmentation of the micro-model could be developed. Within the micro-model differences between categories are relative. Thus, the conceptualization of women moves from intrinsic to extrinsic – it is situational and relative. This mirrors the transformation in sacred space itself, which is no longer intrinsically sacred, but rather situationally sacred.

In the modern period, however, the status of women has been more strongly affected by external cultural models. Within all major movements the relationship between women and sacred space is transformed. In spite of relatively minor transformations within the Orthodox community to this point, it seems likely that women will increasingly be able to gain public access to sacred space. Within all of the communities, however, there is also the paradoxical development of a variation on the intrinsic model of exclusion found in the Temple period. This element is most strongly developed in the concept of קול אשה (a woman's voice). It is likely that this is related to the problem of permeable boundaries which have also led to the egalitarian transformations. With the opening of boundaries the segmentary model no longer creates strong cultural cohesion, thus elements of the centralized model begin to be emphasized.

Notes

1. It is not unlikely that there was variation in practice both geographically and diachronically. This chapter, however, is specifically interested in the model employed to explain the relationship between women and sacred space. It is the model and its conceptual foundations which are relatively consistent throughout this period.
2. Descriptions of noncentralized sacred spaces are also found in the biblical text. The descriptions, however, are not given in sufficient detail to determine the role of gender in access.

3. Ideally only the priests were allowed direct access to the holy precincts.
4. The *Mishnah* addresses several aspects of this question. *Yebamoth* 7:5, for example, discusses the status of a daughter of a priest and some of the reasons why she might not be allowed to eat the Heave-offering. The text is interesting in that it makes a clear analogy between the daughter of a priest and the wife of a priest (assuming she is not of priestly descent). Both are allowed to eat the Heave-offering with the proviso that they are part of the priestly household. This also holds true for a specific type of slave who belongs to the wife of a priest. This supports the view that the daughter of the priest is allowed to eat the offerings on the basis of economics rather than purity.
5. If the first child was female then the family was exempt from this obligation even if later children were male.
6. The priesthood descends through the male line, as did all significant elements during the biblical period.
7. It should be noted that this type of impurity is not only found in respect of women. Men too could be the source of impurity. Leviticus 15:1–25 discusses the various cases of male impurity. Both forms of male impurity and that of female impurity are associated with the sexual organs. In the case of men, however, the impurity is an unusual circumstance, while in that of women it is normal. Thus a man is abnormally impure while a woman is normally impure.
8. This concept is illustrated in the *Mishnah* in *Kiddushin* 4:1. The text divides those who returned from Babylon into ten groups, starting with the priests. Each of these groups is progressively less pure, with the less pure being forbidden to marry the more pure. While it is unlikely that the text describes a real situation, it does offer a model for categorizing people that is similar to that suggested here.
9. Brown *et al.*, 1979: 622.
10. See for example Jastrow, 1985: 878.
11. For a discussion of the access of women to the Temple and other biblical sacred spaces which focuses on practice rather than cognitive models see Grossman, S. (1992) 'Women and the Jerusalem Temple,' in Grossman, S. and Haut, R. (eds) *Daughters of the King: Women and the Synagogue*, Philadelphia: Jewish Publication Society of America, pp. 15–37.
12. A very detailed description of the Temple is given in *Wars of the Jews*, Book 5, Chapter 5.
13. The picture given of the Temple of Herod should be seen as an idealization in a similar way to dynamic sacred space. Most of the texts describing it were written after the Temple no longer existed. The idealized pictures thus allow us to see the mental models of the Temple rather than the Temple itself.
14. Based on Josephus' description of the Women's Court (in *The Wars of the Jews* 5:5) it appears that men did not go through the Women's Court to enter the Inner Court (there was no gate on the west of the Women's Court). Sanders suggests that men and women might have been separated upon entering the Temple Mount. See Sanders, E. P. (1992) *Judaism: Practice and Belief 63 BCE – 66* CE, London: SCM, p. 500. He also indicates, however, that most reconstructions allow passage between the Women's Court and the Inner Court. See also Swidler, L. (1976) *The Status of Women in Formative Judaism*, Metuchen: Scarecrow Press, pp. 88–9.
15. See for example, *m. Sukkah* 5:4, *m. Middot* 2:5–6.
16. See Sanders (1992: 61) for the text of a plaque in Greek forbidding gentiles access to the inner courts on pain of death.

17. This refers to the periods of impurity derived from Leviticus 12:2.
18. The translation of this text is taken from Blumenthal, D. (1978) *Understanding Jewish Mysticism*, New York: KTAV, p. 70.
19. It is not suggested that the element of purity, especially in respect of menstruation, lost all cultural significance, but rather, that it was no longer the primary explanation for exclusion from sacred space. Medieval *halakhic* authorities clearly state that a woman who is menstruating may enter synagogues and pray using God's name. See for example, the Rema's gloss Orah Hayyim 88. For a useful discussion which focuses on the discussions in the *Shulhan Arukh*, see Cohen, S. (1992) 'Purity and Piety: The Separation of Menstruants from the Sancta' in Grossman, S. and Haut, R. (eds) *Daughters of the King: Women and the Synagogue*, Philadelphia: Jewish Publication Society of America, pp. 103–15.
20. The communal element is emphasized in the text which ties God's presence to ten men eating together. Ten men were symbolic of a basic community.
21. For a more detailed discussion of this conceptual transformation see Chapter 3, p. 52.
22. The synagogue, however, as a building, was to be treated with respect. The *Mishnah* and Talmud lay down rules governing both the types of actions permitted in a synagogue and the uses to which a synagogue can be put if it is sold. For example, *b. Megillah* 27b states that when a community sells its synagogue a condition should be included in the sale that the building not be used for a tannery. The fact that the building can be sold, however, indicates that the sanctity of the building is fundamentally different from that of the Temple.
23. See for example the discussion in Sanders, 1992: 197–8.
24. There are some texts in the Talmud which describe the nature of buildings used as synagogues. *B. Berachot* 34b, for example, states that a synagogue must have windows.
25. For a useful discussion of the access of women to synagogues during the early rabbinic period, see Safrai, H. (1992) 'Women and the Ancient Synagogue' in Grossman, S. and Haut, R. (eds) *Daughters of the King: Women and the Synagogue*, Philadelphia: Jewish Publication Society of America, pp. 39–50.
26. Texts which may be significant include *b. Sukkot* 51b – 52a which highlights the separation of men and women in the Temple, *j. Sukkot* 55b, and *b. Kiddushin* 81a which mentions the use of jars or reeds to separate men and women.
27. For an interesting discussion regarding women's access to the synagogue from an Orthodox perspective, see Litvin, B. (ed.) (1987) *The Sanctity of the Synagogue*, Mt. Clemens: Baruch and Ida Litvin. This book includes papers by many important Orthodox rabbis arguing in favour of preserving the separation between men and women in synagogues.
28. It is possible to support this contention from two perspectives. First, in analogy with the structure of the Temple, synagogues may have been modelled on the Temple structure, and indeed many of the symbolic elements suggest this, e.g. the Ark is symbolically associated with the Holy of Holies. Thus a women's section would have been analogous with the Ezrat HaNashim of the Temple. Second, both the *Mishnah* and Talmud exempt women from the obligation to pray at a specific time, thus freeing them from the obligation of communal prayer. This might indicate that women would not generally pray in synagogues.
29. See for example Kraemer, R. S. (1991) 'Jewish Women in the Diaspora World of

Late Antiquity' in Baskin, J. R. (ed.) *Jewish Women in Historical Perspective* Detroit: Wayne State University Press, pp. 43–67

The archaeological evidence during the period under Roman rule shines some suggestive light on the role of women in synagogues. Lishitz, for example, demonstrates that women acted as synagogue patrons, with public recognition. While these inscriptions do not prove that women were allowed to take public leadership roles as well, they do suggest the possibility. See Lishitz, B. (1967) *Donateurs et fondateurs dans les synagogues juives: Répertoire des dédicaces grecqures relatives à la construction et à la réfection des synagogues,* Paris: J. Babalda et Cie; and Brooten, B. (1982) *Women Leaders in the Ancient Synagogue,* Brown Judaic Studies 36, Atlanta: Scholars Press.

30. This interpretation is based on the rabbinic understanding that God addressed the men and women separately on Mount Sinai, offering the Torah to the women first. The text states that God did this due to the fact that the men would follow where the women led.

31. It should be noted, however, that the nature of this exclusion is transformed not only in regard to the conceptualization of women, but also in respect of the transformation in the understanding of sacred space discussed in chapter 3. Several medieval *halakhic* texts suggest that women were excluded only when the sacred space was in use, that is, when it functioned as or was a sacred space. At other times access was not forbidden. Women were therefor even allowed (at least in principle) to hold or touch the Torah. See for example, *Shulhan Arukh,* Yoreh De'ah 282.9.

32. See for example *b. Berachot* 20b and *b. Eruvin* 27a. The general principle is stated in the *Mishnah Kiddushin* 1:7.

33. The Talmud clearly states that women are obligated to pray, for example, *b. Berachot* 31a. The form of such prayer is not specifically defined except in respect of the exemption to recite the Shema. Meiselman (Meiselman, M. (1978) *Jewish Women in Jewish Law* (New York: Yeshiva University Press) suggests that the rabbis distinguished between the public role of men, based on the requirement of ten men to form a *minyan* or quorum for public prayer, and the private role of women. Thus although women are required to pray, they are not obligated to pray in a synagogue. See also, Biale, R. (1984) *Women and Jewish Law: An Exploration of Women's Issues in halakhic Sources,* New York: Schocken Books, pp. 17–21

Maimonides argues that women are obligated to pray, suggesting that prayer was biblically ordained and originally not a time-bound commandment (*Mishne Torah,* Laws of Prayer 1.2–3). Later commentators interpreted Maimonedes' word to imply that women's prayer was therefore outside of the organized public prayer of the community (see *Magen Avraham* to *Shulhan Arukh,* Orach Hayyim 106:2).

34. See for example, Vilna Gaon, *Iggeret ha-Gra Livnei Beito.*

35. Avraham Weiss on the basis of medieval rabbinic texts argues that the home, that is private space, is 'virtually the only place' in which women should function in any respect. See Weiss, A. (1990) *Women at Prayer: A halakhic Analysis of Women's Prayer Groups,* Hoboken: KTAV, p. 5.

36. For further discussion of the *halakhic* opinions on this issue see Meiselman, 1978: 138–40; Biale, 1984: 21–3; and Weiss, 1990: 44–6.

37. This differential treatment is probably due to the significance of women in the Book of Esther. There is, however, disagreement about whether women are obligated to read or to hear the Megillah being read. This has implications in

respect of the *minyan* needed for the reading of the Megillah. Some *halakhic* authorities argued that because women were obligated to hear the Megillah they were eligible to be counted in the *minyan* for that purpose. Although this was not the generally accepted position it is significant in respect of the conceptual understanding of women. It indicates that women are excluded from the *minyan* on the basis of obligation, a relative condition, rather than for any intrinsic condition.

38. This is explicitly stated in the Targum Pseudo-Jonathan which dates from the third to the seventh century CE.

39. The commentators are divided in respect of whether a women should be allowed to wear a tallit. Some, following the text from Pseudo-Jonathan, forbid women from doing so. See for example *b. Menachot* 43b. Others allowed them to, but considered it presumptuous. See for example Isserlis' gloss on *Shulchan Aruch*, Yoreh Deah 17.2.

40. See *b. Rosh HaShanah* 29a.

41. *B. Megilot* 24b, *b. Megilot* 24b, *b. Yoma* 90a, *b. Sotah* 39b, and *b. Gittin* 60a. In each of these cases there is a different reason given for infringement of *k'vod hatzibbur*. The first two relate to disrespectful modes of dress, that is, nakedness and rags. The third regards rolling the scroll (of the Torah) in public which would keep the congregation waiting. The fourth, taking the Ark apart, is forbidden for the same reason. The fifth involves reading from a printed text rather than the scroll. This may be seen to reflect poorly on either the knowledge of a community or their possession of a Kosher Torah. In each of these cases the infringement is not intrinsically wrong. That is, the actions are not sinful in and of themselves.

42. Rachel Biale cites a related text, *b. Berachot* 20b, which may throw light on the use of this term. In that text the rabbis state that a curse shall fall on a man whose wife and children recite *Birkat HaMazon* on his behalf. Although the woman can *halakhicly* recite this blessing, if she does it in her husband's presence it would cast doubt on his knowledge or ritual observance (Biale, 1984: 27).

43. It is suggested below that the use of sexuality as the primary explanation for the exclusion of women may be a feature of the modern Jewish period. This is exemplified by the use of the term קול אשה (a woman's voice), a term emphasizing the intrinsic sexual character which is commonly used in the modern period (by individuals in communities and in legal discussions) to explain the prohibitions. Thus Meiselman's arguments may reflect and be based on this modern understanding.

44. This responsum (Maharam of Rothenburg Responsa No. 47) is sited in Biale, 1984: 27.

45. Sanders states that in the period up to the *Mishnah* the home was a significant place of worship, superseding even the synagogue (Sanders, E. P. (1990) *Jewish Law From Jesus to the Mishnah*, London: SCM, p. 77).

46. The exception to this access is found when a public service is held in the home. Today this is usually done during the period of mourning for seven days after a funeral. Traditionally women would be excluded from this service. This, however, is an incursion of the public into the private as the service must have at least ten men present, that is, the minimum number symbolic of a community.

47. This use of sexuality as a basis for exclusion is used as a means for maintaining dominance and control of women's power within the public sphere. It allows women to only act (and be visible) in the private sphere.

48. The use of the term קול אשה is interesting in this respect. It is not used until the

early part of the modern period and may reflect a new model which excludes women for an intrinsic reason rather than a relative one.

49. These subdivisions include: Ultraorthodox, Modern Orthodox, Conservative, and Progressive (including both Reform and Liberal).

50. Although the term itself is based on earlier usages, it emphasizes the intrinsic aspect and is used in respect of sacred space to a greater extent. In the Bar Elan Database of Responsa, the term is not found prior to the seventeenth- to nineteenth-century database, where it is found once, and then it is found in eight different responsa in the twentieth century.

51. For a good discussion of this phenomenon see Haut, R. (1992) 'Women's Prayer Groups and the Orthodox Synagogue' in Grossman, S. and Haut, R. (eds) *Daughters of the King: Women and the Synagogue*, Philadelphia: JPS, pp. 135–57.

52. Several American Orthodox rabbis have suggested in private conversation the possibility of elements of the Orthodox community ordaining women rabbis within the next 50 years.

53. This document is quoted in Plaut, W. G. (1963) *The Rise of Reform Judaism: A Sourcebook of its European Origins*, New York: World Union for Progressive Judaism, pp. 253

54. See for example a statement by Isaac M. Wise which emphasizes the need for women's involvement in all aspects of communal and ritual life. This text is quoted in: Plaut, W. G. (1965) *The Growth of Reform Judaism: American and European Sources until 1948*, New York: World Union for Progressive Judaism, pp. 339.

55. See Plaut, 1965: 334.

56. Whereas the previous relations with the external world and the associated transformations can be defined as negative or oppositional, this transformation can be characterized as positive and relational.

57. It is interesting to note that this explanation is based on a misinterpretation of Jewish law. The Torah can never become impure.

58. It should be noted, however, that purity is very rarely (or perhaps never) the reason used by the local rabbi to explain the exclusion. They often refer to either the rules of the congregation or traditional practice.

59. See Hauptman, 1992: 159–81.

7 The Shape of Jewish Sacred Space

This book has addressed many of the key models used in shaping the Jewish understanding and use of sacred space. The primary focus was on the way in which these models were transformed during the course of Jewish history in response to new cultural contexts. One of the consistent themes appertains to the interrelationship between centralized and decentralized sacred space. It is demonstrated that although both of these ritemes are present in all periods, they are differentially emphasized depending on the specific context. These ritemes are also seen to be significant features in shaping the use of pilgrimage and the role of women in Jewish culture.

Centralized and Decentralized Ritemes

Throughout Jewish history the centralized and decentralized ritemes have been the primary models used in shaping sacred space. The two ritemes are variations on the same structural model, that is segmentary opposition. The centralized model emphasizes the external boundary. This emphasis is necessary due to the weakening of external boundaries and the related issue of endogamy, that is, open boundaries challenge the need for, or the validity of endogamy as a cultural preference. The centralized model focuses on the widest level of opposition, and therefore minimizes internal segmentation. The only aspects of internal segmentation which occur, mirror the pattern of emphasis. In the same way that Israel is set in structural opposition to the nations, subgroups within Israel are set in opposition to each other, the Levites to the Israelites, the *Cohanim* to the Levites (and the rest of the Israelites), and finally the High Priest to the *Cohanim*. Each level of structural recapitulation strengthens and validates the external impermeable boundary between Israel and the world. The model in respect of human beings is also found regarding space. The centralized model emphasizes the boundary between sacred space and profane space; the two are mutually exclusive. This widest boundary is found either on the ideological level, at the perimeter of the camp or on the functional level, at the borders of the land of Israel. It is important to emphasize that at this widest level the pattern of structural opposition ends; Israel (the land and people) as conceptual categories are set in opposition to the nations (lands and peoples). There is no sacred space outside of the Israel conceptual category.

The dynamic nature of the Tabernacle and the camp as an ideological conceptualization is important in understanding both the centralized and the decentralized models. The Temple as a sacred space appears to suggest that land as separate from people can have intrinsic sanctity. Ideally the dynamic form of centralized sacred space, however, separates sacred space from particular places. The sacred space moves with the camp; the camp does not move to intrinsically sacred spaces. This suggests that an essential aspect of sacred space is defined or created by the presence of the camp, that is by the people rather than by location. This feature, however, may also be present, in albeit a de-emphasized form, in static centralized sacred space. The Temple was built in the midst of Israel, with the tribes placed round about it. In this sense it is somewhat analogous to the structure of the camp, which placed the tribes of Israel in formation around the Tabernacle.

The decentralized form takes this dynamism to its logical extreme. Although decentralized sacred space does utilize particular locations, these places are not sacred in and of themselves. The synagogue and the home, representing the community and the family, become sacred space through the presence of people and the performance of commandments (it is also suggested below that time, that is specific times, are also a feature in creating sacred space). In decentralized sacred space, there is no intrinsic sanctity; sanctity is relative and temporary.

Decentralized sacred space emphasizes the smallest, or lowest level components of the segmentary system. It is focused on the home and the synagogue. As in the case of the centralized model, there is a direct relationship between space and people; the lowest level components regarding human beings are the family and the community. It is argued that the decentralized model is emphasized when external boundaries are not problematic – either in respect of culture or marriage (endogamy). It is particularly strong when the widest boundary, between Israel (the people) and the nations, is externally enforced. This situation allows the lower levels of segmentation to come into play.

The decentralized model emphasizes the qualitative unity of Israel. Although each segment is distinct and set in opposition to the other segments, with endogamy encouraging marriage as close to the patrilineal family as possible, the segments are also equivalent one to the other. The hierarchical elements which are a feature of centralized sacred space, recapitulating the qualitative distinction between Israel and the nations, are no longer necessary internally, as the external boundary is self-validating. Thus apparent internal hierarchies, like the nature of the space itself, are relative.

The centralized and decentralized models are also a significant factor in pilgrimage. The Israelite/Jewish variant of the prototypical model of pilgrimage is associated with the centralized model of sacred space. The pilgrimage to Jerusalem was an additional feature emphasizing the boundary between Israel and the nations; only Israel was required to make the pilgrimage. Unlike the pilgrimages described by Victor Turner, Israelite prototypical pilgrimage was obligatory, uniting all Israel in opposition to the nations. In the modern period, with the development of a variant on centralized sacred space, a new form of prototypical pilgrimage is practiced, focusing on secular sacred space. It is suggested that only secular sacred space can unite the various segments of the community as it exists today.

Decentralized sacred space is associated with the medieval and archaic forms of pilgrimage. These forms typically consist of multiple sacred spaces, serving highly segmented communities. This segmentation mirrors the basic structure of the decentralized model. Each particular pilgrimage site, like the synagogue and the home, serves to unite small segments of the community in a pattern of internal segmentary opposition. Like the model of space and people, there is no necessary hierarchy of pilgrimage sites. Decentralized sacred space, however, is associated with a variant of prototypical pilgrimage; the Passover Seder, which replaces one of the three pilgrimage festivals, can be understood as a form of static, symbolic pilgrimage. This new form is discussed below.

Intrinsic and Relative Sanctity

Analysis of the role and access of women regarding sacred space highlights the nature and quality of the sacredness. Depending on the period and the model used, women were differentially conceptualized. In those texts which discussed or used the centralized model, women's impurity and therefore their exclusion from sacred space was perceived as being intrinsic. This intrinsic quality is seen as being a defining characteristic of centralized sacred space.

The Temple's sanctity was in part connected with place, which itself was intrinsically sacred through its architectural structure; culminating in the Holy of Holies, it also embodied an inherent aspect of holiness, which at least symbolically culminated in the Ark of the Covenant. The divisions within humanity were also based on intrinsic characteristics. Israel was purer than the nations; the Levites purer than the Israelites, again culminating in the High Priest.

Within the decentralized model, however, women were not perceived as being intrinsically impure. The texts emphasize that they are excluded for extrinsic, relative reasons, for example the honor due to the community. Similarly, the other ritemes which are found in the decentralized model also work outside of intrinsic characteristics. The sanctity of the space is relative and actional – related to use rather than location. The distinctions between the different categories of people are also relative. All Jews (male), and all places in which they live, are in the same structural category – differences are based on extrinsic qualities.

One interesting development discussed in this study are the transformations which are occurring in the conceptualization of women during the last century. Within both the Orthodox and to a lesser extent in the non-Orthodox communities the conceptualization of women is returning to a model based on intrinsic qualities. This is seen most clearly in the use of the term קול אשה (a woman's voice) which is seen as being intrinsically seductive and dangerous. It is also seen in those Reform synagogues in which women are excluded from access to sacred spaces on the basis of impurity.

Liminality and *Communitas*

Liminality, or more precisely the transformation of the liminal, is a significant riteme developed in many of the models of sacred space. This is most clearly developed in respect of raised and lowered spaces. In both cases the space is perceived as potentially bridging categories, that is acting as a positive mediator. Within the Israelite underlying structural equation, however, such mediation is problematic. Liminal spaces are therefore transformed. Raised liminal spaces become positive space and lowered liminal space become negative. Sacred spaces, within the biblical text, are usually associated with raised, therefore, positive space. This pattern is carried over into rabbinic texts in the requirement that synagogues be taller than any other building. It is also preserved in the use of raised space within the synagogue to indicate the most significant locations, that is, the Ark and the *bimah*.[1]

It is in respect of pilgrimage that the issue of liminality is most significant. Unlike the model of pilgrimage proposed by Turner in which liminality was an essential feature, Israelite/Jewish pilgrimage typically has little or no liminality. In Turner's model liminality was found on two levels, within the pilgrim as he moved from one status to a new status, and within the pilgrimage, as the pilgrim moved from a profane to a sacred place. In the pilgrimage examined here neither of these elements is developed. On the personal level there is no significant transformation. If transformation occurs, it occurs in all Israelites, emphasized by the obligation to go on pilgrimage yearly. Similarly, the journey to the pilgrimage site appears to be unimportant. Unlike descriptions of some Christian pilgrimages which emphasize the journey almost more than the arrival and actions at the pilgrimage site, descriptions of Jewish pilgrimage always focus on the pilgrimage site itself. If an aspect of liminality is present in Jewish pilgrimage, it is only found in a positively transformed form in the pilgrimage site itself.

This absence of significant liminality is also a feature of the related phenomena of *rites de passage*. Whereas *rites de passage* in many societies are characterized by a sometimes extensive liminal phase which mediates between the two societal roles, Jewish *rites de passage* are immediate. For example, the Bar Mitzvah, which symbolizes a boy's becoming an adult Jew, has no liminal phase; the transformation occurs instantly. Technically, the moment the boy is thirteen years old he moves from one status to the other.

The ritual recognizes or symbolizes the transformation but does not effect it. It is significant that like the transformation which occurs in pilgrimage, that of the *Bar Mitzvah* is shared by all male members of the community. Even if no ritual is performed, all male members of the community become adults on their thirteenth birthday.

Communitas also works in a different way in Jewish pilgrimage than found in Turner's general model. Whereas Turner discusses the development of *communitas* among a particular group of pilgrims, which creates an antihierarchical sense of unity in opposition to those of one's own society who have not performed the pilgrimage. Within the pilgrimages discussed here *communitas*, at least in principle, is extended to a much broader level. The prototypical pilgrimages to the Temple in Jerusalem and to the secular modern state of Israel emphasize not the separateness of the pilgrim from the community, and his opposition to it, but rather create a broader sense of unity which contains many aspects of *communitas*. If opposition is developed it is on the macro-level in opposition to those who are not obligated to go on the pilgrimage, that is, the nations. Jewish pilgrimage is typically not antihierarchical. It is a movement to the cultural center which supports rather than undermines preexisting structures.

Transformation

One of the key features associated with sacred space in many cultures, especially with regard to pilgrimage, is individual transformation from one spiritual state to another. This aspect, however, tends not to be found in respect of Jewish sacred space due to the underlying structural equation of A (not) B, which does not allow elements to move from one qualitative category to another. Thus pilgrimage does not lead to any intrinsic transformation or distinction. The pilgrimages are obligatory and must be performed frequently. The pilgrimage emphasizes the communal covenant with God rather than an individual relationship.

The Passover, Shavuot, and Sukkot: A Static Pilgrimage

The Passover Seder brings together many of the ritemes examined in the earlier chapters of this book. In many respects it includes elements which make it analogous to pilgrimage, albeit static rather than dynamic. It is also one of the primary rituals connected with the home and is thus an exemplar of decentralized sacred space.

As it is currently practiced, the Seder is similar to prototypical pilgrimage. The ritual is directly associated with the Exodus from Egypt, the retelling of which forms the basis of the Passover Hagaddah.[2] The ritual, however, includes a strongly experiential aspect. Each stage in the Exodus is both discussed and experienced. The period of slavery is emphasized by the eating of bitter herbs, *marror*. This usually consists of horseradish which

is eaten raw. The unleavened bread, *matzah*, is also initially used to emphasize the experience of slavery.[3] Ultimately, the *matzah* is transformed into
the bread of redemption, and in part represents the final redemption and
the transformation of the world. Other foods are used to allow the participant to experience other aspects of the Exodus. The wine riteme (four
glasses of wine are ritually drunk during the course of the Seder) is a
unifying symbol, set in opposition to liturgical elements, for example
enumeration of the ten plagues. This riteme moves through a series of
transformations from the redemption in Egypt to the final messianic
redemption, symbolized by the cup of Elijah.[4] This cup of wine is left
untouched, representing the hope rather than the actuality of redemption.

The *matzah* riteme is interesting from a theoretical perspective. It is used
and transformed contextually throughout the Seder. As mentioned, it
initially represents the experience of poverty or slavery; it is then transformed into the bread of freedom, tied to the unleavened bread made
during the Exodus itself, and finally into the bread of redemption. In effect,
the *matzah* represents the stages of transformation gone through by the
participant and all Jews. Moving from slavery to freedom, and ultimately
(at some point in the future) to the time of the final redemption and
transformation of the world.

It is through the Seder that the Jewish people reenact the events connected with their origins and thereby reaffirm their covenant with God. The
Seder itself emphasizes this point by stating that 'in each generation each
person should see themselves as participating in the Exodus from Egypt.'
On a broader level the Passover Seder begins a larger process which
culminates 49 days later in the festival of Shavuot, which commemorates
the receiving of the Torah from God on Sinai. The relationship of both
Passover and Shavuot to prototypical pilgrimage is highlighted by their
origins as pilgrimage festivals.

Unlike the dynamic pilgrimages discussed above, the journey aspect of
pilgrimage is significant in the Passover Seder. The narrative and rituals
emphasize the movement from slavery to freedom. The journey also
includes obstacles and trials, most clearly found in the bitter herb. However,
unlike the pilgrimages described by Turner, Passover is obligatory, all Jews
are required to perform the Seder, and all Jews are equally transformed.

Some rituals connected with the Seder in some Jewish communities
further emphasize the connection of it with pilgrimage. In the *Mishnah*, and
in the biblical text, the leader, at the minimum, is meant to be dressed as for
a journey, with his staff in his hand. In other communities, for example
Syrian Jews, the participants ritually walk around the table, physically
reenacting the Exodus. In Moroccan communities the leader comes to the
table holding a staff and carrying the *afikomen* in a napkin on his back.[5] It is
also possible that the searching for the *afikomen* practiced in many communities also serves a similar function (this, however, may also have a mystical
or messianic referent).

The Passover Seder also includes aspects of liminality and *communitas*.
All participants are meant to sit in a reclining position. This was meant to be

similar to the way which free people sit.[6] To a degree, this was moving out of their normal position in society as a subject people, and taking on a temporary new social position and reflects the almost classless aspect of pilgrimage. This is also illustrated in the custom of never pouring the wine for oneself, which is said to be an imitation of the custom of kings (making all people the equivalent of kings). *Communitas* is demonstrated in a second respect. It is traditional to invite guests, often people too poor to have a Seder, as read in the words of a prayer in the *Hagaddah*, 'let all who are hungry come and eat.' This reflects a theme in the Seder which emphasizes the unity of the Jewish people within the covenant and the Exodus. *Communitas* is also found in a liturgical statement implying the unity of Israel, the '*Midrash* of the Four Sons.' This text describes four different types of children (symbolizing types of people), wise, wicked, simple, and young. Based on four biblical verses it suggests that each type of person be taught in an appropriate way, depending on their personality. Although the wicked son is criticized, he is still included in the Seder (one still tries to teach him). The text is usually interpreted as a statement that all kinds of people, whatever their nature, are part of the community in relation to God.

Like the dynamic pilgrimages discussed, the aspect of obligation and transformation in the Passover Seder differs from Victor Turner's model. All adult Jews are equally obligated to fulfill the commandments connected with Passover, thus participation in the Seder, rather than distinguishing particular people, creates a broader sense of unity. The transformation effected by the Passover Seder is also significantly different. Like all Jewish pilgrimage, the Seder must be repeated. The Seder is performed twice each year, on the first two nights of Passover, by traditional Jews outside of Israel and only on the first night by Jews in Israel.[7] It is thus not a once in a lifetime event which leads to a permanent transformation. The transformation in the Seder is not qualitative; it is rather a restatement or affirmation of the covenantal relationship with God.

The Seder emphasizes the association of the home with the Temple, and therefore decentralized sacred space. Rabbinic texts emphasize that the Seder table replaces the altar of the Temple, and the Seder meal is thus equivalent to the offering of the Pesach sacrifice, which was the culmination of the pilgrimage to Jerusalem. The leader of the Seder is also directly associated with the priests of the Temple through the double ritual of washing of hands which comes at the beginning of the Seder. In *Ashkinazic* communities this is further emphasized. The leader wears a *kittle*,[8] which makes a symbolic association with the robes worn by the priests in the Temple.

Many of the foods eaten or symbolically placed on the Seder table also make this association. The Seder plate includes two items which directly symbolize elements of the Temple service.[9] A shank bone represents the Pesach offering and the roasted egg represents the festival offerings, offered in the Temple on Erev Pesach (they, however, are not eaten, perhaps suggesting that although the home replaces aspects of the Temple, the association is not complete). The *matzah* also has a symbolic association with the Temple. The three piece which are placed on the table represent the three divisions of Israel significant to centralized sacred space, that is, *Cohanim*, Levites, and Israelites. They also represent the shewbread used in the Temple service. The Seder, therefore, exemplifies the role of the home in decentralized sacred space. Through the performance of the ritual, the house is symbolically associated with the Temple and thereby becomes a sacred space.

The Passover Seder also makes an association between sacred space and sacred time. It is suggested above (see page 48) that Jerusalem, as a symbol, in the statement 'Next year in Jerusalem,' at the conclusion of the Seder does not represent the earthly Jerusalem, sacred space, but rather represents the heavenly Jerusalem or the time of the messiah, sacred time. It suggests that time and space are related.

The other pilgrimage festivals, Shavuot and Sukkot, also transform dynamic pilgrimage into static pilgrimage, and use time as a means of transforming space. Sukkot works in much the same way as Passover. It takes the symbols of the original pilgrimage, particularly the *sukkah*,[10] and brings them into the home, emphasizing its association with the Temple. All of the ritemes of Sukkot emphasize the aspect of pilgrimage, and suggest that like Passover, Sukkot has elements of the prototypical model. During the festival Jews are meant to live (sleep and eat) in the *sukkah*. The *sukkah* is symbolically associated with the temporary dwellings made by the Israelites during the 40 years in the wilderness. It is also understood as bringing together the present and the future. The temporariness of the *sukkah* emphasizes that life in the present is also a journey, a pilgrimage toward the messianic future.

The festival of Shavuot has until recently been of less significance, with fewer ritemes associated with it. The aspect of prototypical pilgrimage has been maintained by its association with Passover. The 49 days between Passover and Shavuot, called the *Omer*, which represents the period between the Exodus and receiving the Torah on Mount Sinai, are ritually counted on each night. During this period there are also restrictions on behavior which are similar to practices connected to mourning. This period can be seen as symbolically liminal, reenacting the original transformation of the Israelites. The aspect of transformation, however, is not emphasized, and the mourning practices are explained by other historical events, for example, the death of Rabbi Akiva's students.

The Reform Movement in the United States has developed the pilgrimage and transformational element of Shavuot itself. It has, however, removed the liminal aspect represented by the *Omer*. Although in some temples the *Omer* is counted, none of the liminal practices are observed. The transformational element is found in the confirmation of teenagers. This ritual, which recapitulates aspects of the *Bar Mitzvah*, represents the acceptance of the Torah and is in essence a reenacting of the events at Sinai. Like pilgrimage the confirmation has a strong element of *communitas*, emphasizing the connections within the group which undergo the ceremony and their connection with all of the Jewish community. Shavuot is perceived as uniting the events at Sinai, the reacceptance of the Torah in the present and the ultimate transformation of all the world. This aspect of uniting past, present, and future, is one of the key elements of many Jewish celebrations (and commemorations). It emphasizes the close connection between sacred space and sacred time.

Sacred Time, Sacred Space

This association between time and space is a significant feature of decentralized, dynamic sacred spaces. In respect of Passover, three elements must conjoin to create the sacred space: the home as a locus for the ritual, the ordained time, and the performance of the correct commandments. It is the second and third elements that inject the dynamism into the system; they allow any locus to become a sacred space.

These same elements are present regarding the synagogue and the home in connection with the celebration of Shabbat.[11] The Shabbat as a point in time in part confers sanctity on the celebration and the location. This concept was expressed by A. J. Heschel who called the Shabbat a 'palace in Time.' He describes the Shabbat as a great cathedral and Yom Kippur as the Holy of Holies. Heschel argues that Judaism is essentially a religion of time. Although his suggestion that the Bible is more concerned with sacred time than sacred space may be an exaggeration, it certainly becomes a significant feature of the rabbinic understanding of the sanctity of space.[12] Time as an element of sacred space is a logical expression of the dynamic model. The use of time as a feature of the model allows the association of sacred spaces with both the Garden of Eden and the paradise of the world to come. Many rabbinic texts suggest that the beginning of time and its end are actually the same point (a concept built into biblical Hebrew grammar). They make a play on the word for paradise, which is related to the Hebrew word meaning orchard – seeing the orchard as the garden. The Shabbat becomes a taste of the world to come, thus symbolically transforming the sacred space for the moment in time into paradise.

Personal Dynamic Sacred Space

The dynamic aspect of sacred space is developed in a related way in the Hasidic community. The *tzadik* or *rebbe* has become a new locus of sacred space, based on intrinsic rather than extrinsic qualities.[13] Within the Hasidic community the *tzadik* has become the new center of pilgrimage. In many respects he takes on characteristics of the Temple; this is emphasized by the expectation of pilgrimage to his court on the three pilgrimage festivals. It is also supported by many Hasidic tales in which different *tzadikim* describe themselves as reincarnations of the High Priest.[14]

The holiness of the *tzadik* is intrinsic. Although originally, within the Hasidic movement, the role of *rebbe* was based on personal charisma, within a generation it was transformed into an inherited position, based on inherent charisma. The *tzadik* was understood to be a conduit joining heaven and earth. In effect, he was the primary (or only) place through which the Hasid could communicate with the divine.

The model of sacred space found in the Hasidic community therefore includes many elements of the centralized model. Like the dynamic centralized model, however, it is not based on any particular location. It centers around the person of the *tzadik*, which like the Tent of Meeting and the camp moves with him. The significance of the *tzadik* as the locus of centralized sacred space is exemplified by the Lubavicher Hasidim and the *Rebbe*. The *Rebbe* lived in Crown Heights in New York City. Hasidim interviewed stated that, in spite of problems of space, their preferred place of residence was in Crown Heights in order to live in close proximity to the *Rebbe*. Residence in Crown Heights was even preferred to living in Israel. It is said that the movement has built a house for the *Rebbe* in Israel, in which he never lived, which is identical to his home in Crown Heights. This suggests an interesting inversion in focus. Israel is tied to New York and the *Rebbe* rather than the reverse.

The developments in sacred space in the Hasidic community, and particularly the Lubavich, is therefore a variation on centralized sacred space. It is likely that this is in part related to the transformations in the Jewish cultural context which led to similar developments, that is variations on the centralized model, in other parts of the Jewish community. Like the Reform movement, the Hasidic community developed during periods in which there was a progressive opening of cultural boundaries, especially in respect of external intellectual and cultural influences. The Hasidic community, however, in response to these pressures moved in the opposite direction to the Progressive movements, emphasizing traditional practice rather than modernization. In spite of this difference in direction, the underlying model found in the two is similar.

Secular Sacred Space

The State of Israel is central to an understanding of modern sacred space. It provides a center for all of the diverse elements of the modern Jewish community. It is significant that its importance is predominantly secular rather than religious. This is emphasized by the nature of prototypical pilgrimages to it, which focus on the secular and the historical rather than the religious. It is likely that the secular aspect is emphasized because the religious aspects would emphasize the divisions in the community rather than the unity of the people as a whole. The State of Israel as sacred space fits into the centralized model. It allows the Jewish community to create a focus of identity which allows the creation of an external boundary.

These secular aspects are emphasized in the mission statement of the World Zionist Organization. It lists the goals and aims of Zionism and the State of Israel:

1.   The unity of the Jewish people and the centrality of Israel in Jewish life;
2.   The ingathering of the Jewish people in its own historic homeland ...
     through *aliya* from all countries;
3.   The strengthening of the State of Israel which is based on the prophetic
     vision of justice and peace;
4.   The preservation of the identity of the Jewish people through the
     fostering of Jewish education and of Jewish spiritual and cultural
     values.[15]

It is significant that the spiritual aspect of the land, as sacred space, is left to
the end. The mission statement emphasizes the centrality of the land in
relation to the national secular existence and unity of the Jewish people.

The transformation from religious to secular sacred space is also developed in the term *aliyah*. The term literally means 'go up,' and is related to
positively transformed liminal space. In religious sacred space the term was
used to describe going up to the *bimah* to read from the Torah, or to
participate in the Torah service. In modern secular usage it refers to
immigration to the State of Israel. Thus an equivalence is made between
secular and religious sacred spaces.

There is an interesting transformation in respect of Jewish thought that
mirrors this transformation in model to a more highly centralized model
and use of Israel as the primary sacred space. Earlier in the twentieth
century the model for discussing creativity in Jewish thought and culture
was essentially bipolar, with the United States (and perhaps Europe) being
one pole and Israel being the other. In recent years there is a slight shift in
favor of a centralized model, with Israel being perceived as the creative
center – thus mirroring the model of sacred space. This transformation is
reflected in a paper published by the World Union for Progressive Judaism
in which the authors suggest that the bipolar model is a depreciation of
Zionism as the vital preservative and creative force of Jewish life.[16]

The central role of Israel in relation to the diaspora is also emphasized on
the political and economic levels. Although at some controversial points in
Israel's history, for example the invasion of Lebanon and the *intifada*,
diaspora Jews have been publically divided in support or opposition to
Israel's actions, in general there is a consensus to present a unified public
front in support of Israel. This creates a notional boundary in relation to the
non-Jewish world. It also emphasizes the Jewish community's perception of
its relationship to Israel. This is also seen on the economic level. A major
part of fund-raising in the diaspora is for Israel and Israeli institutions.

Alongside Israel as a secular sacred center, various conceptual foci have
also developed which have served to unite the wider Jewish community.
One of the most successful was the campaign for Jews in the Soviet Union.
This issue allowed all elements of the Jewish community to work together
and present a united front, thereby creating an external boundary. The
cognitive use of the Soviet Jewry issue provides a model of methods
separate from a particular political (or religious) entity of creating a unifying cognitive (and therefore dynamic) sacred space.

During the last several years, particular religious agendas, for example differing methods of determining Jewish identity, have increasingly begun to fragment the united communal stand in regard to Israel. There has also been some fragmentation due to the controversy engendered by political decisions in Israel. This has led to a renewed emphasis on other foci being used to unite the Jewish community, especially since the issue of Soviet Jews is no longer a significant problem.

One new focus is on Jewish continuity or existence. It emphasizes the concern with the continued strength and existence of the Jewish community. It includes a renewed focus on identity building, for example Jewish camps, lifelong education, and reinvigorated spirituality. Many of these elements represent a cultural involution and rejection of western models. Thus the continuity movement fits in with the trends discussed as an attempt to recreate boundaries and clearly demarcated identity. It will be interesting to follow these developments, especially in light of movements within the more traditional Jewish communities to redefine themselves by increasingly marginalizing the non-Orthodox communities.

Notes

1. In spite of the fact that the women's section is a gallery in many Orthodox synagogues, it should not be assumed that it is specifically or specially holy. Rather, it can be seen as creating a separate space which is not essentially part of the sanctuary.
2. The Hagaddah is the book which is read during the Seder. It has been written and rewritten over the last 2000 years. It focuses on the Exodus and the interpretation of it.
3. When it is first mentioned in the Hagaddah it is called 'the poor bread.'
4. The wine is a complex riteme bringing together the concept of redemption, emphasized by the sweetness of the wine, with concepts of retribution. This association is expressed in a prayer which uses the analogy of pouring out wine to express God's punishment of Israel's enemies; the death of Israelite children in Egypt, symbolized by the color of the wine; and the suffering of the Egyptians, represented by the drops of wine removed during the recitation of the Ten Plagues. Some of these aspects are discussed in *v. Pesachim* 10:1.
5. The *afikomen* is half a piece of *matzah* which is saved until the end of the Seder. It must be eaten before the Seder can be concluded. There are two main versions of the ritual connected with the *afikomen*. In one variant the *afikomen* is hidden by the parent, with the children searching for it. It must be found and eaten. The child who finds it is usually given some reward. In the other variant, the children steal the *afikomen* and the parents have to ransom it back before the Seder can end.
6. In imitation of the Roman practice.
7. Due to problems relating to the calendar, traditional Jews in the diaspora celebrate each festival for an additional day, while Jews in Israel (and Reform Jews) only celebrate one day.
8. The *kittle* is a white robe which represents the robes worn by the priests. It is also worn on Yom Kippur, the Jewish Holy Day most associated with the Temple and its service.

9. The Seder plate, which is placed at the head of the table, contains many of the symbolic elements used during the Seder. These include the *marror*, the shank bone and egg, green herb (a symbol of spring), and the *charoseth* (a sweet paste which symbolizes both the mortar used to build the pyramids, or the Temple, and the manna).
10. The *sukkah* is a small temporary hut which was originally built in the fields during the harvest or during the pilgrimage around Jerusalem during Sukkot.
11. This is also partially true for any service held in the synagogue or home.
12. See Heschel, Abraham Joshua (1951) *The Sabbath: Its Meaning for Modern Man*, New York: Farrar, Straus and Giroux, pp. 3–10.
13. As mentioned above, the terms *tzadik* and *rebbe* refer to the leader of an Hasid community. Although the term *rebbe* is used by all Hasidic communities, it is often used today to refer specifically to the leader of the Lubavich community.
14. See for example two statements to this effect quoted by Mintz: Mintz, J . (1968) *Legends of the Hasidim: An Introduction to Hasidic Culture and Oral Tradition in the New World*, Chicago: University of Chicago Press, pp. 182–3.
15. This statement is quoted in Hirsch, R. (1993) *The Israel-Diaspora Connection*, Geneva: World Union for Progressive Judaism, p. 14.
16. Hirsch, 1993: 14.

Bibliography

Albeck, H. (1959) *Shesh Sidre Mishnah, Seder Zeraim* (The Six Orders of the Mishnah, Seder Zeraim). Jerusalem: Mosad Byalik.

Alexander, B. (1991) *Victor Turner Revisited: Ritual as Social Change*. Atlanta: Scholars Press.

Alon, G. (1984) *The Jews in Their Land in the Talmudic Age*. Jerusalem: Magnes Press.

Alter, R. (1981) *The Art of Biblical Narrative*. New York: Basic Books.

Ashley, K. (ed.) (1990) *Victor Turner and the Construction of Cultural Criticism*. Bloomington: Indiana University Press.

Barth, F. (1981) *Process and Form in Social Life*. London: Routledge & Kegan Paul.

Baskin, J. R. (ed.) (1991) *Jewish Women in Historical Perspective*. Detroit: Wayne State University Press.

Bell, C. (1992) *Ritual Theory, Ritual Practice*. New York: Oxford University Press.

Ben-Ami, I. (1981) 'Folk Veneration of Saints among the Moroccan Jews.' In Morag, S., Ben-Ami, I. and Stillman, N. (eds) *Studies in Judaism and Islam*. Jerusalem: Magnes Press.

Benjamin of Tudela (1983) *The Itinerary of Benjamin of Tudela*. Malibu: J. Simon.

Biale, R. (1984) *Women and Jewish Law: An Exploration of Women's Issues in Halakhic Sources*. New York: Schocken Books.

Bloch, M. (1986) *From Blessing to Violence: History and Ideology in the Circumcision Ritual of the Merina of Madagascar*. Cambridge: Cambridge University Press.

Bloch, M. (1989) *Ritual, History and Power: Selected Papers in Anthropology*. London: Athlone.

Blumenthal, D. (1978) *Understanding Jewish Mysticism*. New York: KTAV.

Brooten, B. (1982) *Women Leaders in the Ancient Synagogue*. Brown Judaic Studies **36**, Atlanta: Scholars Press.

Brown, F., Driver, S. and Briggs, C. (1979) *The New Brown-Driver-Briggs-Gesenius Hebrew English Lexicon (BDB)*. Peabody: Hendrickson Publishers.

Clifford, R. I. (1972) *The Cosmic Mountain in Canaan and the Old Testament.* Cambridge: Harvard University Press.

Cohen, E. (1992) 'Pilgrimage and Tourism: Convergence and Divergence.' In A. Morinis (ed.) *Sacred Journeys: The Anthropology of Pilgrimage.* Westport: Greenwood Press.

Cohen, S. (1992) 'Purity and Piety: The Separation of Menstruants from the Sancta.' In Grossman, S. and Haut, R. (eds) *Daughters of the King: Women and the Synagogue.* Philadelphia: Jewish Publication Society of America.

Cohn, R. (1981) *The Shape of Sacred Space: Four Biblical Studies.* Ann Arbor: Scholars Press.

Commission for the Wailing Wall (1968) *The Rights and Claims of Muslims and Jews in Connection with the Wailing Wall at Jerusalem.* Beirut: Institute for Palestine Studies.

Crapanzano, V. (1973) *The Hamadsha: A Study in Moroccan Ethnopsychiatry.* Berkeley: University of California Press.

Crumrine, N. Ross and Morinis, A. (1991) *Pilgrimage in Latin America.* New York: Greenwood Press.

De Vaux, R. (1961) *Ancient Israel.* New York: McGraw-Hill.

Douglas, M. (1966) *Purity and Danger: An Analysis of Concepts of Pollution and Taboo.* London: Ark.

Douglas, M. (1975) *Implicit Meanings: Essays in Anthropology.* London: Routledge & Kegan Paul.

Dwyer, D. (1978) *Images and Self-Images: Male and Female in Morocco.* New York: Columbia University Press.

Eade, J. and Sallnow, M. (1991) *Contesting the Sacred: The Anthropology of Christian Pilgrimage.* London: Routledge.

Eilberg-Schwartz, H. (1987) 'Creation and Classification in Judaism: From Priestly to Rabbinic Conceptions.' In *History of Religions* 26, n. 4, 357–8.

Elbogen, I. (1993) *Jewish Liturgy: A Comprehensive History* (trans. R. Scheindlin). New York: JTSA.

Eliade, M. (1954) *The Myth of the Eternal Return, or Cosmos and History.* Princeton: Princeton University Press.

Eliade, M. (1961) *The Sacred and the Profane.* New York: Harper and Row.

Fohrer, G. (1968) *Introduction to the Old Testament.* London: SPCK.

Freehof, S. (1980) *New Reform Responsa.* Cincinnati: Hebrew Union College Press.

Freelander, D. (1994) 'Why Temples Look the Way they Do.' In *Reform Judaism* 23.1, 35–7.

Gell, A. (1992) *The Anthropology of Time: Cultural Construction of Temporal Maps and Images.* Oxford: Berg.

Gellner, E. (1969) *Saints of the Atlas.* London: Weidenfeld & Nicolson.

Green, A. (1979) *Tormented Master: A Life of Rabbi Nahman of Bratslav.* New York: University of Alabama Press.

Grossman, S. (1992) 'Women and the Jerusalem Temple.' In Grossman, S. and Haut, R. (eds) *Daughters of the King: Women and the Synagogue.* Philadelphia: Jewish Publication Society of America.

Grossman, S. and Haut, R. (eds) (1992) *Daughters of the King: Women and the Synagogue*. Philadelphia: Jewish Publication Society of America.

Gurock, J. (1987) 'The Orthodox Synagogue.' In Werthheimer, J. (ed.) *The American Synagogue: A Sanctuary Transformed*. Cambridge: Cambridge University Press.

Haran, M. (1960) ' "Ohel Moedh" in Pentateuchal Sources.' In *Journal of Semitic Studies* **5.1**: 50–65.

Haran, M. (1978) *Temples and Temple-Services in Ancient Israel: An Inquiry into the Character of Cult Phenomena and the Historical Setting of the Priestly School*. Oxford: Clarendon Press.

Hauptman, J. (1992) In Grossman, S. and Haut, R. (eds) *Daughters of the King: Women and the Synagogue*. Philadelphia: Jewish Publication Society of America.

Haut, R. (1992) 'Women's Prayer Groups and the Orthodox Synagogue.' In Grossman, S. and Haut, R. (eds) *Daughters of the King: Women and the Synagogue*. Philadelphia: JPS.

Heilman, S. (1973) *Synagogue Life: A Study in Symbolic Interaction*. Chicago: University of Chicago Press.

Heschel, A. J. (1951) *The Sabbath: Its Meaning for Modern Man*. New York: Farrar, Straus and Giroux.

Heschel, A. J. (1985) *The Circle of the Baal Shem Tov*. Chicago: University of Chicago Press.

Hirsch, R. (1993) *The Israel–Diaspora Connection*. Geneva: World Union for Progressive Judaism.

Hoffman, L. (1979) 'The Synagogue, the Havurah and Liable Communities.' In *Response* **38**: 37–41.

Hoffman, L. (ed.) (1986) *The Land of Israel: Jewish Perspectives*. Notre Dame: University of Notre Dame Press.

Hoffman, L. (1987) *Beyond the Text: A Holistic Approach to Liturgy*. Bloomington: Indiana University Press.

Hoffman, L. (1994) 'In Search of a Spiritual Home.' In *Reform Judaism* **23.1**.

Hollis, C. and Brownrigg, R. (1969) *Holy Places: Jewish, Christian, and Muslim Monuments in the Holy Land*. New York: Praeger.

Hugh-Jones, S. (1979) *The Palm and the Pleiades: Initiation and Cosmology in Northwest Amazonia*. Cambridge: Cambridge University Press.

Humphrey, C. and Laidlaw, J. (1994) *The Archetypal Actions of Ritual*. Oxford: Clarendon Press.

Jacob, W. (1987) *Contemporary American Reform Responsa*. New York: CCAR.

Jastrow, M. (1971) *Dictionary of the Talmud*. New York: Judaica Press.

Jenson, P. P. (1992) *Graded Holiness: A Key to the Priestly Conception of the World*. Sheffield: Sheffield Academic Press.

Jha, Makhan (ed.) (1985) *Dimensions of Pilgrimage*. New Delhi: Inter-India Publications.

Jick, L. (1987) 'The Reforms Synagogue.' In J. Werthheimer (ed.) *The American Synagogue: A Sanctuary Transformed*. Cambridge: Cambridge University Press.

Kraemer, R. S. (1991) 'Jewish Women in the Diaspora World of Late Antiquity.' In Baskin, J. R. (ed.) *Jewish Women in Historical Perspective*. Detroit: Wayne State University Press.

Kunin, S. (1994) 'The Death of Isaac: A Structuralist Analysis of Genesis 22.' In *JSOT* **64**, 57–81.

Kunin, S. (1994b) 'Perilous Wives and (Relatively) Safe Sisters.' In *Journal for Progressive Judaism* **2**: 15–34.

Kunin, S. (1995) *The Logic of Incest: A Structuralist Analysis of Hebrew Mythology*. Sheffield: Sheffield Academic Press.

Kunin, S. (1996) 'The Bridegroom of Blood: A Structuralist Analysis.' In *JSOT* **70**: 3–16.

Lavie, S., Narayan, K. and Rosaldo, R. (1993) (eds) *Creativity/Anthropology*. Ithaca: Cornell University Press.

Leach, E. (1961) *Rethinking Anthropology*. London: Athlone Press.

Leach, E. (ed.) (1967) *The Structural Study of Myth and Totemism*. London: Tavistock Publications.

Leach, E. and Aycock, A. (1983) *Structuralist Interpretations of Biblical Myth*. Cambridge: Cambridge University Press.

Leigh, M, (1973) 'Reform Judaism in Britain (1840–1970).' In Marmur, D. (ed.) *Reform Judaism: Essays on Reform Judaism in Britain*. London: Reform Synagogues of Great Britain.

Levenson, J. (1985) *Sinai and Zion: An Entry into the Jewish Bible*. San Francisco: Harper & Row.

Lévi-Strauss, C. (1963) *Structural Anthropology*. New York: Basic Books.

Lévi-Strauss, C. (1966) *The Savage Mind*. Chicago: University of Chicago Press.

Lévi-Strauss, C. (1969) *The Raw and the Cooked*. New York: Harper & Row.

Lévi-Strauss, C. (1976) *Structural Anthropology II*. New York: Basic Books.

Lévi-Strauss, C. (1988) *The Jealous Potter*. Chicago: University of Chicago Press.

Lishitz, B. (1967) *Donateurs et fondateurs dans les synagogues juives: Répertoire des dédicaces grecquers relatives à la construction et à la réfection des synagogues*. Paris: J. Babalda et Cie.

Litvin, B. (ed.) (1987) *The Sanctity of the Synagogue*. Mt. Clemens: Baruch and Ida Litvin.

Lockwood, Allison (1981) *Passionate Pilgrims: The American Traveller in Great Britain 1800–1914*. New York: Cornwall Books.

Maier, E. (1975) 'Torah as Movable Territory'. In *Annals of the Association of American Geographers* **65**, 18–32.

Marmur, D. (ed.) (1973) *Reform Judaism: Essays on Reform Judaism in Britain*. London: Reform Synagogues of Great Britain.

Meiselman, M. (1978) *Jewish Women in Jewish Law*. New York: Yeshiva University Press.

Milgrom, J. (1970) 'The Shared Custody of the Tabernacle and a Hittite Analogy.' In *JAOS* **90**: 204–9.

Mintz, J. (1968) *Legends of the Hasidim*. Chicago: University of Chicago Press.

Morag, S., Ben-Ami, I. and Stillman, N. (eds) (1981) *Studies in Judaism and Islam*. Jerusalem: Magnes Press.

Morinis, A. (ed.) (1992) *Sacred Journeys: The Anthropology of Pilgrimage*. Westport: Greenwood Press.

Myerhoff, B. (1993) 'Pilgrimage to Meron: Inner and Outer Peregrinations.' In Lavie, S., Narayan, K. and Rosaldo, R. (eds) *Creativity/Anthropology*. Ithaca: Cornell University Press, pp. 211–22.

Orlinsky, H. (1986) 'The Biblical Concept of the Land of Israel.' In Hoffman, L. (ed.) *The Land of Israel: Jewish Perspectives*. Notre Dame: University of Notre Dame Press.

Pechilis, K. (1992) 'To Pilgrimage It.' In *Journal of Ritual Studies* **6.2**, 59–91.

Peters, F. E. (1986) *Jerusalem and Mecca: The Typology of the Holy City*. New York: New York University Press.

Plaut, W. G. (1963) *The Rise of Reform Judaism: A Sourcebook of its European Origins*. New York: World Union for Progressive Judaism.

Plaut, W. G. (1965) *The Growth of Reform Judaism: American and European Sources until 1948*. New York: World Union for Progressive Judaism.

Primus, C. (1986) 'The Borders of Judaism: The Land of Israel in Early Rabbinic Judaism.' In Hoffman, L. (ed.) *The Land of Israel: Jewish Perspectives*. Notre Dame: University of Notre Dame Press, pp. 97–108.

Rabinowicz, H. (1988) *Hasidism: The Movement and its Masters*. Northvale: J. Aronson.

Reader, I. and Walter, T. (eds) (1993) *Pilgrimage in Popular Culture*. London: Macmillan.

Rosenfeld, E. (1994) 'The New Intimate Sanctuary.' In *Reform Judaism* **23.1**, 38–42.

Roth, J. (1986) *The Halakhic Process: A Systemic Analysis*. New York: Jewish Theological Seminary.

Sacks, J. (1990) *Tradition in an Untraditional Age: Essays on Modern Jewish Thought*. London: Vallentine, Mitchell.

Safrai, H. (1992) 'Women and the Ancient Synagogue.' In Grossman, S. and Haut, R. (eds) *Daughters of the King: Women and the Synagogue*. Philadelphia: Jewish Publication Society of America.

Sallnow, M. (1981) 'Communitas Reconsidered: The Sociology of Andean Pilgrimage.' In *Man* **16**, 163–82.

Sallnow, M. (1987) *Pilgrims of the Andes: Regional Cults in Cusco*. Washington: Smithsonian Institution Press.

Sanders, E. P. (1990) *Jewish Law from Jesus to the Mishnah*. London: SCM Press.

Sanders, E. P. (1992) *Judaism: Practice and Belief 63 BCE – 66 CE*. London: SCM Press.

Scholem, G. (1967) *Major Trends in Jewish Mysticism*. New York: Schocken.

Scholem, G. (1974) *Kabbalah*. New York: New York Times Books.

Scholem, G. (1977) *On the Kabbala and its Symbolism*. New York: Schocken.

Smith, J. Z. (1982) *Imagining Religion*. Chicago: University of Chicago Press.

Smith, J. Z. (1987) *To Take Place: Towards Theory in Ritual*. Chicago: University of Chicago Press.

Sperber, D. (1975) *Rethinking Symbolism*. Cambridge: Cambridge University Press.

Spiegel, S. (1979) *The Last Trial*. New York: Behrman House.

Stahl, Nanette (1995) *Law and Liminality in the Bible*. Sheffield: Sheffield Academic Press.

Strack, H. L. and Stemberger, G. (1991) *Introduction to the Talmud and Midrash*. Edinburgh: T. & T. Clark.

Swidler, L. (1976) *The Status of Women in Formative Judaism*. Metuchen: Scarecrow Press.

Talmon, Sh. (1976) 'המשווה והשיטה "הארץ טבור" ' (Tabûr Ha'arez and the Comparative Method). In *Tabriz* **45**: 163–77.

Tambiah, S. J. (1985) *Culture, Thought and Social Action: An Anthropological Perspective*. Cambridge: Harvard University Press.

Tomes, R. (1996) ' "Our Holy and Beautiful House": When and Why was 1 Kings 6–8 Written.' In *JSOT*, **70**.

Turner, E. (1993) 'Bar Yohai, Mystic: The Creative Persona and his Pilgrimage.' In Lavie, S., Narayan, K, and Rosaldo, R. (eds) *Creativity/Anthropology*. Ithaca: Cornell University Press, pp. 225–52.

Turner, H. (1979) *From Temple to Meeting House: The Phenomenology and Theology of Places of Worship*. The Hague: Mouton Publishers.

Turner, T. (1977) 'Narrative Structure and Mythopoesis: A Critique and Reformulation of Structuralist Concepts of Myth, Narrative and Poetics.' In *Arethusa* **10.1**, 103–63.

Turner, T. (1985) 'Animal Symbolism, Totemism and the Structure of Myth.' In G. Urton (ed.), *Animal Myths and Metaphors in South America*. Salt Lake City: University of Utah Press.

Turner, V. (1967) *The Forest of Symbols: Aspects of Ndembu Ritual*. Ithaca: Cornell University Press.

Turner, V. (1969) *The Ritual Process: Structure and Anti-Structure*. Chicago: Aldine.

Turner, V. (1974) *Dramas, Fields and Metaphors*. Ithaca: Cornell University Press.

Turner, V. and Turner, E. (1978) *Image and Pilgrimage in Christian Culture*. New York: Columbia University Press.

Urbach, E. E. (1979) *The Sages*. Cambridge: Harvard University Press.

Wagner, R. (1981) *The Invention of Culture*. Chicago: University of Chicago Press.

Walter, T. (1993) 'War Grave Pilgrimage.' In Reader, I. and Walter, T. (eds) *Pilgrimage in Popular Culture*. London: Macmillan.

Weiss, A. (1990) *Women at Prayer: A Halakhic Analysis of Women's Prayer Groups*. Hoboken: KTAV.

Werthheimer, J. (ed.) (1987) *The American Synagogue: A Sanctuary Transformed*. Cambridge: Cambridge University Press.

Wolfe, G. and Fine, J. (1978) *The Synagogues of New York's Lower East Side*. New York: New York University Press.

Index